NEW AND NAKED LAND

NEW AND NAKED LAND

MAKING THE PRAIRIES HOME

RONALD REES

Western Producer Prairie Books
Saskatoon, Saskatchewan

Cover design by Warren Clark/GDL
Cover illustration: "Homesteader" by Wesley C. Dennis. Courtesy Saskatchewan Property Management Corporation, Artwork Program.

Printed and bound in Canada

The publisher acknowledges the support received for this publication from the Canada Council

Western Producer Prairie Books is a unique publishing venture located in the middle of western Canada and owned by a group of prairie farmers who are members of Saskatchewan Wheat Pool. From the first book in 1954, a reprint of a serial originally carried in the weekly newspaper *The Western Producer,* to the book before you now, the tradition of providing enjoyable and informative reading for all Canadians is continued.

Canadian Cataloguing in Publication Data

Rees, Ronald, 1935–

New and Naked Land

ISBN 0-88833-260-2 (bound).

1. Prairie Provinces — Emigration and immigration — History. 2. Prairie Provinces — Social conditions — To 1905* 3. Prairie Provinces — Social conditions — 1905– * 4. Prairie Provinces — Economic conditions — To 1905.* 5. Prairie Provinces — Economic conditions — 1905– * I. Title

FC3237.R43 1988   971.2   C88-098007-9
F1060.R43 1988

I wish to thank the Social Sciences and Humanities Research Council of Canada for the grant that enabled me to write this book. I am also indebted to librarians and archivists in many parts of the country. I owe particular debts of thanks to those at the Glenbow Museum, the Saskatchewan Archives, the Public Archives of Canada, and the Archives of the Canadian Pacific Railway.

"A man is, of all sorts of baggage,
the most difficult to be transported."

Adam Smith, 1776

CONTENTS

INTRODUCTION

PART ONE: THE NEW LAND

Chapter One
EXPECTATIONS OF THE NEW LAND   4

Chapter Two
THE WEST ON THE EVE OF MASS EUROPEAN
    SETTLEMENT   28

Chapter Three
REACTIONS TO THE PRAIRIE   35

Chapter Four
CHOOSING A HOMESTEAD, MAKING A SHELTER   45

Chapter Five
THE SURVEY AND THE SETTLEMENT PLAN   60

Chapter Six
ALTERNATIVE PATTERNS OF SETTLEMENT   68

Chapter Seven
NOSTALGIA FOR THE HOMELAND   86

PART TWO: MAKING A COUNTRY

Chapter Eight
THE CULT OF THE TREE   95

Chapter Nine
PLANT PROPAGATION AND CULTURE   107

Chapter Ten
GARDENS, PARKS, AND SHELTERBELTS   123

Chapter Eleven
RANCHERS AND THE PRAIRIE LANDSCAPE   136

PART THREE: THE PRAIRIE AS HOME

Chapter Twelve
IMAGINATIVE INTERPRETATIONS OF THE
    LANDSCAPE   155

THE NEW LANDSCAPE   167

INTRODUCTION

The Greek physician Hippocrates noted, about 400 B.C., that whenever people from one country were sent to another of markedly different terrain, "terrible perturbations" always followed. From this he concluded that people absorb topographical influences from the moment of birth and that separation from them could be perilous. These perturbations we now know as nostalgia (from the Greek *nostos,* to return, and *algos,* to suffer) and homesickness (from the German *Heimweh*). The first known sufferers in modern times were seventeenth century Swiss mercenary soldiers in the pay of European potentates; they were overcome by lassitude and melancholia at sounds and smells that reminded them of Switzerland. Cowbells and the strains of the Swiss melody *"ranz-des-vaches"* are said to have disarmed Swiss soldiers as effectively as any enemy manoeuvre. Europeans first knew the ailment as the "terrible Swiss disease," but it struck at every nation once the Industrial Revolution and the opening of the new worlds began to scatter the old world population.

Throughout the eighteenth century *Heimweh* was treated as pathological, but today it is regarded no more seriously than a protracted cold. Population movements, both voluntary and forced, have become so commonplace, and travel and long distance communication so rapid, that it is easy to forget how stationary people used to be and how insurmountable distances were. People were tied to localities in ways we can no longer appreciate, and shifts of even a dozen miles could be disturbing. Displacements as great and irrevocable as emigration were extremely stressful and could be disabling. Migration to any distant place was difficult and usually painful, but if Hippocrates was right then

1

migrants who found themselves in unfamiliar terrain had the most difficult adjustment. Settlers in the eastern parts of North America at least had the solace of an environment made from the same ingredients as the one they had left, however different the mix and the proportions. But settlers west of the Mississippi and the Canadian Shield encountered an environment stranger than most of them could ever have envisioned. Government and railway advertising had suggested that the new land would not be radically different from the old one. Instead, settlers found a land that was flat, dry, sparsely treed and, by old world standards, empty of people. For Europeans and eastern North Americans arrival on the plains was almost as strange as landing on the moon, as the novelist R. M. Ballantyne intimated in the 1840s. Ballantyne's analogy may seem fanciful, but it was endorsed in our own times by the directors of NASA. So that the astronauts chosen for the moon landing might have some idea of what it is like to confront an alien environment, they were required to read Walter Prescott Webb's classic study of the settlement of the American West, *The Great Plains.*

The problem for settlers on the American plains and the Canadian prairies was how to make a home of the strange new land. Farms had to be laid out, roads made, houses and fences built, and the land ploughed. But greater than the problem of physical control, according to the historian Henry Steele Commager, was the problem of spiritual adjustment. "Home" is not just a physical space that has been ordered and subdued, but a familiar place — as small as a house or as large as a country — to which we feel we belong. How migrants reacted to the prairies and made them home is the main subject of this book. What follows is an essay about one aspect of the pioneer condition rather than a chronicle of pioneer life and settlement. No effort has been made to present a rounded history of the settlement nor to incorporate the responses of all the national or religious groups who came to the prairies. The book begins with an estimate of the expectations, based on the nature of government and railway advertising, that immigrants might have had of the new land, and ends with an assessment of their efforts to make a home of it.

For readers unacquainted with Western Canada, a note on regional terminology might prove useful. The Canadian prairies are the northern section of the grasslands that once covered the interior of North America between the 100th meridian and the Rockies, the region known as the Great Plains. The American grasslands are usually described as the plains, the Canadian as the prairies or prairie. The prairies are divided into two parts: a northern parkland of grasses and poplar bluffs about a hundred miles wide, and, south of the parkland, a broader region of grasslands which were treeless except for a few wooded hills and valleys. The grasses are short in the dry south and south-west and longer in the east and north. In everyday speech people seldom distinguish between parkland and grasslands. In deference to popular usage, I have used the words prairie and prairies to describe the region as a whole, specifying parkland and grasslands only where necessary. Also in deference to common usage, the phrases "West" and "Western Canada" refer to the flat, open country drained by the Red, the Assiniboine, and the North and South Saskatchewan rivers that lies between the Canadian Shield and the Rockies.

Principal sources of information not cited in the text are listed alphabetically by chapter at the end of the book. Many of the observations made by the pioneers themselves were taken from manuscript sources chiefly in the Glenbow Museum (Alberta) and in the Saskatchewan archives. These have not been cited.

PART I

THE NEW LAND

Chapter One

EXPECTATIONS OF THE NEW LAND

The normal human impulse is to cling to the familiar and the known, the home place and the home country. Even for adventurers, part of the pleasure in setting off for the unknown lies in the anticipation of a safe and joyful return. For ancient Greek sailors the high point of any voyage was the first sight of the temple to Poseidon at Cape Sunium that guarded the approaches to Athens and home. If people who aren't oppressed are to be permanently separated from their homelands, the expected gains must be enticing enough to offset this powerful homing instinct. Promoters of settlement in new lands have always had honeyed tongues, perhaps none more so than the legendary Pied Piper who, according to recent speculation, might well have been a twelfth or thirteenth century "locator" employed to find settlers for the pioneer lands of eastern Germany. The youth of Hamelin may have been lured away by sweet talk of Arcadia beyond the Elbe, not by the sound of magic pipes.

The more distant and inhospitable the land, the greater the blandishments necessary to attract settlers to it. Cold, dry, treeless plains half a continent and — for Europeans — an ocean away were hardly alluring, the offer of free homesteads notwithstanding. According to Ray Billington, the American historian, the effort to settle the Great Plains inspired the greatest advertising campaign ever to influence migration. Even the Garden of Eden, Billington remarked wryly, would have looked seedy compared to the images of the West conjured up by the promoters. His remarks

4

were chiefly about American promoters, but their colleagues in Canada were hardly less restrained. Advertisers of the Canadian West had American experience to build on, and with a more difficult product to market and greater barriers of consumer resistance to overcome, they were driven to even more extravagant flights of hyperbole. Prairie winters were longer and colder than winters in the American West and the growing season correspondingly shorter. The Canadian prairies were also more remote. The American East and West may have been worlds apart, figuratively speaking, but they were connected by a band of settlement that was more or less unbroken from the Atlantic to the edge of the grasslands. But between Manitoba and southern Ontario lay a thousand-mile stretch of waterlogged and virtually uninhabitable Canadian Shield — Captain W. F. Butler's "immense marsh."

Out of the Wilderness

To add to their disadvantages as prospective homes for settlers, both regions had reputations to live down. For the first half of the nineteenth century "The West" had been celebrated as a wilderness — a "romantic horizon"* that allowed travellers and adventurers to escape, as Butler put it, "life rusting routine" and "the servitude of civilisation." The Canadian prairies and parklands had been seen either as a northern extension of the Great American Desert or as a southern extension of the Arctic. Vast and uninhabited, save for a few scattered bands of Indians and a handful of European fur traders, they nourished the Romantic imagination and eased a malaise then endemic in over-civilised Europeans: *Europamüdigkeit,* sickness or weariness with Europe.

Only a handful of Europeans had been able to afford a wilderness cure, but all had been able to read the books of James Fenimore Cooper, R. M. Ballantyne, and William F. Butler, and some might have seen exhibitions of paintings by George Catlin, Paul Kane, and Frederick Verner. The title of Butler's most popular book, *The Great Lone Land,* entered the language of the day, and no reference to Western Canada had seemed complete without it. The book ran through nineteen official printings — four in a single year — and an unknown number of pirated printings in Canada and the United States. In Britain alone the book had been read by several hundred thousand people.

As well as stimulating the European imagination, a wilderness image for the West had also served the purposes of the region's long-standing lessee, the Hudson's Bay Company, whose fur-trading interests could only have been damaged by an influx of settlers. The lease of the vast territory of Rupert's Land had been due to expire in 1870. With an eye to securing a renewal, the Governor of the company, Sir George Simpson, declared

* The phrase is William Goetzmann's

that the prairies and parklands west of Lake Superior "were not well adapted for settlement." Similar views were held in Britain and Canada. Ben Hawes, the British Parliamentary Under Secretary, ridiculed the idea of settling a "dreary territory" when there were more attractive lands to go to, and a contributor to the Toronto *Globe* had dismissed the West as a land where "no friendly expanse of forest will shelter [the settlers] from the full sweep of the famine borne wind and no useful timber trees afford them winter's firing."

In spite of contrary winds, the vane of public opinion pointed steadily in the direction of settlement. The growing shortage of "wild" land in Ontario, the need to settle at least some of the country between Ontario and British Columbia, and the fear that if Canada and Britain didn't do so America would, were persuasive arguments. Butler's *The Great Lone Land* was in effect a requiem for a region that was about to be engulfed, as he put it, by the immense wave of human life then rolling ineluctably from Europe toward America. Butler's heart may have been in the wilderness but his head was ruled by a dutiful recognition of the need to settle the West.

To meet the expectations of British and Canadian supporters of expansion, the West had to be re-assessed; the old image clashed with the new interests. Reconnaissance parties sent out after 1850 were required to assess the agricultural potential of the region and to look for possible routes for a transcontinental railway. Captain George Palliser and the naturalist Henry Youle Hind, who led expeditions to the interior in 1857 and 1858, respectively, came down decisively on the side of settlement. Palliser's party had been sent out by Great Britain and Hind's by Canada. By staying south of the 54th parallel both men severed the West from its associations with the Arctic and sub-Arctic, and in their reports they introduced the notion of an agricultural or, in Hind's phrase, "fertile belt" coterminous with the parkland. Neither held out much hope for the settlement of the grasslands (Palliser's Triangle) in southwest Saskatchewan and southern Alberta. Dry and, according to Hind, without a shrub or bush thicker than a willow twig, they were deemed unfit for permanent habitation by civilized humanity.

The doors to settlement, nudged open by Palliser and Hind, were opened still wider by subsequent observers and commentators. A. J. Russell, Inspector of Crown Agencies in Canada, deplored "negative generalizations," and in a book published in 1869 he suggested, without having seen the West, that Hind and Palliser might well have underrated the agricultural potential of the grasslands. G. M. Dawson, the gifted young geologist and naturalist from Montreal who had gone West in 1873 to work on the International Boundary Survey, confirmed Russell's opinion. He examined the soil and surface materials of the southern prairies and concluded that a great area "was well suited for pastoral occupation and stock farming."

He also thought that some parts might even be cultivated. Palliser's triangle, that thorn in the flesh of the Canadian expansionist movement, was gradually being withdrawn.

The final removal of the triangle, and with it the taint of desert, had been the achievement of John Macoun, a government botanist and ardent supporter of Canadian expansion. Like A. J. Russell, he questioned the views of Palliser and Hind before setting foot on the grasslands; when he did survey them, in 1879 and 1880, his suspicions were confirmed. The 1870s were relatively wet years on the prairies and at the time of Macoun's reconnaissance the vegetation might well have been deceptively verdant. As a botanist, Macoun placed great store in plants as indicators of fertility. He was so confident of his judgement that, in a speech in 1881, he dismissed the idea of a fertile belt altogether; the West, he declared, was "all equally good land."

In *Manitoba and the Great North-West* (1882) Macoun pointed out that if rainfall were considered only in relation to the spring and summer months, "the period of vegetation" and the "harvest months," then the grasslands were well enough watered. Drawing on climatological theory then current in North America, he argued that humid air drawn inland by the heat and aridity of the central United States was wrung dry on mixing with cooler Canadian air. Thus, cold and northerly latitudes, traditionally the twin scourges of Canada, were turned to advantage. The result of this happy conjunction of air masses was a climate "not only exceptional as regards character" but, from the point of view of agriculture, "unsurpassed in any other part of the world."

Macoun's flattering assessment of the grasslands passed quickly from the official into the popular thought of Canada. The Governor General, Lord Lorne, visited Manitoba and the North-West during the summer of 1881. At a subsequent lecture in Ottawa, he noted that until the publication of Macoun's maps the grasslands south of Battleford had been consigned to the Great American Desert, whereas in fact they constituted a region that "could not be excelled for agricultural purposes." Restraint had collapsed. A region known to be spare, dry, and cold became "the flower garden of the continent" whose climate was "very much the same as it was in England thirty years ago."

Henry Youle Hind, who had advocated "a gradual process of cautious settlement, consistent with the extreme character of the climate and the very scanty fuel and water resources," was so disturbed by the excesses generated by Macoun's assessment that he emerged from semi-retirement in Windsor, Nova Scotia, to mount what proved to be an extraordinary attack on a set of scientific conclusions. In a series of published letters, previously written to government officials, he accused Macoun of falsifying climatic data, misquoting responsible authors, making spurious generalizations, and describing enormous tracts of country that he had never seen. The larger enemy — Macoun's employer, the Department of the Interior — he accused of subverting science to create a more favourable image of the West. Although disturbed by what he saw as the "progressive depravity of a once proud department," Hind's greater concern was for the prospective victims of government excesses: the "hundreds and thousands of unconscious immigrants waiting to be decoyed by the glozing tongue of the 'agent' with 'official' report in hand."

The Promoters

Against the hosannas that greeted Macoun's new map of the West, Hind's lone steadying voice stood no chance. The new map was a promoter's dream, a *tabula rasa* on which proponents of immediate and rapid settlement, now freed from awkward physical realities, could create the West of their dreams. The promoters-in-chief were the Dominion government and the Canadian Pacific Railway who, with no advertising experience of their own to draw on, followed American precedent and practice. American land and railroad companies recognized that, whereas the humid lands of the Mississippi Valley had virtually sold themselves, only pressure would sell the semi-arid lands of the plains. Through its London office, the C.P.R. bombarded the British and continental presses with information on Western Canada, and its agents trained a supporting fire of pamphlets, folders, and posters in Gaelic, Welsh, German, Dutch, and Norwegian onto the towns and cities of Europe. Prospective emigrants who might have escaped the salvos of print were hunted down by "travellers" who carried the gospel of emigration into far countrysides. No corner of Britain was left untouched; no station wall or hotel lobby was safe from one of the C.P.R.'s poster maps.

Hard on the heels of the travellers came special lecturers armed with a new and persuasive device, the lantern slide, which they were only too willing to lend to anyone keen on advancing Canadian interests. Before leaving Canada spokesmen for the company had been primed with information so that, on arrival in Europe, they were, as one English immigrant put it, "walking encyclopaedias" programmed to recite facts and figures at the merest flicker of interest. "Canadian crackers," as the agents were sometimes called, weren't allowed to advise people to emigrate, but they could spin webs of words to enmesh the unwary. Mary Hiemstra described the agent who had "mesmerised" her father as an intense man from whom words unwound steadily "like string from a ball."

For people in cities there were even more powerful lures. The airy offerings of the "crackers" were easily turned aside but even sceptics had to take note of the material evidence of the West's bounty. Decorated with paintings and photographs and samples of prairie soil and grain, C.P.R. immigration offices were seductive parlours designed to trap

A Canadian Government poster, no date, directed at the universal need for home. (Public Archives Canada, C 126302)

passing pedestrians. They were always placed in busy, fashionable quarters. Located near London Bridge and the Southern railway terminals, the London office was at one of the busiest pedestrian nodes in the empire. More people saw it, claimed a spokesman for the C.P.R., than either Mansion House or the Bank of England.

As well as the paintings and photographs on permanent display in the company offices, there were circulating collections that were hung in mechanics institutes, hotels, town halls, and marquees at agricultural fairs. Harvesting scenes were said to be particularly effective, and many a steamship agent traced his bookings to a photograph or a painting of a bountiful harvest. Country people who might never have visited an immigration office or seen a circulating collection, were reached by a wholly new kind of exhibit: the C.P.R.'s horse-drawn exhibition van. Decked out with prairie products, the van became a familiar sight on the country roads of England. To attract as many viewers as possible, the towns had been papered with handbills to announce the coming, and the van was then brought in on market days. In 1893 it attracted 1.75 million viewers in 593 different places.

In its promotion of the West the Dominion government was at first content to follow in the wake of the C.P.R. Early government advertising had been undertaken by the Departments of Agriculture and Immigration, but in 1892 government responsibility for advertising the West passed to the Ministry of the Interior. Four years later that Ministry acquired a new and dynamic head, the young Manitoba lawyer, businessman, and lay preacher, Clifford Sifton. Up to the time of Sifton's appointment, rates of immigration had been disappointing, in spite of the mammoth efforts of the C.P.R.; by 1896 they were almost at a standstill. Most European emigrants had chosen to go to the United States or Australia. Even Argentina and Brazil had proven to be more popular than Canada.

A Canadian government emigration office, Charing Cross, London, 1911. (Public Archives Canada, C 63257)

On taking office, Sifton took a large broom to the Department of the Interior — the "Department of Delay and Circumlocution" — and called for an extension of the immigration service and more ardent campaigning. He regarded the West as a commodity, distrusted by the rest of the world, that only vigorous promotion would sell: "Just as soon as you stop advertising and immigration work," he told the Canadian parliament, "the [immigration] movement is going to stop." Agents were exhorted to solicit recruits rather than wait for inquiries, and writers of advertising copy were expected to maintain an unbroken flow of ink. The output of pamphlets took a quantum leap — from 65,000 in 1896 to more than a million in 1900.

As well as increasing the volume of advertising, Sifton sharpened its focus and extended its geographical range. Whereas the C.P.R. had looked chiefly to Britain for immigrants and had recruited hairdressers, shop assistants, clerks, and mechanics in the hope that they would make husbandmen, Sifton cast a larger net with a more selective mesh. His quarry was the experienced farmer. The ideal immigrant, as one of his aides put it, was the man of good muscle who was willing to hustle. Americans were particularly prized. They had no barriers of language or culture to overcome and most had cash, equipment, and experience of prairie or continental conditions. They could be transplanted with a minimum of shock. To encourage them to move, Sifton set up immigration offices in the northern states.

His most imaginative departure from C.P.R. practice was to look for immigrants outside Canada's traditional hunting grounds. Britain continued to be the major focus of attention, but the British response had been disappointing. Sifton wondered whether even Scottish or northern English farmers would be able to tackle the most difficult Western lands: the heavy bush country on the northern edges of the park belt. Prospects for recruitment were no better in the other northern countries. Germany had virtually banned emigration, while Scandinavians had eyes only for the United States. The Mediterranean countries might have responded to a call for immigrants, but Sifton regarded southern Europeans as poor pioneer material for a cold continental region. Hardiness was the key, and Sifton judged that there was no shortage of it in the northern Slavs. He set his sights, therefore, on the crowded and impoverished peasant lands of the Austro-Hungarian empire. His intention raised the racial hackles of the Anglo-Saxon majority, and to suppress them he uttered his now-famous dictum: "I think a stalwart peasant in a sheepskin coat, born of the soil, whose forefathers have been farmers for ten generations, with a stout wife and half a dozen children is good quality." For good measure, he added that it takes two generations to convert a town bred population into an agricultural one, and that a country in urgent need of settlers "has no time for that operation."

To recruit Ukrainians and European peasants the Department of the

Interior had to resort to subterfuge. Most European governments regarded solicited immigration as theft, and outlawed emigration agencies.The void had been filled by steamship agents, who stood to profit from the traffic, and the practice evolved of paying bonuses to agents who directed emigrants toward Canada. With Sifton's approval, the Department of the Interior went a step further and organized a select group of shipping agents into The North Atlantic Trading Company. From Hamburg and Bremen hundreds of agents representing the company and the shipping lines fanned south and east into the villages of Galicia, Ruthenia, and Bukowina, where they fixed posters on church gates, distributed printed handbills, advertised in local newspapers, and spoke in village halls and country taverns. All promised free land; the less scrupulous added grants for subsistence and gifts of cattle and tools. No message had ever fallen on more receptive ears; within months emigration fever was coursing through the villages of eastern and south-eastern Europe.

Although the Dominion government and C.P.R. carried the brunt of the advertising, they had help from other quarters. The British government was also anxious to settle the West, and from time to time it urged Governors General to make promotional tours. The most publicised tour was engineered by Prime Minister Disraeli. Disturbed by slow rates of immigration, by the coolness of the British press toward Canada, and by the encroaching American settlement, Disraeli concluded that the best remedy would be a well-publicised tour by the young and attractive Marquis of Lorne, who was Queen Victoria's son-in-law as well as her representative in Canada. Lord Lorne entreated the editors of influential British newspapers and magazines to send their best reporters. Several obliged, but some were less than enthusiastic. John Walter of the *Times* thought that life in Canada was too commonplace to provide interesting copy, but in the end he relented and sent Charles Austin, one of his best men. The antithesis of Walter was William Luson Thomas, editor of the *Graphic,* a popular illustrated magazine. A staunch imperialist, Thomas regarded the West as a safe destination for British capital and as a safety valve for a population growing so rapidly that it threatened to burst the nation's seams. He devoted the *Graphic's* entire North American coverage to the settling of the Canadian West, and was only too pleased to send along his best artist-reporter, or "special," Sydney Prior Hall. The only Canadian reporter on the tour — Mr. Williams of the pro-West Toronto *Globe* — was a gate-crasher. As an uninvited guest he had to make his own travel arrangements and was frequently a day or two behind the main party.

Other help in promoting the West came from public-spirited individuals. Two of the most influential were John McDougall and George Munro Grant. McDougall, a Methodist missionary to the Cree and Stoney Indians, wrote half a dozen books on the West. Like Butler he loved the wilderness and feared for the Indians, but because he thought European settlement would prove beneficial in the long run, he travelled through Ontario as early as 1867–68 regaling audiences with first-hand accounts of the West and its resources. His contemporary, George Grant, was equally energetic and even more enthusiastic. Grant had been the recording secretary for the Sandford Fleming Expedition despatched in 1871 to find a route for the transcontinental railway. Disturbed by the slow rate of immigration, Grant wrote *Ocean to Ocean* in 1873, using notes made on the expedition, and followed it with *Picturesque Canada* in 1882. Both books were undisguised panegyrics.

The West as a prospective home for emigrants also attracted professional writers and observers. One of the earliest was Washington Frank Lynn, journalist, painter, and a founding member of Britain's Royal Colonial Institute. Lynn visted Ontario in 1868 and returned to Britain a vigorous supporter of emigration to Canada. In 1871–72 he visited both the American and the Canadian West, and he was as pleased with the latter as he was distressed by the former. He was critical of the U.S. Government for its neglect of immigrants on the journey west and for inequities in the system of land allocation. He was also disturbed by the prevalence of malaria. Lynn eventually settled in Manitoba, but before doing so he wrote pamphlets warmly recommending the colonial life.

After the completion of the C.P.R. in 1885 hardly a year passed without at least one travel book on Canada appearing on the lists of British publishers. Not all writers approved of what they saw, and the best-known may well have checked emigration. Rudyard Kipling raised the spectre of cold with his phrase, "My Lady of the Snows," and Rupert Brooke may have given traditionalists pause by remarking that in Canada the European would find nothing to satisfy the hunger of his heart. Canada had no haunted woods; no ghosts of lovers walked in Canadian lanes. But other writers were encouraging. Edward Roper, the English naturalist and illustrator, crossed Canada on the C.P.R. in 1887 and recorded his impressions in his book *By Track and Trail*. Roper was a keen imperialist and on his return to London he lectured under such titles as "What does it mean to Emigrate?" At his lectures he exhibited oils and watercolours of Western Canadian life.

But the most persuasive advertisers of the West, as Sifton had realised, were the settlers themselves. Whereas the organized literature was often distrusted, few questioned the veracity of letters from emigrant friends and relatives. "Let no one here listen to anybody but his own relatives whom he has here in this golden America," wrote a Scandinavian immigrant in Minnesota. Only a fraction of the letters written by immigrants have survived, but an examination of these suggests that they, too, would bear careful reading. Patently false were letters commissioned by steamship and emigration agents urging their countrymen to come to Canada. But even bona fide letters were often misleading. After the upheaval of departure, few were disposed to admit that emigration was painful, far less a mistake. Letters home tended to be justifications of the new life, and if, as sometimes happened, they found their way into the hands of skilled editors, they were easily transformed into near-panegyrics of life in the new land. But true or false, the letters usually had great currency. Passed from hand to hand and read aloud at family gatherings and village meetings, they spread the pro-emigration message in ways the official propagandists couldn't hope to match. In the Ukrainian provinces they helped create a "Canada fever" that was just as infectious as the America fever produced in Scandinavia by the "America letters" written by emigrants in far off Minnesota and Wisconsin.

A New Climate

The immediate task for promoters of settlement was to soften the image of the West. Travellers and adventurers might revel in "romantic horizons," but immigrants need settings that comfort and nurture. The first and most obvious target was the invidious prairie winter. Though the Palliser and Hind expeditions had dissociated the West from the Arctic and sub-Arctic, Western Canada was still widely regarded as a cold, dry plain that wouldn't break easily to the plough. Americans knew it as "a land of ice, snow, drought, and disillusionment," while for the English it was "the Siberia of the British Empire." London's merchant bankers and an important segment of the British press were far from convinced that the Canadian prairies were a safe home for British capital or British emigrants. The *Times* refused to endorse a region with "so rigorous a climate" and warned its readers against investing too heavily in Canada. A respected Dublin journal, *Nation,* described Manitoba as "a kind of Siberia" while the London journal *Truth,* in an editorial on the Canadian Pacific "Bubble," warned that if the railway was ever finished it would run through a "death dealing" country which was frost-bound for seven or eight months of the year and where to survive the people had to imitate the habits of the "Esquimaux."

Although the tones were sometimes alarmist, there was a kernel of truth in most of the observations. On the cold, windswept plains, settlers would have done well to build, if not igloos, then compact, streamlined dwellings. In most parts of the prairies the frost-free season is less than a hundred days, and Winnipeg's twin, climatically speaking, is the city of Irkutzk in central Siberia. But a Siberian connotation then was even less supportable than it is today.

After taking office, one of Clifford Sifton's first acts had been to ban the publication abroad of Manitoba temperatures. When his aides pointed out that a suggestive silence might be even more damaging than disclosure, Sifton relented, but not until he had forbidden all references to snow and cold in official publications. Snow-covered scenes were banned from immigration offices. Cold became a taboo word to be replaced by euphemisms for character-building discomfort, such as "bracing" and "invigorating." Earlier, the ebullient Sir William Van Horne had campaigned against the West's wintry image. He announced in London that the coldest weather he had ever known was in Rome and Florence, adding a rider of breath-taking audacity: "I pine for Winnipeg to thaw me."

In government publications climatic extremes were usually buried in monthly, seasonal, or yearly averages. The announcement of a mean temperature of 5 degrees F. for January, or 15 degrees F. for the winter season, disguised the fact that temperatures might frequently be a great deal colder and could even fall to 40 degrees F. below zero, the defining temperature that in Canadian folklore separates winters that are really cold from winters that are merely cold. A similar ploy was used with rainfall. Totals for the season of growth, which on the prairies is the more humid season, disguised the fact that annual amounts (14–20 inches) were meagre by eastern or European standards.

For Canada's chief rival in the immigration stakes the length and severity of the prairie winters was an obvious ace, and American editors, who feared a northward drift of their own settlers, used it to advantage. Manitoba and the Territories were vilified as "sandy, sterile wastes where vegetable growth [was impossible]" and where "snow and ice covered the ground for nine months of the year." Manitoba and the Territories responded by quoting the American climatologist Lorin Blodgett, who asserted that distance from the equator was not the only arbiter of temperature, and that the prairies were in fact a latitude-defying gulf of warmth.

The belief that all places on the same parallel of latitude have the same climate and produce the same plants had been popular since classical times. In his book *The Climatology of North America* (1857), however, Blodgett pointed out that ocean currents, continental masses, and winds also affect temperature. Using the relatively new concept of isothermal lines — that linked places with the same seasonal or annual temperatures — Blodgett demonstrated that in summer the North-West was warmer than places farther east: "In the interior, the public appreciation of the climate has been greatly at fault. By a peculiarity of configuration which exists in no other part of the temperate latitudes, it grows warmer in going northward in the interior. From Fort Massachusetts at the limit of the cultivated portion of New Mexico, at 37.5 N. latitude, to the plains of Saskatchewan at the 52nd parallel, the mean temperatures and the cultivable capacity steadily advance. On the Platte it is warmer and more cultivated than on the Upper Rio Grande; on the Missouri at Fort Benton, it is superior to the Platte, and on the Saskatchewan the country is better than on the Missouri, and all these points lie in prairie districts, yet the prairies of the Saskatchewan and the Assiniboine are equal if not superior to the others in fertility."

Blodgett concluded that mid-latitude crops could be grown successfully at these higher latitudes and, but for the "pernicious views" of fur traders bent on preserving them as wilderness, they would have been opened to civilization long since. The English journalist Washington Frank Lynn took the argument an unscientific step further by suggesting that the prairies were a gulf of stillness as well as a gulf of warmth. Lying in a basin protected by mountains to the West and the Shield to the north and east, the prairies, he argued, were spared "the gales so common in Kansas and Nebraska."

Though cold was the spectre most feared by promoters of the West, it was only one in a gallery of unfriendly ghosts. In spite of Macoun's blandishments, doubts remained about the adequacy of rainfall for farming in the drier parts of the grasslands. Unable to deny that rainfall might be only marginal for agriculture, the government sought to eliminate a source of potential embarassment by suppressing all references to dryness in government publications. Drought, like cold, became a taboo word.

Even the powerful William Pearce, the so-called Czar of the West, was made to heed the government veto. In an address to the Association of Dominion Land Surveyors in 1891, Pearce, who was then the Superintendent of Mines for the Department of the Interior, had recommended that guidelines be prepared for the legislation and control of irrigation water in the southwest. Shaken by the suggestion from a prominent official that nature might have been less than generous with water in the southwest, the government implored Pearce to make no more public statements about the need for irrigation, and forced him to cancel an address on the progress of irrigation in Canada that he was to have given to an international congress. Pearce's imputations also disturbed Sir William Van Horne who complained to the government that talk of water shortages in the southwest threatened the C.P.R.'s foreign securities and inhibited land sales.

Though effective in silencing its own officials, the government's embargo failed to contain the West's reputation for cold and drought, and news of them spread abroad. So, reasoned the promoters, if the West's cold, dry image couldn't be dispelled, might it not be turned to advantage? Alert to every opportunity, they lighted on the new science of climato-therapy. One of the central tenets of the science, based on observations dating at least from the time of Hippocrates, was that dry, cool air is healthier than warm, humid air. According to then-current medical theory, the decompositon of organic matter, which is more rapid in warm, humid regions than in cold, dry ones, created atmospheric gases or "miasmata" that endangered health. This particular correlation of the climato-therapists was later rejected, but there appeared to be no reason then to doubt its validity. Ague or malaria was most common in the warm, humid parts of the continent. It was the scourge of the Mississippi Valley in the nineteenth century, and it is likely that well over half the population south and west of New England suffered from it at one time or another. Although the disease had nothing to do with bad air *(mal-aria)* or miasmata, its carrier, the anopheles mosquito, liked breeding in wet, low-lying areas.

One of the first Canadians to attack the warmer, humid conditions south of the border was the well-known expansionist Charles Mair. America, Mair had warned, was the haunt of the deadly malarial mosquito and the source of poisonous exhalations from stagnant waters. He stopped just short of recommending plague masks as an appropriate prophylactic: air from the south had "danger on its breath" and brought with it "the dim edge of fever, the dread of pestilence and famine." Subsequent promoters of the West sustained the attack on the fetid American atmosphere, but they lacked Mair's dramatic intensity. The Marquis of Lorne advised immigrants to avoid regions "notorious for their cyclones, snakes and centipedes, or for ague and fever" and bade them remember "how healthy the conditions of life in the North are, and to what a great age men usually live [there]."

Alexander Begg, head of the C.P.R.'s Immigration Department, adopted a philosophical tone: "What use to the immigrant are fair fields and meadows, beautiful crops and the acquistion of wealth if, to obtain them, he is obliged to sacrifice his own health and that of his family." Safer by far to settle in Manitoba where "the almost total absence of fog or mist; the brilliance of the sunlight; the pleasing succession of the seasons all combine to make Manitoba a climate of unrivalled salubrity, and the home of a healthy, prosperous, and joyous people." One of the boasts of the Red River settlers was that the climate was so healthy that "a cough is scarcely ever heard among us." Nor, if the promoters are to be believed, was there ever a sneeze. According to one brochure there was no ragweed in the Canadian West and consequently no hay fever. "The air is fresh and clear. . . . The only sounds in summer are those of birds singing, cattle lowing, bees humming." The prairie was an Elysian field where, as one wag noted, undertakers had to kill in order to get a customer.

In his *Atlas of Western Canada* (1901), Sifton praised the climate in the brisk, take-it-or-leave-it tones that had become the hallmark of his administration. The Department of Circumlocution had been laid firmly to rest. "The climate of Western Canada, as described by those who have lived there for some years, is said to be very agreeable. Disease is little known, while epidemics are unheard of. Spring commences about the first of April. Some seasons, however, seeding is begun early in March, the snow having entirely disappeared." And: "The climate [of Saskatch-ewan] is healthy, and free from endemic or epidemic diseases. It is bracing and salubrious, and is undoubtedly the finest climate on earth for con-stitutionally healthy people. Average summer temperature about 60 degrees." Van Horne also championed the climate. Trapped in wet, dank Europe, he sighed for a beakerful of prairie air: "The atmosphere in the far West intoxicates you, it is so very invigorating."

A New Landscape

Although winter, the threat of drought, and sheer distance from Europe and the east were the chief deterrents to settlement, informed easterners and Europeans must also have had misgivings about the landscape. Most travellers and commentators had found the parkland appealing, but the grasslands had been almost universally displeasing. Even the parkland, whose similarities to the planted landscapes of England had enchanted early travellers, took on a different complexion when looked at through the eyes of prospective settlers. Edward Roper, the travel writer, noted that the open bluffs of the parkland gave the land a homelike and pictur-esque look, but the feeling in them, nevertheless, was one of loneliness. To attract settlers it was necessary to create the illusion of landscape not radically different from the one left behind. All emigrants expected to be able to make a home in the new land. The common vision, revealed in a ditty sung in Britain about the time of the First World War, was of a comfortable home in a congenial setting:

> *Will you come to Canada!*
> *To Canada! To Canada!*
> *Will you come to Canada with me?*
> *If you'll be my wife*
> *You'll have a very happy life*
> *In your cozy Canadian home.*

To make the landscape seem more homely, descriptions of it had to reduce the scale and suggest comforting enclosures rather than sublime panoramas. Description also became more detailed because prospective settlers wanted information as close to photographic accuracy as possible. Generalized descriptions couched in sonorous prose gave way to something far more comforting and comprehensible. A letter solicited by the Department of the Interior from a Mennonite delegation to Sas-katchewan in 1898 diminished the landscape and converted it into a cliché of groves, meadows, and cultivated fields: "The grass grows very close, and the growth is wonderfully nutritious, which was to be seen by the fat cattle in the neighbourhood. The newly planted wheat seemed in splen-did condition and promises a rich crop. Altogether the whole district is very encouraging and hopeful to us. It is a nice prairie, covered with beautiful grass, and dotted here and there with little poplar forests which give the whole a very romantic appearance. The settlers whom we visited look forward to a very happy and contented future, and we thank God that He laid the way open for them to erect their houses in this part of the earth."

For readers with literary inclinations this remarkable conconction appeared in Sifton's *Atlas of Western Canada:*

> *A Drive Never to be Forgotten*
> *The heavy dew of the night before lay like a veil of gray chiffon over the landscape, and as the lazy mid-summer sun lifted itself from a rose-coloured cloud-bed, the veil shivered and sparkled as though sprinkled with diamond dust. Through tangled copsewood we drove for hours, now and then skirting a "slough" (pronounced slew), encircled with a great belt of rushes, standing with uplifted torches of velvety brown. . . . Again emerging from the wonderful jungle, our eyes were dazzled by a veritable field of cloth of gold, the transparent petals of the graceful prairie sunflowers showing acres of molten gold against the sky-line of deepest blue.*

The most sustained attack on the image of the West as an empty, intimidating land was made by George Grant, one of the earliest promoters of settlement. *Ocean to Ocean* (1873), published within a year of Butler's *The Great Lone Land,* was a landmark in the history of perceptions of the West. Whereas Butler had directed his book at "prisoners of civilization," Grant aimed his unerringly at the prospective farmer. Although scornful of "buncome," i.e. the "irresponsible promotion of lands unsuited to agricultural settlement," Grant was a positivist whose guiding principle was that positive evidence is much more valuable than negative. The doctrine was convenient because it allowed him to see only what he thought he should see. Nuisances such as the locust and dreaded mosquito could be overlooked: "myths as far as we could learn." Winters were more pleasant than in Ontario, Quebec, and the Maritimes and — in an oblique reference to wheat grown in missions to the north of the North Saskatchewan River — the way to avoid frost was to go north. The only fault he could find was, in effect, a virtue: in places the soil was so rich and fat that grain grown on it produced too much straw.

Unlike adventurers and romantic travellers, whom only wild nature pleased, Grant had eyes only for the picturesque, the pleasant, and the productive. When he looked at the prairie he saw a soft and gentle garden needing only the ploughs of settlers to stir it into productive life. "Come plough, sow, and reap us" whispered the urgent prairie winds. He wrote of the valley of the North Saskatchewan: "A lovely country, well wooded, abounding in lakelets, swelling into softly rounded knolls and occasionally opening into a wide and fair landscape. . . . We were in a country that could easily be converted into an earthly paradise." A few years earlier John McDougall had beheld a similar vision. He, too, was anxious to dispel the image of the West as a place of "immense meadows" and like Grant, took the view that human occupation was beneficial, "We drove early and late through the northern slope of the Great Saskatchewan Valley . . . through its rich pastures and over it rich soils . . . it is easy to imagine this reclaimed part of our heritage dotted with prosperous homes. All day long . . . I was locating houses, and selecting sites for village corners."

In *Picturesque Canada* (1882) Grant extended the Arcadian vision. Thanks to John Macoun's recent delivery of the grasslands from the grip of semi-aridity the entire region, Grant avowed, could now be proclaimed the Garden of the World. In time, images of the West as a productive land dominated the advertising. Sifton, for example, concluded that the most effective way of wooing immigrants was to concentrate on the West's tangible assets — the rich soils, the summer heat, and the long summer days. Descriptions of wooded valleys and coulees, of charming alternations of woodland and grassland, were gradually dropped from government publications. By 1903, in Sifton's *Evolution of the Prairie by the Plow,* the prairie west of Winnipeg had become a gigantic wheatfield: "Travel from Winnipeg westward, it is all the same story; nothing between your eye and the skyline but wheat, wheat. . . . Here and there rise the tall, red, hump-shouldered elevators, where settlements have clustered into villages, but across the fenceless, unbroken expanse, nothing but wheat, wheat, wheat."

Drawings, paintings, and photographs of the prairie made or taken after 1880 simply affirmed the image of a land that was both productive and picturesque. The pattern was set by F. B. Schell who did the illustrations for *Picturesque Canada.* Schell's drawings show wooded stream courses and settled, productive landscapes. Horizon lines set high diminished prairie space, and foregrounds filled with flowers and clumps of grass masked the emptiness of the landscape. Schell's prairie was cribbed and confined. Most of his prairie drawings were made in Manitoba where the garden image had an ideal vehicle in the villages built by Mennonites who had come, a few years earlier, from southern Russia. Villages were not characteristic of prairie settlement. Clusters of picturesque houses, windmills, and herds of cattle tended by cowgirls in traditional European dress gave the lie to Butler's conception of the prairie as a great lone land.

Schell's methods of reducing prairie space became standard in the promotional material. Drawings, paintings, and photographs in posters and pamphlets issued by the government and the C.P.R. seldom betrayed the true nature of the prairie. Landscapes were limited, inhabited, and

The cover of an emigration booklet circulated in Holland in the mid-1880s. (Glenbow Archives, Calgary, Alberta)

"A Prairie Farmstead, the Northwest Manitoba," Picturesque Canada, *1882.*
F. B. Schell's methods of diminishing prairie space became standard in the pro-
motional material. Horizon lines were kept high and empty foregrounds were
filled in. (Public Archives Canada, C 82967)

productive. Captions from the photographs in Sifton's *Atlas* are instructive: "Representative Homes of Those Who have Succeeded," "Some of
the Great Mills and Elevators," "Giant Roots and Vegetables," "A Western
Canadian Orchard." Occasional drawings in the sketchbooks of the special
artists who worked for the illustrated magazines showed expanses of
empty prairie, but if submitted to their editors they were never published.
The "specials" had some feeling for emigrants who would give up home
and country for pioneer life and most, too, were well aware of the persuasive power of pictures. "Sketches," wrote Sydney Prior Hall of the
Graphic, "set a person to thinking and they might convey ideas which
written description would not, and prompt people to become better
acquainted with the country."
    Yet, however strong the desire to be objective, the "specials" and their
fellow journalists were victims of context. Most worked for magazines
that were strongly imperialist, and they all travelled as guests of the
government or the C.P.R. Often, too, they accompanied Governors
General on promotional tours of the West. Their role had been to record
the civilizing of a once wild land by people of predominantly Anglo-
Saxon stock. In keeping with such a desirable event, their sketches were
cheerful and lively and their reports flattering. In a July 1881 issue of

"A Settler's Home near Carberry, Assiniboia," Edward Roper, 1891. Drawings and paintings in travel books and the illustrated press usually romanticized pioneer life. (Public Archives Canada)

the *Graphic,* Sydney Prior Hall wrote that the North-West was "a glorious heritage, and comprises the best and most desirable lands now open for free settlement in any quarter of the globe." A month later the reporter for the London *Daily Telegraph* noted that Manitoba, far from being a northerly, inhospitable land and a paradise for the Esquimaux, was "softer in climate and more fertile than many of the wide-stretching lands very far south of it; that owing to certain atmospheric causes not yet quite determined, it is never troubled by the excesses of frost and cold of other countries in the same latitude."

Commentators who managed to retain a sense of proportion were so few that their voices were drowned by the trumpetings of the promoters. Josef Oleskow, a soil scientist, agronomist, and promoter of Ukrainian emigration, had tried to prepare his countrymen for what lay ahead of them in Canada. In his lengthy booklet *O Emigratsii* he advised the penniless not to emigrate and warned of the need to adopt new patterns of behaviour and dress, and new standards of hygiene. He had also been forthright about the Western Canadian climate. He thought the winters too cold for fruit and orchards to survive and the summers too short to ripen cucumbers and beans. Oleskow had also been careful to point out that the word "homestead," for which there was no exact equivalent in Ukrainian, was an area of undeveloped land. In other immigrant literature the word had been replaced by the neologism *farma,* which was not always distinguished from the Ukrainian word for farm (*hospodarstvo*) with its connotation of buildings and cultivated fields. Similarly, the use of the Ukrainian word *pole* to describe non-wooded areas might also have been misleading. In the Ukraine, *pole* indicated open land or a field, and it seems likely that some emigrants would have expected to get cultivated as distinct from cultivable land. In the provinces of Galicia and Bukowina it had been widely rumoured that immigrants to Canada were provided with a farm, a home, and even cattle.

Edward Roper also had few illusions about the hardships of pioneer life. He warned that the price of prosperity was immediate loneliness, and that for every successful settler there was another who succumbed to the summer heat, the awful winter cold, and mosquitoes. Roper found the grasslands desolate: "cold, bare, bleak in the extreme — no gardens, no fences, no roads . . . loneliness, utter loneliness." Yet his paintings conveyed one of the desolation that he sometimes felt. Like most observers he concentrated on the improved rather than the primitive landscape, painting farmsteads and ploughed fields chiefly in the parkland. Roper's one painting of the grasslands showed not "the most monotonous country" of the text but a substantial farmstead flying the Union Jack. When he picked up his brush Roper, too, shared the common vision of a plain divided by hedges and fences into regular fields and sprinkled liberally with groves of trees and substantial dwellings.

"A Home in the Great West," Canadian Illustrated News, September 11, 1880. (Public Archives Canada, C 7561l)

The misleading nature of the promotional material drew some contemporary criticism. Probably the most severe critic was John Donkin,
a young Englishman who served for four years as a corporal with the
North-West Mounted Police. Though he himself was only adventuring
in Canada, Donkin saw clearly what the settlers were up against. In
Trooper and Redskin (1889), his vivid account of service with the
N.W.M.P., Donkin tried to offset the misleading fare of the promoters.
He was particularly critical of visiting journalists who saw the West only
through the windows of heated and upholstered Pullman cars. Treated
with unbounded courtesy and feted at every halting place en route, it
would have been churlish of them, he noted, not to place their pens and
pencils in the service of the "wondrous glories of the great North-West."
They saw nothing of what lay behind the scenes, and because of their
"arrowy flight" they knew nothing of the vast stretch of wild and lonesome
land that lay beyond the railway. Yet ignorance, Donkin noted acidly,
didn't prevent them from sending forth their impressions with much
dogmatic assertion. Donkin died tragically in a workhouse shortly after
his return to England, and it is unlikely that his book was widely read.

More studied criticism of the promotional literature came from the
noted Canadian scholar Adam Shortt. Shortt contended in 1895 that the
promotional literature was grossly deceptive, and that instead of help-
ing the country it was proving to be its most serious drawback. In particular, he feared that reckless advertising south of the border would
backfire by attracting only undesirable immigrants—the unstable, the
mortgage-eaten, and the poverty-stricken. The industrious, the shrewd,
the thrifty, the enterprising, and the self-reliant were not likely, he wrote,
to be caught by the promoter's chaff. Even Clifford Sifton had said that
he was disturbed by the rhetoric of government and C.P.R. advertising
and, on taking office in 1896, he advised his aides that statements about
the West should be "fair, not too favourable." His aim had been to impress
the ordinary, and perhaps sceptical, farmer with "the sense of reality."
But in the heavily oxygenated atmosphere of the turn-of-the-century West,
maintaining a sense of reality was far more easily said than done.

There is no way of knowing precisely what immigrants to the prairies
expected to find on arrival, but what is clear is that few could have anticipated the reality. For every immigrant who might have read one of
the few disinterested travel books or, even less likely, a scientific report,
there were a thousand whose image of the region had been framed by
propaganda produced by government, the Canadian Pacific Railway, and
public-spirited authors and journalists.

No one today would quarrel with Edward McCourt's assertion that
the advertising literature was the purplest prose ever written about Western
Canada. It was flattering at best, wilfully misleading at worst, and it
could be condemned out of hand. Yet a more tolerant view is possible.

The promoters operated in a context of high emotion and high expectations. Canada wanted the West settled, and quickly, and no means was seen as too questionable to bring about that desirable end. It was a time in the history of the Europeanized world when, as George Orwell contended, wealth and material progress were admired to the point of being confused with moral virtue. Vulgarity reigned, perhaps a little more obviously in Western Canada than elsewhere. With wheat prices rising after the depression of the 1890s, and good land available for the taking, the future of the West looked golden. When the promoters looked about them they saw the prairie as it would become, not as it was. The vision was millennial, and almost everyone was dazzled by it.

Chapter Two

THE WEST ON THE EVE OF MASS EUROPEAN SETTLEMENT

Settlers from Ontario, Quebec, Iceland, and southern Russia who arrived in the 1870s and 1880s, in advance of the main settlement, found a land touched only lightly by human beings. Save for their trails, the Indians had left the prairie unmarked and, after signing the seventh and final treaty, in 1877, all their territories were reduced to reserves. Europeans and Métis were numerous only in Manitoba, and most of their settlements clung to the banks of the Assiniboine and Red Rivers. The largest group were the Métis, sons and daughters of Saulteaux, Cree, or Assiniboine mothers and French fathers. They had lived for more than fifty years in uneasy balance between civilization — a fixed residence and a potato patch along the Red River — and seasonal movements onto the western plains or northern waters to work as huntsmen, tripmen. and guides. Each summer and fall entire Métis communities, except for the old and the disabled, ventured onto the plains in search of buffalo that were killed for their meat and their skins. As tripmen, the Métis carried furs and trade goods on the York boats of the Hudson's Bay Company, or they contracted to carry freight by cart along the Red River to St Paul, or along the North Saskatchewan to Fort Carlton and Edmonton. Tripping was seasonal, casual, and varied.

Alongside the Métis lived the descendants of colonists who had come from Europe and eastern Canada early in the nineteenth century. They included French Canadian voyageurs from Quebec, Orkneymen who had come out to work for the Hudson's Bay Company, and the luckless Scotch and Irish settlers who had followed the impractical Lord Selkirk. Selkirk had made no provisions for their arrival — "not a plough or a harrow" — and in June 1815 more than half the colony left for Ontario.

Whether Métis, French, or Scotch, the settlements were physically alike. Whitewashed log cabins and houses of the more substantial Red River frame construction lined the banks of the rivers, while behind them stretched the long, narrow lots derived from the river ranges of old Quebec. The original lots were about five hundred feet wide and two miles long, and to each was added a hay-cutting "privilege" that gave each property a *de facto* extension onto the prairie. Behind the houses ran corduroy roads that bound the individual dwellings into tight communities. The sight of the settlements heartened the English journalist and painter, Washington Frank Lynn, who first saw them from the deck of a slow-moving Red River flat-boat which was taking him from the terminus of the St Paul and Pacific Railroad to Winnipeg in 1872. For the previous two weeks Lynn had seen nothing but empty and daunting Red River lowland, a "flat and uninhabited waste, stretching away to a blue line on the horizon." But after Pembina, when the Red River settlement came into view, his heart leapt up and for an instant he was reminded of rural England: "The plastered houses looked so white and neat with their haystacks and outbuildings and patches of corn and vegetables around them. Small herds of cattle were browsing on the plain or were being driven home to their corrals by picturesquely garbed and dark-skinned little half-breed boys."

As a group only the Selkirk Scots had farmed seriously, but because drought, flood, grasshoppers, and hail caused frequent crop failures, they, too, had taken part in the buffalo hunts. Farm produce didn't replace pemmican — a mixture of fat and dried, powdered buffalo meat — until after 1870, and even Winnipegers depended upon it when crops failed. As in the highland villages of Scotland, only the river lands were cultivated. The best drained land was on the raised natural banks or levees close to the river. Behind the levees were low-lying flats that dried slowly in the spring; they were useful for rough grazing and haying, but poor drainage and a cover of tough sod discouraged cultivation. Farming methods on the river lands were primitive. The Scots had left home before the new agriculture that revolutionized English farming in the nineteenth century had taken root in the Scottish highlands. When dry enough in the spring the land was broken with ploughs of oak and iron and sown with wheat that was broadcast and then harrowed into the ground. Barley, oats, potatoes, and perhaps some Indian corn, followed. Vegetables, including melons and pumpkins, were garden crops.

Farmers clung to the rivers even in well-drained areas, despite the obvious advantages of farming open prairie. A contributor to the *Manitoban* noted in September 1871 that on the prairie there was no need to prostrate the monarchs of the forest, nor grub for soil amidst burly roots, nor wait years for sun and rain to rot charred stumps. He concluded that the Manitoban farmer began where the eastern Canadian farmer ended after years of toil. Yet the need for water, shelter, and wood for fuel were paramount, and these were available only in the valleys. The universal reluctance to move away from the rivers placed such pressure on available land that subdivision of the long lots reduced some of them to mere slivers. The narrowest on record was forty-five feet wide and four miles long. Settlement reached as far south as Pembina near the American border before it extended a mile from the rivers. Overland trails and the Red River cart reduced dependency on the waterways as a means of communication, but the rivers did make travel easier, and the settlements strung like beads along the banks satisfied the desire for neighbourhood. Weigh these advantages against the difficulties of life on the "main" prairie, and the appeal of the Red and the Assiniboine Rivers is easily understood.

West of the Red and the Assiniboine the prairie, in what was then the Territories of Assiniboia, Saskatchewan, and Alberta, was still held, as John Donkin put it, in the "hush of an eternal silence." Except for smaller game such as deer, prairie chicken, and ducks, the "mighty pastures" were empty. The buffalo had been hunted to the point of extinction; the Indians had withdrawn onto reserves. The confinement of the Indians brought to an end the aboriginal way of life. To advocates of agricultural settlement, the Indian culture was simply an anachronism that stood in the way of material progress. They might have admired the nature craft of the Indians and wondered at their prescient or, as they sometimes put it, "uncanny" knowledge of the prairie, but there was no question of savage instinct being allowed to stand in the way of civilized progress. Painter/ethnographers such as George Catlin and Paul Kane had recognized that Indian ways of life represented a fine adjustment to the prairie environment. So, too, had French and Scottish fur traders and Red River settlers, who adopted many Indian practices. But for later immigrants, schooled in nineteenth-century science and technology, Indian culture must have seemed infinitely remote. The contrast between the Indian's knowledge of the prairie and his consummate ability to survive, and the ignorance and incapacity of the homesteader, is a striking discontinuity in Western Canadian history.

To survive by hunting and gathering, prairie Indians had to be familiar with the habits and haunts of the animals they hunted, and to know where they might find drinking water, edible roots, berries, and wild rice. Indian names — Many Berries, Clearwater, White Mud Creek, etc. — were always descriptive of the places to which they applied. Under normal conditions game was abundant, and within the tribal hunting grounds it was common property. Fish swarmed in the lakes and rivers, and beaver, muskrat, rabbit, and wildfowl were plentiful. Buffalo, elk, deer, and antelope were also available in large numbers. Buffalo were the mainstay of the prairie tribes. The great herds provided food, shelter, clothing, wrappings, containers, thread, rope, implements, toys, and even fuel in the form of buffalo-dung chips.

Virtually everything that grew had some use. Berries and fruits were an important supplement to the diet although not considered real food (*natapi waksui*) by the Blackfeet. Dried or fresh saskatoon berries were added to soups, stews, and meats; wild strawberry and raspberry leaves were used to make tea; wild mint was a flavouring for meat and pemmican, and the sap of the Manitoba maple provided hard cakes of sugar. Arrow shafts came from the straight stems and branches of the western snowberry, chokecherry, and saskatoon, while bows were made of yew and ash. A framework of cottonwood covered with buffalo hide was the Blackfoot saddle; the bark of the cottonwood was a remedy against alkali-tainted drinking water, and the buds of the cottonwood a source of yellow dye. The inner bark of the aspen was winter feed for horses; sedges and grasses stuffed into moccasins were a protection against extreme cold; soft moss was used to line cradles and, with pads of cattail down, served as diapers. The boiled roots of the cherry tree and the saxifrage plant were a recognized cure for diarrhoea; earth moulds were a treatment for wounds while the dry, powdery interior of certain toadstools was used as a styptic to stop bleeding. Plant medicines were legion.

When buffalo were plentiful and their movements predictable the living might not have been easy, but it was, as Commissioner Sir Cecil Denny of the N.W.M.P. remarked, "self supporting, almost rich, and certainly contented." When serving as a captain in southern Alberta he found that, when they had meat in the lodges, no people were happier than the Blackfeet. Alex Johnston, a modern student of Indian life, came to a similar conclusion: "The way of life the Indians created after the acquisition of the horse was such that few men anywhere in the world had known more independence or greater security." But by 1880 their independence and security had gone. The buffalo and much of the smaller game had been eliminated, and the Indians had lost most of their former hunting grounds. A people who had once enjoyed "the full confidence of glorious liberty," as the English officer Henry James Warre noted, were shuffled onto reserves where they camped in river bottoms and scratched the earth to grow a few vegetables.

The Territories were also the home of Métis refugees from Manitoba. As mystified as their full-blood cousins by the principle of property in land, and with their livelihood threatened by the arrival of steamboats and railways, many had come west after the uprising of 1869–70 in the hope of maintaining their semi-nomadic way of life. As Roman Catholics they had been attracted to the missions of the Oblate Fathers; near them they reconstituted the kinds of farm villages they had known on the Assiniboine and Red Rivers. From the villages they made frequent excursions onto the prairies while there were still buffalo. They also fished in the lakes and streams for pike and whitefish, gathered wild rice and berries, and grew potatoes and cabbages on their river lots. Gardening and small-

"Red River cart and Half Breed Camp," W. M. Notman, 1889. Though they owned river lots, Métis had no real grasp of the notion of land as property. (Notman Photographic Archives, McGill University, 2031)

scale farming took up only a few weeks in the summer and were seldom pursued vigorously. Ideas of industry and learning that the Oblate Fathers tried to instill failed to impress the Métis, who could see no reason to exchange a carefree, if precarious, existence for a careful one.

Even less convinced of the virtues of a settled, industrious life were the entirely nomadic Métis, the winter-rovers or *hivernants,* who had no permanent settlements. The most Indian of the Métis, they moved around in all seasons, not just in the winter as their name suggested. They preferred portable skin lodges to cabins, and they set up their winter camps in wooded hill ranges and valleys that ran through the buffalo pasture regions. The valleys of the South Saskatchewan, the Red Deer, and the Whitemud were especially attractive to them. Elk and bear were plentiful in the valleys, and antelope moved in great numbers across the aprons of the hills. Beaver, mink, otter, and muskrat were available in the smaller streams, and as late as 1873 a party spent several days riding twenty to thirty miles a day through a placidly grazing buffalo herd. But by 1880 the buffalo had gone, and the replacement of the York boat and Red River cart by steamboat and railway cut at the roots of native life. Cribbed and confined, their means of sustenance gone, Indian and Métis alike were about to join the buffalo as former residents of the prairie, at least in any vital way. By 1885, the year of the railway, all that remained of native ways of life was a mesh of trails cut by the hooves of horses, oxen, and buffalo, and the wheels of Red River carts.

European life in the Territories was restricted to a handful of Hudson's Bay and N.W.M.P. forts, a few clusters of civilian settlement along the rivers, and the route of the C.P.R., and some scattered ranches in southern Alberta and Saskatchewan. To a large extent, the civilian settlements had complemented rather than clashed with native culture. Locations had been chosen without government or other institutional restraints, and in this sense they were "organic." The settlements were all on creeks and rivers, and usually near woodland. But homesteaders who arrived after the land had been surveyed and subdivided were frequently directed to particular locations by land agents and; survey markers determined the shape and orientation of their fields and farms.

The activity that most complemented the native way of life and disturbed the prairie environment least was ranching. As a form of stock raising, it differed from eastern stock farming both in the rancher's use of the horse and in the need for large unfenced acreages where cattle could graze freely. The earliest ranchers in the Territories had spread northward from the American plains in the 1870s and, as in the United States, they were the first Europeans to make economic use of the grasslands. The government favoured them at first. Anxious to establish a supply of meat and fulfill its promise of provisioning the Indians, the Canadian government presented the Territories as God's gift to cattlemen, granted leases of up to 100,000 acres at a nominal rent of one cent per acre per year, and introduced and underwrote a stock-breeding programme. Purebred stock were carried free of charge by the C.P.R.

Rancher responses to the prairie will be examined later but it may be noted here that ranching, like hunting and gathering, was an adjustment to the prairie, never a ravage. Indians and ranchers practiced what we would now describe as adaptive ways of life, and both, for that time and place, were out of date. Ranchers, of course, fared better than Indians, but they, too, had to make way for the homesteader, the standard bearer of progress. Civilization, as we understand the term, was the creation of sedentary — that is, farming — societies and their attendant towns and cities. Nomads leave no monuments. Ranchers and Indians might have appealed to the romantic imagination, but by resisting sedentary ways of life they threatened civilized values. The spirit of the age was against them; they were no match for the homesteader. Their legacy, a filigree of trails that spread tentatively over the prairie, was shunted aside by the arrow-straight lines of road, railway, and farm boundary.

Chapter Three

REACTIONS TO THE PRAIRIE

For settlers from Europe and Eastern Canada, the prairie was not just strange; it was probably stranger than they could have imagined. Except for the Mennonites and the Doukhobors, they had known only landscapes filled with trees and hills and hedgerows, and there had been little in the advertising to suggest that the prairie would be radically different from anything they had known. Evan Davies, an intelligent and literate Welshman who emigrated in 1904, expected to find a landscape similar to the one he had left behind: "We had visualized a green country with hills around and happy people as neighbours — no doubt a naïve outlook . . . but one common to many people emigrating at the time." Other immigrants probably arrived with no expectations at all. Ivan Pillipiw, one of the first Ukrainians in the West, declared that many of his country-men had no idea of what they were coming to: "Our people who left home with the world in their eyes had not even the remotest idea of where they were going. . . . They knew neither the geography nor the language of the country to which they were going."

To many of the immigrants, a great plain covered with grasses or, at best, patches of small, thin trees seemed not just spacious, but vacant: "not a country at all," as Willa Cather's Jim Burden said of Nebraska, "but the material from which countries are made." William F. Butler set the tone for subsequent reactions to the Canadian prairies when he wrote in 1856: "This utter negation of life, this complete absence of history. . . . One saw here the world as it had taken shape from the hands of the Creator." A sense of barely finished nature also assailed Norah Armstrong, Edward McCourt's Irish-born heroine. She saw the hated Saskatchewan prairie as "[a land] from which the hand of God had been withdrawn before the act of creation was complete." And for Marie

35

Hamilton, an unliterary child from Ontario, the prairie was simply "a new and naked land."

To the explorers and early settlers the grasslands seemed so much more like ocean than land that the very nomenclature of the plains came to suggest water travel. A long, low line of sweeping hills was a "coteau," or coast, and short leaps across open prairie were "traverses," the voyageurs' term for a short trip across a wind-swept lake. To be in a landscape in which there were no hills and trees was to be "out of sight of land." As if to anticipate the ocean metaphor, the Indians had referred to open prairie as the "bare land," and from their sheltered campsites in wooded hills and valleys on the edges of the prairie they spoke of distant buffalo herds as "passing far out," like ships at sea. Indian maps, or mental images of the region, suggested that they approached the grasslands warily. When fur trader Peter Fidler sketched a map of the plains based on a description by the Blackfoot Chief Little Bear, he drew a line along the rim of the map and called it "Wood's Edge." The boundary may not have represented the edge of the known world, as did the boundaries of ancient European maps, but it does suggest that the world beyond the woods was less completely known.

For newcomers who found themselves in open, featureless parts of the prairies two anxieties surfaced immediately: fear of getting lost and fear of being caught in open prairie during a fire or a storm. Refuges were few even in the parkland, and the sense of exposure was often acute. It could even be disabling; readers of O. E. Rolvaag's *Giants in the Earth*

"View of the Prairies," pencil sketch (unpublished), Sydney Prior Hall, 1881. Sketches of empty prairie were seldom published by the illustrated magazines. (Public Archives Canada)

will recall how a terrified Beret Holm climbed into a trunk in her cabin during a thunderstorm on the North Dakota prairie. Prairie storms, which tend to be of biblical proportions, were awesome: "wild struggles between earth and sky," as the young James Minifie put it, "not English Midlands fireworks." Lightning was the chief cause of the dreaded prairie fires, against which there was little protection in the early period of settlement. With few natural or artificial firebreaks to overcome, flames at furnace heat raced frighteningly before the wind. Until they had ploughed the prairie and created protective belts of fields around their houses, early settlers dreaded them. "Since coming to the homestead [in Alberta]," wrote Sarah E. Roberts, "I have been in abject fear of two things — of being caught in a prairie fire and of getting lost." A frustrated correspondent to the *Brandon Times* wrote, in 1887, that anyone caught firing the prairie in the fall "would meet that summary justice that would save all legal disputes in the matter."

Without landmarks to guide them, Europeans lost their bearings with disturbing ease. In the bare lands, Indians navigated by relationships, not fixed points, rather like sailors on open sea; they were guided by the position of the sun, by the direction and feel of the wind, and by the lie of the grass. It was said of Jerry Potts, the half-breed police scout, that he knew the prairie better than homesteaders knew their quarter-sections, and that he could pick his way through the strongest blizzard and the blackest night. Subtle changes of scene, of sun, and of wind escaped most Europeans who saw only a featureless landscape. Even when moving they felt they were getting nowhere. Evan Davies noted that in Wales he had usually faced the direction in which he was travelling because he liked to see what lay ahead, but on the prairie it didn't matter because the view was always the same. The anonymity of the landscape struck home when he finally reached his quarter section: "What was there to distinguish it from all the rest of the land we had seen . . . . ? Nothing, nothing at all!"

Though the prairie would acquire fields, fences, elevators, and towns, the patterns they made were so unvaried that they failed to dispel the anonymity of the landscape. Travellers can still feel they are standing still, though moving at high speeds. On certain temperaments, the effects of movement in undifferentiated space can be very disturbing. Dr. Henry Osmond, a former director of the Saskatchewan Mental Hospital at Weyburn, observed in the foreword to *Land of Hope* that "Journeys on the prairies have a nightmarish quality [for town dwellers and those used to small, broken countries], dozens, scores, even hundreds of miles revolve on the speedometer and yet there is the same stretch of stubble and slough, the same ribbon of road and ditch, the same half dozen elevators."

In open prairie, features that offered shelter from the elements and relief from enveloping space were a solace. Wooded hills and valleys pleased everyone. As they approached Saskatoon in 1883, members of

Gerald Willoughby's party thrilled to the sight of "real" trees — Manitoba maples, cottonwoods, and an occasional ash — beside Beaver Creek. After miles and miles of broad prairie, the creek looked "like a touch of home." For Georgina Binnie Clarke, the Qu'Appelle Valley, where she home-steaded alone, was that "exquisite oasis of the prairie." Farther south, on bare uplands in the short grass prairie of southwest Saskatchewan, valleys were havens from scorching winds and a blistering sun. The young Wallace Stegner, whose parents homesteaded on a baking flat in hot, dry country just north of the border, had reason to be grateful for the willow-covered valley of the Whitemud River: "That sunken bottom sheltered from the total sky and the untrammeled wind was my hiber-nating ground, my place of snugness, and in a country often blistered and crisped, green became the colour of safety. When I feel the need to return to the womb, this is the place toward which my well-conditioned unconscious turns like an old horse heading for the barn."

Dry, spare country that neither sheltered nor pleased the eye appealed to few immigrants. A wry cockney in Manitoba told Edward Roper, "there's a lot more scenery wanted in this country, ain't there!" Other settlers reacted more dramatically: "O, the prairie . . . its vastness, dreariness, loneliness is appalling . . . like the sea on a very smooth day, without beginning or end," exclaimed an Englishwoman in Manitoba. Norwegian Iver Bernhard spoke for all immigrants when he wrote: "How could people from beautiful enchanting mountains endure life on this flat moor without even a decent hill to look at? . . . . On this great plain it seemed there could be nothing to aspire to for long. All poetry and yearning were as though left out of life, or would be smothered if they appeared."

Eyes accustomed to near views were distressed by a landscape so flat and featureless that it seemed to be nothing but horizon. On the drive from the railway station to her brother's homestead, Lucy L. Johnson of London at first thrilled to "the peace that comes with the wide open spaces," but some hours later she complained to her brother of the distance they had to travel. He told her to forget the distance. "As if I could! Every time I gazed across the prairie, it looked like the same old place to me. . . . All I could see was sky and straw-coloured grass . . . and a few trees about every million miles."

Frederick Niven, the novelist, told of meeting a distraught young man in a city hotel who had recently decided that he was "through with" the prairie. He gave as his reason the view from his pioneer shack, and to demonstrate this he pointed to a window sill. "If you just focus your eyes on that window-sill," he remarked, "and imagine, you'll have the view from my homestead. The front of the sill is the beginning of the prairie outside my house; the farther side of the hill is the horizon. Got it?" He quit the homestead on a day when he was working outside and,

Settlers from the American plains crossing the prairie of southern Alberta c. 1905. Settlers from Europe and eastern North America came by transcontinental railway. (Public Archives Canada, C 37957. Reproduced with permission from the Glenbow Archives)

desperate for the sight of some object between himself and the horizon, rushed inside to look at a wall. He washed the dishes, then made up his mind to leave.

But by no means all responses to the landscape were negative. Immigrants from the industrial and metropolitan slums breathed fresh air and saw unadulterated sunshine for the first time. P. G. Wotton, who had come from a slum in West Bromwich, exulted in the "joy and pleasure of it. Birds, flowers, [and] fruit in summer." Carl Grunstadt from Norway was overwhelmed by the beauty and silence of the grasslands: "Before us was the most beautiful landscape I had ever seen. As we stood side by side gazing over the level, luxuriant prairie untouched and unspoiled by the hands of man, the soft wind came down from the northwest and gently caressed the tall grasses that grew there, and as they moved their silvery sheen gave one the impression of an endless ocean of fertility." For religious groups escaping the taint of the world, isolation was precisely what they wanted. "There was no living human being for miles around," wrote Peter Windscheigl, a German Catholic who settled near Rosthern, Saskatchewan, "no road, no house, only beautiful virgin prairie dotted with small lakes and poplar groves."

Many settlers also saw the practical advantages of farming open prairie. For G. H. Hambley, who had come from a country of "stones, stumps, hills and poor soils," the prairie was "a revelation." One pioneer woman wrote of her husband: "He fell in love with the Golden West. . . . Few stones, no trees or stumps to contend with . . . no creeks to stop the miles and miles of growing grain." The novelist Frederick Philip Grove told of meeting a settler from Ontario who began ploughing his quarter section on the very day of his arrival.

For some, the sensation of being alone in the world was uplifting. In the empty Buffalo Horn Valley of southern Saskatchewan, Myrtle G. Moorhouse found that she was in another Eden: "I stood in one spot and looked around, especially in the early evening. It was like a huge bowl of blue turned over us. No matter where we turned, we could see the horizon, a complete dome, and I marvelled at it. With a ridge to the west, the waters of springtime divided, flowing to the Gulf of Mexico in the south. On this ridge we could see for ten miles. . . . There was a profusion of beautiful wildflowers, of all unknown varieties. . . . The valleys held a mystic feeling that made me think I was the first human who ever walked there. . . . There were no landmarks, no fences. Just the odd dot of a shack, and at night someone's light." Others thrilled to the melding of the elements. W. J. Ryan marvelled at the way in which the dawn sun — "a great ball of fire in the east" — fused earth and sky, "just like in a painting by J. M. W. Turner."

On others the spell of the plains worked slowly. "Looking back now," wrote Robin Greig, "I do not think the great plains were monotonous after the first month or so. . . . The unbroken spaces were both soothing and uplifting. . . . I have understood the native of the Shetland Islands who was visiting the Lothian district of Scotland and remarked that it seemed to be a fine country, but was spoiled by trees." Mr. Faithorn, an Englishman, came to Winnipeg in 1881 and a year later moved west to Fort McLeod with a survey party. He thought the country the "queerest place" he had ever seen — "mile upon mile of rolling country without a house or fence or living thing." But it was, he decided, "a great setting for a new life."

The parkland, with its almost designed arrangement of poplar groves and grassland, was as appealing to many of the settlers as it had been to the earlier travellers and adventurers. Captain John Rigby couldn't have been more pleased with his Manitoba homestead: "Oak lake is a beautiful sheet of water, clear as crystal and abounding with fish and fowl. I think we could travel the world over before hitting another spot to equal Manitoba and this locality in particular." Bertram Tennyson — nephew of the Poet Laureate Alfred Lord Tennyson — who spent a few years at Moosomin in the 1890s, was enchanted by the country around Wood Mountain: "A beautiful country gemmed with scarlet tiger lilies and golden marigolds, the champaign broken here and there by clumps of the universal aspen poplar, which give a park-like look to the scenery." The graceful poplar appealed to many of the settlers; the slender trunk, the delicate green of the leaves in the spring, and — thanks to a flexible stalk attachment — leaves that dance in the wind and catch the sun were irresistible attractions.

Other views of the West were determined by utility. Immigrants from the wood-scarce Ukrainian provinces could hardly believe that stands of trees were available for the taking, and for them the parkland was a magnet. Germans, on the other hand, were as unimpressed with the slender, short-lived poplar as the English had been with the gum tree or the eucalyptus in Australia. Poplar was too soft to be of much use as timber, and if grown in marshy places it was liable to rot within. As fuel it was not very satisfactory because its special quality is that it is resistant to fire. German immigrants were inclined to dismiss the poplar groves as *busch,* reserving the dignified *wald* for the stronger woods of the north.

Though parkland was generally appealing, in the more heavily wooded northern districts settlers were disturbed by the absence of paths and trails. Whether made by animals or humans, a trail is comforting. It signals the presence of life and suggests purposeful, cooperative behaviour. As Gaston Bachelard once remarked, a trail is a beckoning feature that invites us to come out of ourselves. For settlers craving comforting associations, a landscape without trails was unbearably foreign:

> *I found no path, no trail*
> *But only bush and water*
> *Wherever I looked I saw*
> *Not a native land — but foreign*
> *I found no path, no trail*
> *Only green bush*
> *Wherever I looked I saw*
> *A foreign country*

By the same token, the making of trails and paths gave great satisfaction, even in cities. "I knew that path so well," wrote W. G. Herklots of Winnipeg. "I knew and was proud of that little twist by which instead of being a mere track that crossed a vacant lot it became a path directing *me* to my door."

Most of the comments on landscape were about the compelling plain, but usually the first direct contact with the West was not with the country but with the town or city where the immigrant got off the train. Before setting out to choose a homestead, or to locate one already chosen, most immigrants would have spent several days in a hotel, boarding house, or hostel. For people accustomed to comely villages and towns, built from local materials and occupying sites that offered discernible commercial, climatic, or strategic advantages, prairie towns and cities were disconcerting. They were a reminder, if one was needed, of the raw condition of the land. Whereas European towns and villages looked as if they had been set into the landscape, most prairie towns appeared to have been arbitrarily set down upon it. For Rupert Brooke, who crossed the prairies in 1909, they wore the same air of discomfort as a man trying to make his bed on a level and unyielding surface such as a lawn or a pavement: "He feels hopelessly incidental to the superficies of the earth." Brooke thought that all towns should be on hills or in valleys.

Buildings in the newer towns were made from imported lumber or prefabricated parts, to eclectic designs, so they were in no sense products of place. Forty years after their erection, Edward McCourt could still describe them, collectively, as "alien eruptions upon the face of nature." Many of them were shoddily built, unpainted, and made all the more forlorn by false fronts designed, ironically, to give them a look of solidity and worth by concealing the pitched roofs behind. To add to their discomfort, they were set beside main streets broad enough to be avenues but which were, in effect, merely unsurfaced spaces between boardwalks. In short, the towns were the characteristic and inevitable products of pioneer districts, no worse and no better than pioneer towns in America or Australia. Their function was to tranship wheat and provide basic goods and services; the only buildings that invariably were well constructed and maintained were the grain elevators, railway stations, and banks. Almost everything else was makeshift.

Even seasoned travellers were shaken by the roughness. Washington Frank Lynn, the artist-reporter, found the streets of Winnipeg to be in "only . . . the merest embryotic condition." Even on Main and Portage,

Main Street, North Battleford, 1906. The unpainted buildings, unpaved streets, and boardwalks of the small towns frequently upset European immigrants. (Public Archives Canada, C 23351)

sidewalks and pavements were "a few broken bits of planking, with long and, in wet weather, muddy intervals between." Hotels were "rough in accommodation, as might be expected," and expensive, so newcomers were often forced to put up temporary shelters in the tent towns that occupied the waste lands scattered around the town. Immigrants were frequently shocked by the condition of the towns. One described them as "clapboard monstrosities," while to a Barr colonist Saskatoon was a town of "large boxes rushed up without regard to architecture and comfort." But perhaps more disturbing than current failings, which were to be expected, was the gnawing suspicion, articulated by Rupert Brooke, that as products of a dynamic, restless age, prairie towns might never mature and so never acquire "that something different, something more worth having."

The visible landscape drew the first responses, but comments about the weather and climate followed quickly. Immigrants from the industrial cities were exhilarated by air that was clean and dry, and by a world that seemed perennially fresh. But as the crisp and sparkling days of fall gave way to the iron nights of winter, the climate took on a different complexion. Temperatures that could actually threaten life were a disturbing novelty for immigrants from Western Europe. In a letter to his Dutch compatriots, Willem de Gelder remarked that, when working outside in the coldest weather, "we continually had to watch each other's noses and cheeks to warn of the possibility of frostbite. . . . Sometimes I still have cold feet, even wearing 3 pairs of warm winter socks, a pair of sheepskin-lined mocassins, and over all that elkskin mocassins. To give you another example of the cold, you can't keep your hands warm in gloves, so you have to wear mitts, and it's extremely dangerous to take them off even for a second."

The length and severity of the prairie winters unnerved even Central and Eastern Europeans. Russian winters were neither as hard nor as long. When Easter came without the accustomed signs of spring, Ukrainians in particular were anguished. Easter in the Ukraine is a celebration of the rebirth of life as well as of the Resurrection of Christ. "All is blooming everywhere / Beauty in the meadows lies" a well-known Easter poem began. The date of the festival in the Julian calendar could be as much as five weeks later than the Gregorian, but even in years when the holiday fell in late April or early May it could still be too early to celebrate spring. The first nostalgia, wrote Myrna Kostash, was the longing for early spring and blossoming plum and cherry trees, while all around were only poplar saplings, willow bush, and native grasses under the snow.

In open prairie, where nothing held back the swooping winds, winter conditions could be frighteningly harsh. Marie Hamilton spent a few years in Regina when it was still a huddle of shacks and tents on a plain as "flat and featureless as deal boards." Over the unprotected town the wintry winds "whooped and shouted," and when they died temperatures fell to Arctic depths, the sky took on a metallic sheen, and boards warped and cracked like pistol shots. Wind and the cracking of boards were the only natural sounds apart from the mournful cry of the coyote. Winter for much of the time was silent and lifeless, but it could unleash storms that made the stoutest hearts quail. John Donkin described a blizzard as "a storm peculiar to the prairie regions, almost indescribable in its deathly power. It is the most terrible wind that rages upon earth; a cloud burst of powdered ice, accompanied by a violent hurricane, with the thermometer away below zero. I am utterly impotent to describe the cold. During one blizzard in 1884 the thermometer in the barracks showed thirty-seven degrees below zero [F], or sixty-nine degrees of frost, and the velocity of the wind — as measured by the anemometer on top of the quartermaster's store — was fifty-five miles an hour." Had Donkin been able to calculate the wind chill, he would have arrived at a sensible temperature — i.e., the temperature the body feels — of 90 below zero [F].

Chapter Four

CHOOSING A HOMESTEAD, MAKING A SHELTER

For settlers who wanted to farm, the first task was to choose a homestead or, if no homestead land was available, land that could be bought. Practical considerations, such as quality of soil and availability of wood and water, were usually paramount. Even Lord Selkirk, not the most practical of men, had exhorted his agent to choose a location that would allow his settlers to enjoy "the advantage of wood, water, and open lands fit for immediate cultivation." The first settlers had clung to the rivers, but by 1870 virtually all the river land had been taken up; newcomers were forced onto open prairie, where they settled as close as possible to poplar bluffs. Ontarians, who arrived in considerable numbers after 1870, French Canadians from the New England states who came in 1874, and Icelanders in 1875 all sought wooded or lakeside land. In Ontario, thick vegetation or well developed woodland had long been supposed to be an indicator of soil quality and, according to John Macoun, the Ontario farmer in the 1880s believed that land covered with forest was "new" and therefore richer than prairie.

Wood was also prized as fuel, so much so that one early pioneer in the grasslands recalled seeing telegraph poles with hour-glass figures, the result of travellers taking chips from the bases to start camp fires. Only in the 1880s, when barbed wire was available for fencing and deep well-drilling guaranteed a supply of water, was there any willingness to settle on open prairie. Even then the movement was limited to those who could afford fencing and fuel.

The most considered selections of land were usually made by settlers intent on commercial grain farming. These saw at once the advan-

A homestead in parkland near Atwater, Saskatchewan. Wood and water were magnets for settlers from Europe and eastern parts of Canada and the United States. (Public Archives Canada, C 14967)

tages of having land ready for the plough. Most Americans, for example, sought locations in the grasslands or the drier margins of the parkland where there were no trees to fell and where they could employ dry-farming techniques learned in the mid-West. Most had funds for fuel, fencing material, and well-digging equipment, and if they couldn't find suitable homestead land within striking distance of a railway they didn't hesitate to buy from the C.P.R., a land company, or the Hudson's Bay Company. The more prosperous Americans hired a settler's box car from the C.P.R. and arrived with tools, household effects, and lumber for building.

For settlers who thought of the West more as a place where they might make a life, not just a living, the desire for a comfortable setting and familiar features was just as important as practical considerations. If most settlers arrived with no clear idea of what to expect of the prairies, all carried with them an image of the kind of surroundings in which they would like to live. We are all marked by the first world that meets our eyes, and we carry that imprint as a permanent image of the way the world should be. Memories of the homeland, or idealized versions of them, became templates for the future. "Heredity being in the saddle," recollected Marjorie Wilkins Campbell of Yorkshire, "it was natural for us to think of farming in terms of our Old Country experience. . . . After the ordeal of the voyage and the long train trip it was rather comforting to visualize a cozy farmhouse snuggling with its outbuildings in a windbreak of trees and flanked by productive gardens and fields of grain and fodder. Imagination even managed to stock the many acres with herds of sheep and cattle, and the paddock with horses. Poultry were there as a matter of course." According to Gabrielle Roy, whose father — a settlement agent — had worked with many groups of Slavs, Doukhobors beheld a similar vision: "They did their best to see it [the plain] covered with little whitewashed houses, with pens for the chickens, vegetable gardens, fences, milk pails upside down on the fence posts, busy comings and goings, and even their seesaw wells, like the ones at home in the Caucasus."

There was little prospect of settlers matching the landscape in the mind's eye with the one actually confronting them, but many were still drawn to familiar or recognizable features. In strange settings we gravitate instinctively to what we know. A known plant, land form, or animal could bring home closer. Vilhelm Moberg recounts how finding a *sippa* near a brook in Minnesota was a singular discovery for Norwegian immigrants. The sippa is Norway's national flower, and although the Minnesotan sippa was the smallest and spindliest the immigrants had ever seen, and had no smell, it still seemed to link Norway and America. In some cases even a name with familiar associations would attract settlers. An American, "dried out" in South Dakota in 1911 and determined to try his luck farther north, chose Wood Mountain in Saskatchewan, which he had seen only on a map, because he liked the sound of the name. Neither he nor his family was disappointed on arrival. "Every coulee," his daughter Aquina Anderson recollected, "had its share of poplars and willows. . . . Wild roses were in bloom everywhere and high hills on either side of the valley gave a look of protection and grandeur. Cool springs flowed down from the wooded coulees."

John Kennedy from the Gatineau Hills of Quebec was equally pleased with his quarter in the Qu'Appelle, "the Eden of the West." In the coulees there were springs, white poplar for building and fuel, and an abundance of wild fruits (saskatoons, chokecherries, cranberries, raspberries, and hazel nuts). It was, said Kennedy, an ideal place to make a home. But the Qu'Appelle was exceptional. The sides and floors of most valleys were too steep or too uneven to be of much use for farming. For some settlers, too, the scale of the Western valleys was simply too large. Mary Hiemstra's mother, a Barr colonist, found the Saskatchewan River far too big and wild. "What she wanted," said her daughter, "was a friendly little river like the Spen at home."

The desire for a familiar setting was sometimes so strong that immigrants would pass up good land for poorer that contained some recognizable feature. "A little muskeg now and again," remarked Eugene Van Cleef, "is not unwelcome to a Finn." Yet for Beecham Trotter, a horseman who felt at home on open prairie, behaviour that resulted in impractical choices was decidedly "ornery." "One of the strangest land seeking phenomena," he wrote, "was the way in which experienced farmers, after trailing over innumerable townships in which there was nothing to offend the plough, would choose some stony lot which, compared to what they might have had, was too poor to raise a disturbance." Two cases in point were a group of land-seeking Doukhobors, to whom Gabrielle Roy's father had been assigned, and Evan Davies's companion, David James. To Mr. Roy's consternation, the Doukhobors chose rough valley land over smooth and fertile prairie because the terrain reminded them of the Caucasus Mountains. Directed by a similar instinct, David James chose a quarter section that had on it patches of stone and a small ridge. He could have chosen a cleaner quarter close by, but "I rather fancy," noted a bemused Evan Davies from the rich lowlands of Cardiganshire, "that he chose the piece with the ridge on it because the flatness of the other pieces was abhorrent to his Glamorgan nature."

One of the most colourful choices was made by the landscape painter Augustus Kenderdine. To be close to the English Barr colonists at Lloydminster, Saskatchewan, Kenderdine filed on a homestead at nearby Lashburn. The quarter was on rolling parkland on a bench overlooking the Saskatchewan River. After he had built a house, Kenderdine was captivated by a nearby lake, and by the "highest hill in the country." Determined to have a view of the lake, Kenderdine raised the house onto skids and with a team of oxen hauled it to a point on the hillside where it overlooked the lake. "It didn't seem to matter," his daughter May recollected, "that that hill — 'Pike's Peak' — took up the whole 160 acres leaving only a fringe to be cultivated. We all loved the place." The new homestead also contained a comforting piece of prairie history. The old Fort Pitt–Battleford trail, along which the Kenderdines loved to ride, lay along the edge of the lake.

Probably the most striking example of land chosen for non-agricultural reasons was the Ukrainians' unfailing selection of heavily wooded parkland that was sometimes stony and poorly drained. Only occasionally, as J. G. McGregor remarked, did they stumble onto first class land. But behaviour that many observers dismissed as naïve was in fact rational and considered. Like other European settlers, they were attracted by woodland and water because these features were familiar. "We chose to settle [in the Dauphin region of Manitoba]," said Dmytro Romanchych, "because the woods, streams, and meadows very much resembled our native Carpathian scenery." But woodland and water were also useful. "When I came out here," said one Ukrainian immigrant, "I saw a creek — there's water! A bush, there's fire! We didn't have that in the old country. And the bush wouldn't be there without the soil."

O. Woychenko relates how Wasyl Zahara, the first Bukowinan settler in Canada, had his mind set on land containing plenty of woods, a river, and some prairie. The fact that the land he chose was also swampy and stony and its agricultural potential so unpromising that it had been passed

"The Homestead: Pike's Peak," A. F. Kenderdine, 1922. The lake that held such attraction for Kenderdine is just visible in the background of the painting. (Collection of Glenbow Museum, Calgary, Alberta)

up by other settlers did not discourage him. "To become a proprietor of a large tract of woodland and a meadow adjacent to a river," noted Woychenko, "was a chance he grasped at quickly and avidly." For Wasyl Zahara, the river was a certain source of water for himself and his cattle, while the marsh provided slough grass for winter feed and thatching as well as a habitat for game birds. In the surrounding woods he would find wild fruits, nuts, berries, mushrooms, and the ingredients for folk medicines. For a peasant farmer thinking of subsistence rather than profit, wilderness is paradise enough.

Although woodland appealed to most of the settlers, to the Ukrainians it was irresistible. In the homeland every twig had been owned by the landlords, and woodland was harboured so fiercely that for peasants wood became the scarcest of resources. For the immigrants, an abundant supply of it was at least as valuable as any crop they could put in its place. The heavier the bush, the more attractive the land. Peter Schevcook tells of his father going into the Mundare district of Manitoba and picking "the bushiest land he could find," while a member of Dr. Oleskow's first contingent of settlers wrote that "all wanted to have as much wood on their land as possible." This insistence on obtaining woodland puzzled Anglo-Canadians, among them land commissioner W. F. McCreary. He wrote to Deputy Minister James A. Smart in 1897: "These Galicians are a peculiar people. They will not accept as a gift 160 acres of what we consider the best land in Manitoba, that is first class wheat growing prairie land; what they particularly want is wood, and they care but little whether the land is heavy soil or light gravel; but each man must have some wood on his place." By 1904 the Ukrainian predilection for woodland was so well recognized that C. W. Speers, the General Colonizing Agent, could write that bushland north of Prince Albert was "especially adapted for Ruthenian colonization" while "beautiful open country [with] good soil" farther south was "well suited for German people." By the end of the century, government settlement agents routinely consulted the leaders of each ethnic group to find out what kind of land they preferred. In other cases the agents attempted to match the immigrants with terrain they thought to be representative of their homelands, or with terrain chosen by the first settlers of each group. James A. Smart, for example, thought that the coniferous zone along the prairie fringe in the Red Deer area was well suited for Finnish settlement.

As well as gravitating toward familiar features and places, immigrants were also attracted to people of their own kind. For non-English-speakers in particular — for whom customs, laws, and in some cases even Latin script, would have been unfamiliar — the presence of neighbours they could talk to was as powerful an attraction as any material attribute. By the 1890s the government had recognized that block or colony settlement was a means of diminishing the general hardships of pioneer life, whatever its effects upon the process of assimilation into Anglo-Canadian society. Blocks of land were set aside for particular nationalities, and quarter sections allotted to applicants.

The concession was particularly suited to groups like the Ukrainians who tended to migrate *en masse* or in successive waves. By sending encouraging letters home, emigrants could trigger chain reactions that virtually drained villages and districts. The letters were frequently misleading, but they were nearly always trusted. Those eager for news of absent relatives took every opportunity to share the letters with family and friends, often reading them aloud at community gatherings, and thus spreading the immigration message far more effectively than the official propagandists could ever have dreamed of. The "Canada fever" that swept through the Ukrainian provinces was every bit as infectious as the America fever that had engulfed Scandinavia as a result of similar communications from emigrants in Minnesota and Wisconsin.

Concentrations of kinsmen and fellow villagers were so marked a feature of the Ukrainian settlement that a Yorkton (Saskatchewan) lawyer claimed he could identify the home villages of his countrymen simply by looking at where they settled. Significantly, Ukrainians who emigrated to Siberia at roughly the same time didn't display the "hiving" instinct to nearly the same degree, even though they settled in country much like the prairies. In Siberia the common Slavic culture seems to have allayed anxieties and reduced the tendency to group together. Russians,

The "shells of Ukrainian settlers, Stuartburn, Manitoba 1900–1905. The first houses and farm buildings were sometimes of traditional European design (Public Archives Canada, C 6605)

BeloRussians, and Ukrainians quickly developed a common dialect, a sectional outlook, and a common appellation. All became "Siberniks."

The desire to be near friends, relatives, or countrymen was sometimes so great that immigrants filed on homesteads without even inspecting the land. Ukrainians in the Stuartburn district of Manitoba exhorted the government to open odd-numbered sections to settlement so that friends and relatives in Galicia could settle near them. That Stuartburn and the Interlake lands were generally regarded as "leftovers," unfit for grain growing or other types of farming, deterred no one — neither the Ukrainians in place nor those about to come. In Sniatyn, Alberta, land dismissed by the first Ukrainian immigrants because it was "all sand and bush and not fit for farming" was taken up by later arrivals who were determined to have Ukrainian neighbours. One group threatened violence when government officers attempted to direct them to Fish Creek, Saskatchewan, when they wanted to to be near friends and relatives in Alberta and Manitoba. C. W. Speers's dramatic telegram tells all:

> *Almost distracted with these people, rebellious, act fiendish, will not leave cars, about seventy-five struck off walking Regina, perfectly uncontrollable. Nothing but pandemonium since leaving Regina. Have exhausted all legitimate tactics with no avail. Policemen here assisting situation — eclipses anything hitherto known. Edmonton, Dauphin or die. Will not even go inspect country, have offered liberal inducements, threatened to kill interpreter. Under existing circumstances strongly recommend their return Edmonton and few Dauphin and get another consignment people special train leaving here this afternoon. Could take them Regina. Answer immediately am simply baffled and defeated — quietest and only method will be their return. Waiting reply. Mostly have money and will pay fare. They are wicked.*

The government's encouragement of block settlement made for contiguity of linguistic groups and, in some cases, actual closeness. When settlers obtained a solid block of land as their reserve, they were able to homestead each quarter section and, by locating their farmsteads at the interior corners of the quarter sections, they were able to create a settlement pattern that was a compromise between the peasant villages of Europe and the dispersed farmsteads of North America. Ordinarily, in any one thirty-six-section township, twenty sections were picked off by the railway and the Hudson's Bay Company. Limited to the even-numbered sections, homesteaders frequently found that their nearest neighbours were a mile away. And in spite of the government's best intentions, linguistic mixes did occur, so that the mile-distant neighbour could be even further removed by a virtually insurmountable barrier of language.

A Ukrainian farm in the Manitoba parkland. For Ukrainians from wood-scarce areas of central and eastern Europe, an assured supply of wood was an invaluable resource. (Public Archives Canada, C 6608)

Making a Shelter

Once a homestead had been chosen, the next step was to build a permanent or semi-permanent shelter. The nature of the shelter depended on
the settler's means and the location of his homestead. One whose
homestead was reasonably close to a main or branch line might bring
in building materials; if he wanted to save himself the trouble of making
a house plan he could simply buy a kit supplied by the C.P.R., Eaton's,
or one of several lumber companies in British Columbia. Settlers of
slender means in the same circumstances could buy a load of lumber
and a few rolls of tar paper at the nearest station. Tacked onto walls
and roof, the tar paper — while it held — made a wind- and rain-proof
shelter.

Settlers who arrived before the railway, or whose homesteads were
some distance from the nearest line, had to make do with the materials
at hand: grass sod on open prairie, poplar logs in the park belt. The
first shelter in both zones was often a dug-out (*zemlyanka* or *burdei* in
Ukrainian), a rectangular opening cut into a slope or bank and roofed
with poplar saplings covered with sod. Both dug-outs and sod houses
were relatively easy to build; they were fireproof, warm in winter, and
reasonably solid. But even with walls covered with sacking or newspaper
they were difficult to keep clean, and without boards, shingles, or metal
sheeting, roofing was a persistent problem. In a dug-out or a sod house
a three-day rain could last a week. Nineteenth-century miners in the
Ukraine, who built temporary shelters, used to say: "The rain is beyond
the hill, but in our *zemlyanka* it is already dripping." The parallel expres-

*A well-roofed tar paper shack, near Shellbrook, Saskatchewan. Good roofing
was a homesteader preoccupation. After a heavy rain, a sod roof could drip
for days. (Public Archives Canada, PA 21735)*

A sod house in the Viking area of Alberta, early 1900s. For settlers in treeless areas sod was often the first building material. (Glenbow Archives, NA-1758-13)

sion in Manitoba was: "When it starts to rain in Winnipeg it is already leaking in our house." Watertight roofing was high on every pioneer's list of priorities.

Log shacks were made of round or squared poplar logs. Properly laid logs fitted snugly and they could be chinked with clay or sodded on the outside. Clay or, where limestone was available, crude sand and lime plaster applied to the inside walls reduced draughts and fended off bugs and flies. Both logs and sod are heat retentive and, because the houses were compact, low to the ground, and had only one door and a few small windows, they could be reasonably warm in winter. But during the summers they tended to heat up if not properly ventilated, and the walls mildewed and became as soft as putty unless they were frequently re-plastered. For poor immigrants on marginal land, living conditions were sometimes atrocious. In his 1898 report on Ukrainian homesteads in the Edmonton district, immigration officer Thomas Spence used repeatedly such phrases as "very poor," "wretched poor house," "destitute," and "no provisions." He reported that children had few clothes, no shoes, and that there was no money for blankets. The houses had mud floors and a great many had hens in them. To the list of miseries he could have added mosquitoes, the scourge of the bushlands. To fend them off settlers were forced to burn "smudges" of green branches and manure which they sometimes carried around in buckets. When smudges failed they wore gloves, face nets, and even sheepskin coats.

The immigrant's progress was measured by the speed with which the sod or log shack was abandoned and replaced by a substantial frame or log house. In Ukrainian districts the first permanent dwelling was usually a squared-log house, with an overhanging hip roof made of thatch, and plastered walls covered with a thin lime wash delicately tinted with a dash of bluing. The houses had two rooms: a bedroom, and a living room which also housed a large oven. In winter the children usually slept on a high, plastered ledge above the oven. The earthen floor was hard-packed, smoothed over with clay, and "waxed" with a solution of dung and water. Until bricks were available, chimneys were made of woven willow branches plastered with mud.

Though cozy in winter and — because of thick walls and a thick, overhanging roof — cool in summer, these traditional houses couldn't compete with the offerings in the catalogues and illustrated magazines. As soon as possible they were replaced with frame, two storey "Angliki" houses which had wooden floors, windows on all sides, a verandah, a living room, and a cast iron stove. Furnishings, too, came straight from the catalogues. As well as being fashionable and easier to keep clean,

An impoverished Ukrainian immigrant and her child, Yorkton area, Saskatchewan. Few photographs of the rural areas showed the extreme poverty of some of the immigrants. (Glenbow Archives, NA-2878-63)

An "Angliki" replacement house, and car, Vegreville, Alberta, 1918. The tradi-
tional house, in the foreground, has become a barn or storage shed. (Public
Archives Canada, C 17574)

the catalogue houses were protective colouring for uncertain Slavic immigrants afraid to parade their ethnicity. At every turn they were reminded
that they spoke an "inferior" language and possessed an "inferior" culture.
Their response was the understandably timid one of a people who lacked
the confidence to express their own traditions or respond to the needs
of the area.

However makeshift and uncomfortable they might have been, sod
houses and log shacks were the prairies' only indigenous dwellings.
Designed by the species rather than by individuals, and made of local
materials, they were the true nests of the West. They were part of prairie
nature in a way that tar paper shacks and upright frame houses could
never be. They may have been solitary but they were never alien. In
the early photographs no sight is more depressing than an eruption of
tar paper shacks on the face of the prairie. Wallace Stegner's first home
in Saskatchewan was "an ugly tar paper box" on a prairie "as empty as
nightmare." Not even the shack's low, rounded roof, built so to give the
wind less to grip, could bind it to the horizontal world. "A soddy that
poked its low brow no higher than the tailings of a gopher would have
suited me better," wrote Stegner.

Log houses weren't much more comfortable than sod, but they, too,
could be reassuring, as the young Scotswoman Elizabeth Mitchell
discovered: "A log house built by capable hands and efficiently plastered

is by far the most beautiful dwelling in the West though it is not considered 'the thing.' The ends of the round beams supporting the roof make a natural ornament, and the individual arrangement and shape of the windows gives each house an expression of its own, like our old cottages. Such a house," she added, "is also warmer than the average lumber house."

Even when well built, the first dwellings were so spartan that civilizing touches assumed a particular grace. Mrs Heimstra, one of the English Barr colonists, hung hand-made antimacassars over the unglazed windows of her log cabin and swept the dirt floor every day with a small handbrush brought from England. So great was the fear of a descent into barbarism that many settlers made a special effort to maintain links with the cultures of Europe and the settled east. They brought with them books, pictures, and musical instruments, and many used some of their scarce cash to subscribe to eastern newspapers and magazines. Walt Whitman's mythic pioneer may have left his past behind, but almost any inventory of pioneer belongings shows that actual pioneers went to great lengths to bring to the new world as much of the old world as they could carry. Almost every house had its Dickens or its Galsworthy — or their European equivalents — some pictures, or a favourite chair or carpet.

Ukrainian houses tended to be particularly well supplied with objects from the homeland. Few women came away without some household treasures: a cloth delicately woven in silver and gold cutwork, a hand-woven rug to spread on the floor, embroidered towels or *rushniki* to hang on the walls. The colours reflected the landscapes from which they had come: bright oranges, yellows, and greens of the Carparthian mountains; maroons, blacks, rich purples, and browns — the dark, earth colours of the lowlands; and silver-greys, browns, soft reds, blues, and golds of the sunny wheat districts of the central Ukraine. In old country houses, went an old Hutzul saying, there were no unadorned spaces: "So that there be no empty spaces, all is decorated." Window sills held pots of geraniums and basil, floors and walls were covered with hand-woven rugs and embroidered rushniki, and virtually every house had its Schevchenko corner where a lithographed portrait of the poet, draped with rushniki, hung above a copy of his collected works.

Women also made an effort to make gardens that grew familiar plants in familiar arrangements. There were garlic, cabbages, and turnips, as in all gardens, but also dill, succulent black beans, cucumbers, and melons. Vegetables, herbs, and flowers, which included poppies and sunflowers, were laid out in neat rows or — in the case of flowers — in beds to imitate Bukowinan embroideries. For government agents, planted flowers were the first sure sign that a settlement had taken.

Robert England gave us this idyllic portrait of a Ukrainian village: "They work patiently in their gardens surrounded by a close twig fence along which bright tall poppies and sunflowers nod in the breeze. The houses, whitewashed, squat with narrow windows, the single doors invitingly open to the farmyard. The men off in farm or town. There is little to suggest that life is lived in another country." The place, which England didn't specify, could well have been the village of "Ukrainia" that stretched along the east bank of the Red River. The houses had been built side by side on old river lots. For several miles the road was lined with picturesque Ukrainian houses with whitewashed walls, red and blue window frames, and pots of geraniums and basil resting on the interior ledges. "Ukrainia" might have passed for a village in the old country.

Chapter Five

THE SURVEY AND
THE SETTLEMENT PLAN

Neighbourly, village-like arrangements of farmhouses were not, however, characteristic of Western settlement. The general pattern of settlement was a dispersed one, each farmer or farm family living apart from neighbours on a rectangular plot of land. To prepare for the settlement, the Dominion Government had begun to survey and subdivide the prairies in 1869. No land survey in history had been as methodical. The model was American, or Jeffersonian, but the great unbroken expanses of the Canadian prairies allowed an even more rigid application of geometrical principles than had been possible in the topographically more diverse American plains. In Canada only the correction lines necessary to compensate for the curvature of the earth, and occasional sags or swells in the survey lines due to the use of chains of the wrong length, interrupted the perfect symmetry. From the edge of the Shield westward to the foothills of the Rockies, large blocks of land were subdivided into near-perfect patterns of squares that would have gladdened the heart of any Cartesian. "If lengths had been correctly measured," wrote the Surveyor General in his annual report for 1913, "the land survey of the Dominion would have been the most perfect and remarkable one in the world."

The object of the survey was to delineate the basic unit of land holding, the 160-acre quarter-section. The quarters were grouped into 640-acre sections, one mile square, and the sections into townships of thirty-six sections each. By numbering the townships north from the principal base line and the "ranges" east or west of the principal meridians, the position of each quarter could be precisely defined. Thus a rural address in pre-post office days might have read: S. E. Quarter, Section 3, Township

Lunch break for a survey party engaged in the most methodical of all land surveys. Southern Alberta, 1913. (Glenbow Archives, NA-2604-16)

10, Range 19, West of the 1st Meridian — the address, in fact, of the first quarter section sold by the C.P.R., about two miles south of Brandon. The principal meridian passed just west of Winnipeg, and other meridians were added as settlement moved west; the first base line was the 49th parallel. The system was uniform, easily understood and, because it was founded upon astronomical observations rather than readings from a magnetic or solar compass, remarkably accurate. Iron stakes driven into the ground by the surveyors to mark the sections, and square holes dug to mark the quarter sections, became reference points for every pioneer. Used in conjunction with the Torrens method of land registration, the rectangular survey eliminated disputes over property rights. The Torrens method, devised in Australia and adopted by Manitoba and the Territories in 1885-6, required by law that land titles and the transactions affecting them be recorded at a land office. To own a quarter section a settler had to live on it for three years, with an absence of not more that six months in any one year, and cultivate at least fifteen acres, of which ten were to be cropped.

The rectangular survey, and the quarter- and half-section farms it was designed to provide, were a critical element in the government's settlement plan for the prairies. From the passage of the American Homestead Act in 1862, any nation hoping to compete for immigrants with the United States had to be prepared to offer quarter-section farms in exchange for a nominal registration fee. Other elements of the plan were a police force to ensure lawful and orderly settlement, a transcontinental railway, and a dense network of towns to provide goods and services for the farming community. The lay-out of the towns and their distribution was as un-complicated as the survey itself: a simple network of square blocks and straight streets hung on a pair of T-shaped axial streets usually served as the town plat. The shorter street, which was one-sided, ran parallel with the railway and the longer at a right angle away from it. Plats were laid out at regular eight- to ten-mile intervals along main and branch lines, so that with a relatively dense rail network no farm would be more than half a day's journey from a town. To cap the exercise, along the Grand Trunk line (now the C.N.R.) the towns were named alphabetically; the most complete sequence began with Atwater, Bangor, and Cana, and ended with Xena, Young, and Zelma. Never was town-planning so mechanical, and it showed in the appearance of the towns. They looked, J. F. Fraser remarked, "as though turned out to the same pattern in the

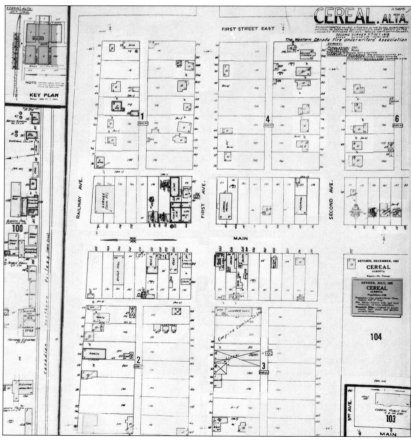

Cereal, Alberta. A rectangular grid of streets adjacent to the railway was the standard plan for small prairie towns. (Glenbow Archives, NA-4106-8)

same machine, as lacking in individuality as factory-made furniture, with no ambition to be pretty, but serviceable, workable, dollar earning." John Donkin was even more forthright. "A prairie town," he remarked, "is a more depressing object than a burnt forest."

In areas where settlement preceded the survey, as at Red River and around forts and missions in the Territories, the Dominion surveyors respected property rights, when asked to do so, by manoeuvring around existing farms and fields and validating the old boundaries. Refusal would have caused the dismemberment of entire communities and the loss of improvements made to land. The older properties were river lots created spontaneously to serve the basic needs of settlers in frontier regions. Unlike the square sections and the roads that divided them, they represented the settlers' assessment of the environment, and although they would not serve machine agriculture and profit-oriented farming nearly as well as square fields and farms, they were appropriate to the time and place. For the Métis, the river lots were also a cultural symbol and, though they were indifferent farmers, they objected violently to the threat of change. The first Métis uprising in 1869 had begun symbolically with a confrontation between Louis Riel, the Métis leader, and a survey party attempting to run a base line across the river lots on the Red River near Winnipeg. But for European farmers, for whom the long lots had no cultural significance, the appeal of a compact holding was irresistible, and they readily adopted the sectional system.

Mechanistic approaches to planning may offend modern sensibilities but the authors of the settlement plan had no other purpose than to prepare the way for the orderly, democratic and, so they hoped, rapid settlement of the West. It was left to the individual settler to make a judicious choice of land, make the necessary adjustments to the physical environment, and bear the social costs of living in an isolated frontier setting. Like all planners of new territory in which the land was flat and reasonably uniform in quality, government officials chose a regular, easily applied, and comprehensive system of rectangles. Seen from a great height, the Regina Plain bears some resemblance to the Po Valley of Northern Italy, subdivided by Roman surveyors in the second century B.C. Because the township survey was conducted without benefit of either a topographical or land classification survey, the surveyors were restricted to mensuration. They were required to take note of the vegetation and the major relief features, and to assess the potential for agriculture, but their only effective task, as critics of the survey have seen it, was to superimpose upon organic nature an abstract and, in some respects, an impractical mathematical scheme.

Thomas Adams, the distinguished British planner who visited Western Canada in 1916, remarked that the survey required no discretion from the surveyors "beyond what was required accurately to define and locate boundaries according to a rigid and inelastic system." The rigidity of the sectional survey, compared with the flexibility of the old river lots and the trails that connected them, had earlier (1883) offended a contributor to the Edmonton *Bulletin,* who questioned the practicality of replacing the Fort Saskatchewan–Edmonton trail by surveyed roads: "If travel is to be obliged to follow the road allowances the distance to be covered will be nearly double that required at present, and besides in many cases the road allowances will pass through swamps, lakes, or across coulees where a passable road can only be made at great expense. The road allowances do not follow the lay of the country as the present trail does."

In modern times, the most severe critic of the rectangular survey has been Paul Shepard, the American ecologist. Shepard concedes that the survey may have reassured anxious settlers by conveying the impression of a landscape possessed and controlled, and that its perfect rectangles may also have satisfied notions of ideal form and the ideal organization of space, but for these gains there were offsetting losses. He argues that, under the guise of providing a framework for the control and improvement of nature, the survey merely sanctioned the removal and destruction of any elements that did not fit the pattern. It was a kind of war against selected objects, species, processes, and forms in the landscape — in short, a form of "nature hating." Except in utterly flat, treeless areas where it would have been churlish not to complement nature's own geometry, the survey interposed an inorganic network of straight roads, field, and farm boundaries between the settlers and their surroundings. The old trails, in Hamlin Garland's phrase, had approached hills with caution, had followed lakesides with leisure, and did not rive, nor uproot, nor crush; but the surveyed roads confronted every obstacle. To preserve the angular pattern, hills were confronted and summarily crossed, and sloughs and lakes were laboriously filled in.

Many years after the survey and settlement had been completed, William Chornlesky, the son of a Ukrainian pioneer, recollected how the pioneers had used a well-beaten trail that followed the shore of a small lake on his father's homestead. The lake, however, lay athwart a road projected by the government surveyors, and when the road was finally built the lake had to be filled in. In those days filling a lake was a "tremendous project" that required fill to be drawn from both ends of the lake by team and slusher or scraper. At that time Chornlesky thought nothing of the alteration, but in a painting of the homestead commissioned later he instructed the painter to remove the road and replace it with the old trail. Surveyed roads, as Hamlin Garland remarked, were mere prose, but trails were poetry.

For the pioneers, the immediate consequences of the sectional survey were that they could have near neighbours only if they built on the interior corners of their quarter sections, making a trail from the centre of the section to the cut-line or road allowance. The alternative was to build at the adjacent corners of the sections facing the road allowance. In practice, however, few arrangements of this kind were made, and most settlers found themselves living in farmsteads that were half a mile or more from their nearest neighbour. At the beginning of settlement, when only the even-numbered sections could be homesteaded, distances between farmsteads were often greater than this. All too often, as Marie Hamilton pointed out, the houses were "lonely landmarks" in a landscape that she found drab and melancholy.

One of the earliest critics of the isolation imposed by the sectional survey was E. V. Smalley, a popular American writer on agriculture. He wrote, in an 1893 issue of *Atlantic Monthly,* that in no other place had the cultivators of the soil adapted their home life so badly to the conditions of nature as in the Northwestern prairies. Life in Europe might have been toilsome, but it was not lonely; country people lived in villages in pleasant landscapes and enjoyed a full social life. Prairie homesteaders, on the other hand, lived alone in settings where "the natural gregarious instinct of man cried out for satisfaction." The isolation of the homesteaders was most acute in winter, when all around lay the silent plain. In winter a journey of even a few hours could be dangerous, and during blizzards settlers left the safety of the cabin only to tend stock and to get fuel. Loneliness bred fears of accident and disease and caused bachelors to share a cabin, even though they might have farmed widely separated quarter sections. Some bachelors spent the winters in rented rooms in the nearest town.

Casual visiting was possible only in summer after the spring ploughing and seeding, and in places where there were knots of settlers. It was satisfying only when visitors and visited could understand each other, and when they had a common past to talk about. Differences in language and nationality prevented true intercourse, and could even intensify the sense of loneliness by reminding homesteaders of how cut off they were from their own kind. To paraphrase Kipling, a neighbour who does not talk one's talk, and who cannot feel one's mind is, however kindly, a neighbour in a limited sense only. In some areas, too, the turnover of homesteaders was probably so rapid that there was no time for bonds to develop. The experience of a settler in North Dakota must often have been duplicated on the Canadian side of the border: "Nobody keeps track of neighbours out here. People come and go; families move in and out, and nobody asks whence they come and whither they go. . . . I have lived here for six years and I do not know who occupies half the surrounding farms, although they are in full view."

One of the sharpest commentaries on pioneer farm life came from Elizabeth Mitchell, a young Scotswoman who spent five months on the prairies in the fall and winter of 1913-1914. Elizabeth Mitchell was a first-class graduate of Oxford University and an early member of Britain's

Garden Cities Association (later the Town and Country Planning Association). After her return to Scotland she had a long and distinguished career in community planning, and was awarded the Ebenezer Howard medal in 1955. During her sojourn in Saskatchewan she was disturbed by the emptiness of much of the prairie and by the widespread dislike, amounting in some cases to a "certain horror," of farm life:

> *In driving about, one could not help seeing these sinister weed-grown abandoned farms, as well as the strangely scattered nature of the actual settled land, with the great unbroken spaces between. Homesteaders could be heard planning to perform the homestead duties for three years, just enough to secure ownership of the land from the Government, and then to go to town and sell the homestead — to somebody. . . . Again and again one heard the tales of disillusioned and discouraged farmers. . . . The loneliness of many parts is still extreme. The farms are large, a quarter mile square at least. In three districts I knew blocks of empty "Company land" [C.P.R. land being held until surrounding settlement drove up the price] were constantly intervening, breaking up the settled country and harbouring gophers. . . . I stayed with an Englishwoman on the borders of an Indian reserve in a most picturesque desolation, and I think she said the nearest Englishwoman was seven miles off; certainly the trail by which we left that farm was bare of habitation. Far worse cases could be found. . . . The prairie madness is perfectly recognized and very common still; the "bachelors" suffer worse, and the women. For even if neighbours are not so impossibly far off, yet the homesteader has to work hard all day, and is in no great mood for exerting himself in the evening to walk to a neighbour's; if he is poor and has only oxen, their slowness is unendurable for a pleasure-trip — they make about two miles an hour. . . . A woman alone in the house all day may find the silence deadly; in the wheat farming stage there may not be even a beast about the place. . . . The husband may be willing and sympathetic, but she may grow shy and diffident, and not care to make the effort to tidy herself up and go to see her neighbour — any neighbour, just to break the monotony. The fancies come, and suspicions, and queer ways, and at last the young Mounted Policeman comes to the door, and carries her away to the terrible vast "Sanatorium" that hangs above the Saskatchewan [River]. There is still that kind of loneliness on the prairie.*

As most people now recognize, during the settlement period the Mounted Police were as much social workers as they were lawmen. While the fictional Mounties may have spent all their time getting their men, the actual ones spent much of theirs occupied with problems less dramatic. One of the chief purposes of their patrols, as J. Wooff remarked, was "to guard against the tragedies of hardship and suffering, and the pure unconquerable hardship of isolation."

The figures for homestead entries and cancellations were a rough measure of the social and economic difficulties of farming on the prairies. After examining the entry and cancellation figures for the years 1870–1927, Chester Martin discovered that forty-one out of every hundred homesteaders withdrew before they had even acquired patents to their homesteads. By province, rates of failure were 20% for Manitoba, 57% for Saskatchewan, and 45% for Alberta. Granted that many of the entrants had no serious intention of becoming farmers, hoping merely to "prove up," sell out, and move on, the rate of withdrawal is still remarkable. V. C. Fowke went farther, noting that the discrepancy between entries for homesteads and the achievement of patent was "so pronounced as to indicate wastefulness little less than shocking."

Even Americans hardened to pioneer conditions met their match in the Canadian West. The Dominion census shows that between 1901 and 1916 the number of American residents in Alberta and Saskatchewan rose from 13,887 to 179,581, a net increase of 165,704. Immigration data, on the other hand, show a total in-movement of 560,389. What, asked the historian Dennis Bicha, happened to the 400,000 Americans who entered Western Canada, satisfied the Dominion officials of their intention to become permanent residents, and could not be found when the census was taken? Bicha looked at all possible explanations and came to the conclusion that nearly two-thirds of the Americans who came and saw the prairies did not stay long enough to conquer. Unlike European immigrants, Americans had a homeland they could return to without much difficulty. Bicha's conclusion is corroborated by the data on homestead entries and final patents. The number of homestead entries made by migrants from the United States varied from a minimum of 164 in 1897 to a maximum of 12,813 in 1910, but in no year did the number of final patents exceed one third of the number of entries made three years before.

The figures are striking, and are given resonance by Bicha's observation that most of the American immigrants were farmers from the mid-West who were accustomed to continental conditions and equipped with the farming techniques to exploit them. Across the Canadian line they found not the fabled Big Rock Candy Mountain but a climate and a general environment that bore down on them with, in Bicha's phrase, "frequent brutality." Spirits that withstood the elements then had to adjust to an economy that depended on a single crop whose price rose and fell at the whim of international markets. In American eyes, the prairie wheat farmer was as vulnerable as the ante-bellum cotton planter.

Chapter Six

ALTERNATIVE PATTERNS OF SETTLEMENT

The loneliness of homestead life disturbed both government officials and disinterested observers. Without special concessions, the sectional survey system and the homestead regulations prevented the development of close settlements. To make these possible the Government granted blocks of land to particular national groups and, in a few cases, it extended the river lot surveys. Long lots of seventy-five to a hundred acres were surveyed along the Saskatchewan River at Fish Creek, and Ukrainian families were placed on them. At the request of the Department of the Interior, river lots were also laid out along the Duck, Pine, and Whitemouth Rivers in Manitoba, and Ukrainians were also located on these. But in terms of the overall settlement, these variations were so minor as to be hardly noticeable.

Observers of the settlement were invariably critical of the sectional survey and the isolated farmstead, and several of them recommended alternative arrangements. Henry Tanner, a professor of agriculture who visited Manitoba twice during the 1880s, urged the adoption of farm villages. Tanner was British and, though he did not himself recommend the re-creation of English farm villages in Western Canada, the English village was the ideal against which other types of rural settlement tended to be measured. E. V. Smalley, the American agricultural writer, was also keen to draw people together into villages, and he argued for the abandonment of the isolated farmstead. He suggested that settlers on the Northwestern plains would be well advised to follow the example of the peasants of the Russian steppes and the village dwellers on the great Danubian plain. He pointed out that in places where homesteaders held title to their lands it would be entirely feasible to divide the land into regions of roughly uniform fertility and then build villages in the centres of four-section tracts. Each of the sixteen settlers would still have 160 acres and no one would be more than a mile from the farthest limit of his farm. Nearer fields could be used for stock and distant ones for grain.

The isolation of life on the homesteads, and the rate at which homesteads were being abandoned, also disturbed Sir William Van Horne. Like Tanner and Smalley, he thought village life would make prairie conditions more tolerable, and he proposed that settlers live in villages placed in the centre of each township, or in hamlets around the villages. In Sir William's plan, radial roads struck across the grid, providing settlers with more direct access to the village than was possible under a rectilinear road pattern.

Criticism of the government settlement plan became more insistent after the turn of the century as British ideas about town and country planning began to reach Canada. The contrast between planning ideals and prairie realities was alarming. A "Closer Community Conference," held in Regina in 1915, was a measure of local concern, as were A. A. Stoughton's articles in the *Manitoba Free Press* in 1917. Stoughton, a professor at the University of Manitoba, was particularly critical of the prairie towns. He dismissed them as "promiscuous groups of shacks" that were so "deformed, squalid and ugly" that they lacked even "the barest necessities for the inspiration of a civic spirit." He was no more pleased with the rectangular survey — "a deadly rectangle of section lines" — and insisted that the grid pattern of roads be replaced by radials leading to towns and villages so planned as to be true community centres. The severity of Stoughton's attack on the survey and the settlement plan was matched by that of another professor, Richard DuWors of Saskatchewan, sixty years later: "The prairies were settled in what was probably the most socially inept system of residence ever used. If one were to be asked what form of settlement . . . made for the greatest isolation and gave the least chance for communal settlements to grow, then the answer would be the form of settlement used in the prairies of North America."

By far the weightiest criticism of the pattern of settlement came from the distinguished British planner, Thomas Adams. In 1916 he had been asked by the Commission of Conservation to examine rural conditions in Canada. Thomas Adams was a past President of the British Institute of Town Planners; at the time of his Canadian visit he was secretary and manager of Letchworth Garden City, the first new town to embody the ideals of the visionary planner, Ebenezer Howard. Though Adams understood the need for a system of land allocation that would allow the rapid and orderly settlement of a vast area, he attacked the survey for its unwavering adherence to mathematical abstraction. Even on flat prairie, he argued, there were local considerations, such as the position of a railway or a river, that ought to have prevented the imposition of a fixed and general system. He was also critical of the towns, noting that the instruction manual for Dominion land surveyors encouraged them to make the directions of the streets and avenues conform to the natural features of the ground while insisting, paradoxically, that they adhere to a system of straight streets crossing at right angles. He also pointed out that the cost of paving main streets ninety-nine feet wide guaranteed that many would remain wildernesses of mud and dust.

Like Professor Stoughton, Thomas Adams recoiled at the isolation of the prairie homesteads and the dreariness of pioneer life. Borrowing Arthur Young's phrase, he charged the government with using the "magic of property" and the "magnet of ownership" to attract people to the land, and then failing to provide the amenities for a social life. The settlement plan he denounced as nothing more than a method of placement. He thought homestead life particularly unattractive for women, and inferred that until it could be made more attractive for both sexes the headlong flight from the land would continue. To substantiate the point, he made reference to an issue of the *Farmer's Advocate* in which it had been reported that homesteaders in the West were leaving the land in thousands.

On the question of improvements, Adams was a realist. He liked the neighbourly arrangement of the early river lots, and he approved the adoption of them in regions of new settlement — e.g., along the Birch and Whitemouth Rivers in eastern Manitoba — but he recognized that in areas already settled the township survey was there to stay. He also acknowledged the farmer's decided preference for compact holdings and square fields, and an arrangement that allowed him to expand his holding by purchasing empty railway lands. In his report to the Commission of Conservation, Adams suggested several methods for planning and re-planning townships. In each case towns and villages were located in the centres of the townships, and the roads led to them as directly as possible. The plans concentrated the settlement and allowed for variations in topographical and physical conditions. Farmsteads arranged in linear patterns along selected roads would make possible a more varied social life and reduce the costs of providing roads and other services.

So appealing was the idea of concentrated settlement, and the mutual aid that was seen to be its corollary, that it eventually found its way into imaginative literature. Dennison Grant's "Big Idea" was a carefully planned cooperative venture that substituted group settlement in villages for the isolated homestead and the rectangular survey. "I propose to form a company and buy a large block of land," said Grant, "cut it up into farms, build houses and community centres, and put returned men and their families on these farms. . . . I shall break up the rectangular survey of the West for something with humanizing possibilities; I mean to supplant it with a system of survey which will permit of settlement in groups —

villages if you like — where I shall install all the modern conveniences of the city." Robert Stead, the author of *Dennison Grant* (1920), had been a colonization agent for the C.P.R.

Yet, in spite of the apparent need for community in the pioneer West, there were relatively few attempts at village life. The homestead laws and the sectional survey did not encourage the formation of villages and, with few exceptions, the farmer's desire for a compact holding whose farthest corners were easily accessible overrode social considerations. It is possible, too, that the advantages of village life were less evident to immigrants than to their observers, who tended to be urban and middle-class. Cyril Genyk, the educated son of peasant parents and the first Ukrainian-born immigration officer, attacked any suggestion or action that might lead to the re-creation of European villages in Western Canada. According to Genyk, Ukrainian villages in the Old Country were notorious theatres for jealousy, quarrelling, and litigation, and places in which ambitions and aspirations beyond the common were routinely stifled. "A village," he remarked, "is not a convenience, it is hell, and we simply cannot have villages here." Even E. V. Smalley was forced to admit that the advantages of contiguity were sometimes more apparent than real. He noted that in the early settlement of Dakota it sometimes happened that four families, each with a quarter-section homestead, built their temporary dwellings on the adjacent corners so as to be near one another. But after a few years, when they were able to put up permanent buildings, they moved to the opposite sides of their claims, giving as a reason that their chickens got mixed up with those of their neighbours. He hastened to add that in most of these instances the people were Americans, in whom generations of isolated living had developed a crustiness that did not take kindly to the familiarities of close association.

Cyril Genyk's fears that villages would grow in all corners of the prairies were unfounded; Western Canada proved no more accommodating to farm villages than the rest of North America. The most durable villages were those built by religious groups, but by 1915, the year of Thomas Adams's visit, many of these had broken up and others were on the point of dissolution.

Mennonite Villages

The first villages, which were also the most instructive, had been built by Dutch Mennonites from — due to the alchemy of East European geography — the Russian steppes. As radical Protestants who refused to bear arms or participate in state affairs, the Mennonites had been driven from the Netherlands early in the sixteenth century and from Prussia late in the eighteenth century. Though politically suspect, they were excellent farmers and able colonists, and in 1788 they agreed to settle Russia's newly acquired "Tartar frontier": the flat, treeless plains along the northern shore of the Black Sea that had only recently been wrested from the nomadic Tartars. The Mennonites were given land (175 acres per family) and guaranteed freedom of religion and exemption from military service.

Their collective response to the steppe was recorded in a memoir: "We looked at each other with fear to find ourselves in a wilderness which as far as the eye could see showed . . . nothing but withered grass. [We had arrived in a world where] the dark winter days and the long nights seem never to end. We were separated from all mankind, and lived miserably in the greatest need." A few tried to return home, but they were turned back by Russian officials. From the Russians and other neighbouring peoples the Mennonites learned how to build subterranean houses — *burdei* or *zemlyanka* — in the black earth of the steppe, and how to fit them with smoke vents and small windows made from animal bladders. With no wood available they invented a heating fuel — *Mistholtz* or manure wood — made from barnyard straw and animal manure. The mixture was moistened, dried in the sun for a year, and then cut into blocks and stored in the same way as firewood.

The Mennonites prospered on the steppes, but by 1870 the Russian welcome had worn thin. Pan-Slavic sentiment threatened the linguistic autonomy of the Mennonite schools, by insisting on the use of Russian in all schools, and the rising militarism of the Germanic states seemed likely to force the Czar to adopt universal military service. But the Mennonites also had internal difficulties. The colonies had outgrown their allocations of land, and landlessness was becoming a problem. Uncertain of the future, the Mennonites began to cast around for possible havens. They looked east to the empty lands of the vast Russian empire and west to the beckoning lands of the New World. Now thoroughly accustomed to the steppes — it was said that a hillock was a thorn in Mennonite eyes — they were particularly interested in the pampas of Argentina and the plains and prairies of the United States and Canada.

Eager to attract the skilled and industrious Mennonites, both the United States and Canada sent agents to Russia to invite delegations to visit their respective Wests. In 1873 delegates visited both regions; most opted for Kansas and Nebraska, whose milder climates would allow the growth of winter wheat and watermelons. Manitoba disappointed them. They were disturbed by the absence of a transcontinental railway, the presence of Indians and Métis, the possibility of drought and, not least, by the aggressiveness of the mosquitoes, whose "forwardness surpassed all limits of decency and moderation." The delegates slept in tents, and at night the mosquito attack was so merciless that neither clothes, hats, nor face nets were proof against it.

In spite of the general reservations, a few delegates — those from the

Bergthal and Keinegemeinde colonies — opted for Manitoba. With their Russian experience in mind, they were swayed by the Canadian government's promise of legislation that would exempt them from military service, and by the government's willingness to modify the homestead laws so that they could settle *en bloc*. They were influenced, too, by the arguments of Jacob Schantz, a prosperous Mennonite businessman from Ontario, who accompanied the Russian delegation. Schantz had visited Manitoba in 1872 and his record of the visit, "Narrative of a Journey to Manitoba," had so pleased the Dominion government that the pamphlet was translated into several languages and distributed widely. The Mennonites were offered eight townships south of Winnipeg and east of the Red River (the "East reserve") with the promise of more should numbers warrant. The first party of settlers arrived in late July 1874, and when the eight-township block of the East reserve was filled the government set aside a new and larger block of seventeen townships (the "West reserve") in open prairie on the west side of the river. Between 1874 and 1880 almost seven thousand Mennonites came to Manitoba.

Although accustomed to steppelands, the Mennonites were distressed by the openness of the West reserve, in spite of assurances that the earth was "excellent good land." Their leaders expressed concern about the absence of wood and hay, and they might well have looked elsewhere for land had Jacob Schantz not reassured them that woodlands along the Pembina Hills would be reserved for the colony. The land of the West reserve between the Red River and the Pembina Hills — "Big Plain" to the Red River settlers — had often been crossed before the arrival of the Mennonites. The Selkirk settlers had crossed it again and again on their hunting expeditions to the Pembina Hills, and in 1875 it was still being crossed by Canadian settlers from Ontario on their way west to rolling country beyond the Pembina Hills community of Mountain City. The historian James Trow noted in 1878 that neither the Scots nor the Ontarians had the least interest in the West reserve, "owing to the scarcity of timber." They had also rejected the East reserve because much of the land was gravelly and poorly drained.

Though upset by the scarcity of woodland, and jarred by the severity of the winters, the Mennonites were wise enough in the ways of the steppe to survive on the Manitoba prairie. Their first primitive shelters had for centuries been the standard temporary dwellings in the grasslands of Russia. A rectangular pit two to three feet deep surrounded by three-foot sod walls, across which poles were extended to support a sod roof, made a dwelling that was proof against the prairie winter. Their clothing was not, however, and they supplemented it with leggings and moccasins made of sacking. In Russia they had learned how to plant trees, and how to make fuel in the absence of wood. They also knew that it was possible to strike water on level ground, though in Manitoba they found well-digging both difficult and dangerous.

A century on the steppe had also taught them the advantages of concentrated or nucleated settlement in exposed, unfamiliar territory. The need for shelter, noted the Mennonite pioneer Harold Funk, was always uppermost in their minds. Linguistically, the Mennonites made no distinction between a village and a shelter: both were *Darp*. They referred to this village, this shelter, this darp. The houses were built side by side and bound together by quick-growing cottonwoods taken along the Pembina River just above the United States border. "Trees were planted," wrote the Mennonite historian Peter Zacharias, "and as the years went by huge cottonwoods lined the street of the village. They tied the whole darp together as it should be bound together. Maples, ashes, elms and evergreens grew in yard after yard. . . . Underneath the shadow of the trees, new houses and barns and summer kitchens linked together to form their own private refuge. Yet on the horizon all these merged together into one, one rising bluff, one prairie shelter." Within the village, visiting or *spazieren* was a confirmed habit, and the word neighbour, or *Nachbar,* encompassed all villagers without reference to the location of their houses. The villagers were usually friends, and in Russia they had been members of the same congregation.

The villages varied in size from a few to a few dozen houses, and on the East reserve there were probably no more than forty-five villages

Cottonwoods lining the village street of Reinhold, Manitoba. Mennonites made no linguistic distinction between a village and a shelter. Both were darp. *(Mennonite Heritage Centre Archives)*

Built in 1906 in Hochfeld, this is a typical example of the type of structures erected by the first Mennonite settlers. Patterned after buildings in the old country, it is reputed to be the only building of its kind in existence in Saskatchewan today. (Mennonite Heritage Centre Archives)

in existence at any one time, although fifty-nine were founded. On the larger West reserve there were seventy foundations, but here, too, abandonment reduced the total so that no more than fifty existed at the same time. The villages were normally laid out in such a way that the buildings of the individual farm units were placed about 200 feet apart and about 100 feet away from the streets to provide ample space for trees, gardens, and fences. Unless a village was laid out alongside a creek, to which all the farmers wished to have access, houses and farm buildings were built on both sides of the street, with lots reserved for schools and churches. Hence they were known as *Strassendorfer,* or street villages. At the end of the village a quarter section or more would be reserved for a common pasture, in which all the animals would be cared for by a single cowherd who, in winter, might also be the village schoolteacher.

The permanent houses were compact, one-and-a-half storey buildings of boards or square timber built, as in Russia, with their gable ends facing the street. Bedrooms were on the street side of the houses, utility rooms and kitchens at the rear. The houses were heated by large ovens of sun-dried brick, about six feet high, built in the very centre of the structures. The ovens, whose sides usually formed part of the interior walls, burned sun-dried manure or *Mistholtz,* twists of straw, and prairie hay. As in southern Russia, house and barn were connected, so that stock could be tended without having to cross the farmyard in winter. Fire was a major hazard because it could, and sometimes did, destroy both house and barn. Disease, infection, and smells were also a problem, but the Mennonites guarded against them through painstaking cleanliness. Manure was never allowed to accumulate in the barns.

Mennonite methods of distributing land were as distinctive as their houses and villages. The village land, or Flur, made up of the quarter sections of each of the householders, was subdivided so that everyone got an equal measure of arable land, woodland, and meadow. Use of land was determined by conditions of slope, drainage, soil quality, and by location in relation to the village. The village was placed in the centre of the Flur. Following the primary division of land, each arable field, or *Gewanne,* was then divided into as many strips or *kagel* as there were households in the village. The usual allotment per householder was about fifty acres of arable land from the various Gewanne. In theory, each householder was free to cultivate his land as he pleased, but in practice everyone followed the same procedure. Crop rotations and the frequency of summer fallowing were arrived at by common consent, so that the same crops (wheat, oats, barley, and flax) were grown at the same time. Cattle were looked after by cowherds, so there was no immediate need to fence the arable fields and haylands. After the harvest, cattle were pastured on the stubble. Each householder was allowed to send out a fixed number of animals with the village herd and to take a fixed amount of hay and wood from the common lands.

Mediaeval in origin, the system was sensitive to human needs and in some ways it was practical; it allowed for differences in the quality of land and, in the early phase of settlement when isolation was felt most keenly, it provided the settlers with community. But not even Mennonite ideals could counter the centrifugal tendencies within North American society; in time, communal farming was abandoned entirely. The strips were too narrow to be farmed efficiently with modern machinery, and the exchange of strips to make compact fields soon progressed to the consolidation of all lands to make individual farms. Farmers found, too, that hauling machinery from the village to distant parts of the Flur took time and caused unnecessary wear and tear. In the East reserve the villages were replaced by dispersed farmsteads; a strong desire for community remained, however, and the dispersal was not always total. To maintain a semblance of village life, compromises were often struck between the two extremes of highly organized village life and the isolated farmstead. Two variations that could be discerned in Manitoba, but which were more noticeable in later Mennonite settlements in Saskatchewan, were the unorganized village and the four-corner hamlet. The unorganized village followed the linear Strassendorfer pattern, but was much looser in form. Lot sizes varied widely, and the spacing of the dwellings was erratic. The four-corner hamlet was made up of three or four farmsteads clustered on adjacent corners of their quarter sections.

The village structure proved to be most durable on the West reserve in Manitoba. More than a dozen Strassendorfer survived the breakdown of communal farming, and each day the farmers went out from the village to work their compact fields. According to the geographer John Warkentin, they had the best of both worlds: the social advantages of village life and the opportunity to farm efficiently and independently on large, consolidated units.

Despite the eventual failure of an ideal, during the forty or fifty years that the villages lasted a small part of Manitoba was as picturesque and as pastoral as any of the West's promoters could have wished. Quaint wooden houses, with plastered exterior walls and roofs of thatched hay; flour mills with huge arms and sails; herds of cattle tended by girls in bonnets or flowered kerchiefs and long, dark dresses; and villages with names to soften the most sceptical heart: Rosenthal (valley of roses), Rosengarten, Rosenfelt, Blumenist (place of flowers). Mennonite women, who loved flowers, introduced the dahlia to the prairies. The Mennonites also loved trees. Immediately after settlement long rows of maple, poplar, and balm of Gilead trees were planted, both for protection and decoration, so that the villages, as one chronicler remarked, were "gems of sylvan beauty."

Tourists, visiting journalists, agronomists, and rural planners were all enchanted by the Mennonite villages. Cora E. Hind left this description of a transplanted world: "The walls are a delicate lilac, the window sashes a dull red, the shutters gray. Wind and rain and sun have stained the thatches a deep brown. A village of these houses, seen when flooded with mellow October sunshine and against a background of yellow stubble fields, presents a wonderful harmony of colour, and is more suggestive of Holland, in the sixteenth, than Manitoba in the nineteenth century." But the greater admiration was for the villagers themselves. The Mennonites had been the first settlers to live away from the shelter of valleys and woodlands, and their villages offered a practical alternative to the isolated homestead. One of the strongest admirers of the Mennonites was Lady Dufferin, wife of the Governor General, Lord Dufferin. She admired their ability to settle so quickly into a woodless place — "which no other people will do" — and to survive a long Canadian winter without wood or coal. She liked the simplicity of their houses, "very plainly built," and the general orderliness of the settlement. "Everything looks neat," she wrote in her Canadian journal (August 1877), "home-made wooden furniture, flowers in the windows, nice gardens, etc. . . . . Think what a gain they are to this country: in three years to have eighteen square miles of country settled by such people."

Doukhobors

Equally as adept at surviving in a prairie environment were the Mennonites' erstwhile neighbours in southern Russia, the Doukhobors.

Another radical Christian sect, the Doukhobors at the beginning of the nineteenth century sought refuge from the molestations of their Orthodox central Russian neighbours in the Tartar frontier just north of the Crimea. Their only settled neighbours were the Mennonites, who preceded them, and the Molokans, who came shortly afterward. Like the Mennonites, they refused to do military service, and in the 1840s an impatient Russian government expelled them to a cold, dry region of the Caucasus. As skilled farmers accustomed to continental conditions, but living uneasily in Russia, the Doukhobors had attracted the attention of a Canadian government anxious to fill the empty lands west of Manitoba. In 1899 more than seven thousand of them were induced to emigrate. They were granted concessions similar to those accorded the Mennonites: reserved land, exemption from military duty, and permission to settle in villages. Their allotment was three large blocks of land, reserved for their sole use, in what was to become Saskatchewan.

Like the Mennonites, the Doukhobors adopted a decentralized pattern of settlement. Villages, built on traditional plans followed in the Ukraine and the Caucasus, were of no more than fifty houses, each house sheltering a family of several generations. Where trees were available they made houses of logs chinked with clay; in drier districts, where the spindly willow was the only woody plant, they resorted to the practice of wattle-and-daub, interweaving the branches and applying inside and out a smooth coating of clay. The first houses were roofed with sod and heated with clay-built stoves large enough for children and the old to sleep on in the coldest weather. The houses were built in a double row, with the street between; behind them were barns, granaries, stables, and outdoor baking ovens. The village street was wide and tree-lined and, in districts where there were no trees, windbreaks and fruit trees were planted.

Traditional houses arranged in street villages, and large open fields worked communally, gave Doukhobor villages more than a passing resemblance to Mennonite villages. But there were differences in the Doukhobor landscape produced by differences in outlook. For Doukhobors, who adhered strictly to the directives of their spiritual leader, Peter Veregin, communality was all. In Russia the connected house-barn had been the traditional farmstead unit, as it had been in the Mennonite settlements, but in Canada Veregin decreed that Doukhobors should lead a strictly communal life. As communal property, crops and livestock were properly to be stored in community barns. Land, too, was regarded as indivisible, and large fields were farmed as single units. There were no individual strips, as in the Mennonite fields.

Doukhobor intransigence over the principle of communality quickly brought them into conflict with the Canadian government. About two thirds of the Doukhobors refused to register their quarter sections and obtain patents for them. They also refused to pledge allegiance to the

Crown, fearing that this might entail military service. To Canadians, Doukhobors seemed very foreign indeed. Within a few years they were labelled "Sifton's pets" by the press, and "the refuse of Russia" by a choleric senator. Mennonites, however, gained universal approval; as law-abiding and inventive farmers they were held up as models to incoming homesteaders. Unwilling to tolerate Doukhobor intransigence, the Canadian government in 1905 demanded that the homesteads be registered on pain of forfeiture. Doukhobors who had rejected the idea of hereditary leadership complied, but the followers of Peter Veregin stood firm, and within a few years they moved west to form communities on land they had bought in the interior of British Columbia.

Secular Communities

Villages, in the sense of a core of dwellings from which the inhabitants moved out daily to their fields, were rare outside the religious communities. Secular communities for the most part were settlements whose aims were social and economic rather than ideological. The best-known experiments were English, and they were motivated not by lofty communitarian ideals but by an arcadian vision: the prospect of re-creating on the prairies the life of well-to-do English farmers. They were versions of what Lewis Mumford once called "Utopias of the Country House."

There were two well-known experiments: the settlement of Cannington Manor and the Barr colony, both in Saskatchewan. As envisaged by its founder, the Reverend Isaac Barr, the Barr colony was to be an all-British settlement of professional men and successful urban artisans. Barr stressed that the settlement would be of "the ordinary kind," but one characterized by companionship, social cooperation, and mutual help. Settlers would farm their own land rather than congregate in villages, but by each locating on a tract of land reserved for the colony they would be spared the isolation that usually accompanied pioneering on the prairies. To provide ballast for a settlement bound to be top-heavy with townsmen, Barr proposed to introduce a few experienced Canadian and American farmers (of British descent) whose farms would be an object lesson for inexperienced British settlers. Only 10% of the Barr colonists had any experience of farming.

In March, 1903, two thousand colonists set sail from Britain in a ship designed to carry five hundred. On reaching the West, they found the way unprepared. Barr had promised to supply the colonists with food and equipment through a merchants' syndicate, but on arriving in Saskatoon the colonists had to fend for themselves. Nor had Barr made adequate preparations for the trek to their reserved land in western Saskatchewan. Instead of the 400 horses promised, there were thirty "cayuses." The "tent hotels" promised for accommodations on the route west were in the end provided by the Department of Immigration, which set up camps with supplies of wood and hay every twenty miles along the trail.

The predicament of the Barr colonists was no different from that of thousands of other immigrants who came unaided to the prairies. It stands out because of the particular ingenuousness of the colonists, their high expectations, and the fanfare that attended their arrival. A number of them, as the settlement agent George Langley remarked, "seemed unable to free themselves from the idea that the whole thing was a sort of picnic," and that they were about to enter a new Jerusalem: "picturesque parkland," as one colonist envisaged it, "with grassy, gently rolling slopes interspersed with clumps of trees, a sparkling stream and possibly a silver lake thrown in, and the whole estate alive with game of all kinds." Though the Battleford area of Saskatchewan, where the colonists settled, is in the parkland, the realities of pioneer farming and the first winter brought a rude awakening. The less determined colonists left for Britain or the cities, but the rest muddled through. Under new leadership and a new name (Britannia) the colony survived, but of course it failed to provide the kind of English country life envisaged by its promoters; in form and function it was no different from any other group settlement on the prairies.

More focused, but just as ridiculed today, was the earlier Cannington experiment. The founder of Cannington was Captain Edward Michell Pierce, an energetic Victorian whose fortunes in England had sunk with a merchant ship that carried the bulk of his investments. Failing health and the prospect of raising a large family on a diminished income made him look to the colonies, and he was attracted to Western Canada. He came to Toronto in 1882, then travelled West with his two eldest sons to look for homestead land. Like all Englishmen, he was captivated by the parkland, and in particular by a location on the lightly wooded slopes of Moose Mountain, a line of low hills that ripple the surface of what is now southern Saskatchewan. The soil was good and the slopes of the mountain offered pleasant prospects, game, and timber for fuel and construction.

But when filing for a homestead, Captain Pierce learned that the district in which it was located, roughly forty miles south of the Canadian Pacific line, was not yet open for settlement. Undeterred, he returned to Ontario, where he determined to beg a dispensation from the Minister of the Interior. Instead, he was granted an interview with the Prime Minister himself, Sir John A. Macdonald. At the interview Captain Pierce disclosed a scheme for founding in Western Canada a settlement of British people of his own stamp. Possibly intrigued by the prospect of a leaven of gentlefolk in what was certain to be an overwhelmingly plebeian settlement, and probably mindful of recent legislation that encouraged group settlement in the West, the Prime Minister granted Captain Pierce's request. He promised to open the district for settlement, allowing Captain Pierce and his three eldest sons to file for homesteads. He also promised to build a branch line that would connect the proposed settlement with the main line of the C.P.R. In addition, the government and the C.P.R agreed to reserve sections adjacent to the Pierce properties for English families.

To attract settlers from his own social class to the district, Captain Pierce sent to English newspapers notices that presented Cannington as a place no "heavily handicapped *paterfamilias*" could reasonably resist. Land was virtually free, there were no rents, rates, taxes, or coal merchant's bills, and there was fine shooting, fishing, boating, and good society. "You will still fancy yourself in England," he promised, "only without England's worries and anxieties."

Captain Pierce's blandishments worked. Middle-class English families were attracted to the district, and these formed the mainstay of the settlement. Not the least of the attractions was the prospect of a congenial social life. James Humphrys, a marine engineer, wrote from Cannington to his wife in England: "I cannot but recognize this all important question of social surroundings for you and the children." The settlement was named Cannington, after the home of the Michell family in Somerset, and, ostensibly to prevent confusion with Cannington, Ontario, the haughty suffix Manor was added.

Incoming families built houses from fieldstone, or squared logs — cut on Moose Mountain by neighbouring Canadian pioneers — or sawn lumber hauled by ox team from the C.P.R. station at Moosomin, forty miles away. Although made from unfamiliar materials, the houses looked reassuringly English. All migrants, the geographer Vidal de la Blache once remarked, like to carry their shells with them. Most of the houses were Victorian villas with spacious hallways, well staircases, French windows, dining rooms and, in one or two cases, libraries. On birthdays and festivals the occupants ate off Wedgewood dinner services with Georgian silverware, and listened to recitals played on a grand piano. To complete the Englishness of the scene, some of the houses were set in lawns and gardens protected from prairie winds by planted trees and shrubbery.

However reassuring they might have looked, Victorian villas were hardly practical in Western Canada. Biting winds tore at their upper storeys, and cold ran amok in the generously proportioned rooms. They were impossible to heat; cutting and hauling wood for the largest house in the community was a full-time job for two men. Servicing the houses was also a problem in the Canadian social climate. Servants brought from England quickly drifted away, the men to homestead on their own and the women to marry Canadian bachelors. In some cases, too, household tasks were complicated by shortages of water. Houses built on high ground so that their owners might enjoy a view were usually far above the water table.

A picnic in the garden of a lakeside cottage near Cannington. The pansies, the climbing vines, and the brick-edged path could be found in almost any English country garden. (University of Saskatchewan Library, Morton Collection)

To realize his dream of a self-supporting community, Captain Pierce encouraged commerce and manufacturing. The community's economic nexus was a cooperative trading company (The Moose Mountain Trading Co.) that built and owned most of the community services. These included a grist mill, a blacksmith's and woodworker's shop, a cheese factory, a pork-packing plant, a hotel — the Mitre — a post office, and a general store. All were placed in the centre of the community on homestead land claimed by the Pierce family. The company also built a church and an assembly hall, which did double duty as a school, and hired the services of a doctor from England. The pork-packing plant actually supplied the London firm of Spears and Pond for a time, but lost the contract when it couldn't maintain a steady supply of meat.

As a supplement to their incomes, Captain Pierce and the heads of other large families struck on the novel idea of founding an agricultural college in which young men from well-to-do English families could learn basic farming practices. They hoped that, once trained, the young men would take up homesteads of their own and so solidify the middle-class nature of the community. To advertise the scheme, letters were placed in the *Times* and the *Manchester Guardian* proclaiming the agricultural promise of Western Canada and offering "expert tuition to young men of good birth and education" for the sum of one hundred pounds a year.

Captain Pierce's proposal evidently answered a need, for the response to it was immediate. Many families siezed the opportunity to place, at no great expense, younger and, in some cases, unwanted sons. The first students arrived within months of the appearance of the advertisements. In spite of its popularity, however, the college never acquired permanent buildings nor a permanent staff. Some of the students were housed in a dormitory attached to Captain Pierce's house while the rest boarded with other members of the community or squatted in abandoned pioneer shacks in the district. Instruction appears to have been haphazard and uninformed, and many of the students seem to have had no serious interest in farming. Several, in fact, had generous remittances and looked upon their stay at the settlement as a carefree interlude between school and adult life. Yet in spite of the failings of the instructors and the general imperviousness of the instructed, a few students managed to learn enough about farming to take up homesteads of their own.

For a few years the settlement of about 150 people prospered. There were thriving choral, dramatic, and art societies, and during the summers the active played tennis, cricket and rugby — the triad of English middle-class sports. By not mixing socially with the surrounding homesteaders, the community maintained its middle-class English character. The bachelors alone adopted the ways of the new country, forsaking standard English dress for pioneer outfits of coarse brown duck, cowboy hats, and Mexican spurs. In spite of these small threats to its social integrity, Captain Pierce must have been well pleased with his settlement. But his enjoyment was brief. In 1888 he died prematurely, and the social leadership of the community passed to a group of rich, pleasure-loving bachelors who were to undermine its serious, if eccentric, purpose.

The bachelors, who lived in a twenty-two room stone mansion replete with a billiard parlour, indulged in the sybaritic sporting life for which Cannington is now a byword in Western Canada. Built of limestone, and with a high gabled roof, bay windows, and a broad verandah, "Didsbury" was easily the most striking house in southern Saskatchewan. Wrote one bemused reporter: "One is rather staggered at seeing such a place on the prairie." Staggering, too, was the interior, with its hand-carved mantles, polished mirrors, Hepplewhite furniture, and Turkish carpets. Beside the house stood a stone-built stables lined with mahogany.

To indulge their sporting interests, the bachelors made a race-track, and they imported thoroughbred horses which raced in meets as distant as Chicago and New York. They also built a cockpit and an elaborate complex of kennels for bull terriers and hounds. The bull terriers were used for badger-baiting and the hounds for chasing the red fox, then plentiful in Saskatchewan. Because there were no fences, and little cover for the fox, hunts were conducted at a gallop. Bertram Tennyson, who was a frequent visitor to Cannington in the 1890s, described the pace of the hunts:

> *For here no fences break the pace, no*
> *Check gives time for breath,*
> *You're in for no long hunting run, we*
> *Ride from view to death.*

At the hunts men wore jackets, top boots, and breeches; women wore riding habits. Each fall the settlement devoted a full week to hunting — if necessary, legend has it, delaying the harvest, regardless of the condition of the crop.

But the frolic was short-lived. By 1900 the bachelors had run through their fortunes and the branch line of the C.P.R. that Captain Pierce had been promised passed ten miles south of the settlement. The owners of small businesses gradually moved out, and were soon followed by the English farming families. A few settled in a new location near the railway, taking with them the "Manor" half of the colony's name. Some returned to England; others, attracted by the mild climate, moved to British Columbia. The bachelors went in several directions: some to professional and business careers in the cities, others to the Boer War and the equally dangerous Klondike goldfields. The few diehards who were still in the district by 1914 returned to England to fight in the Great War.

Members of the Cannington Manor Hunt Club. Hunting was so popular that — according to prairie lore — the harvest was sometimes postponed in favour of the fall hunt. (Saskatchewan Archives Board, R-A 8181)

Cannington today is usually regarded as nothing more than a colourful footnote to the serious business of prairie settlement: a colonial folly, perpetrated by "green" Englishmen, whose failure has served to reinforce the cherished myth of the stalwart pioneer. Yet however eccentric and outlandish the aims of its founders, Cannington should be seen as a significant counterpoint to the settlement at large. In a rural society riven by loneliness, it was a deliberate and, until the death of Captain Pierce, serious attempt to defy the ideals of individualism inherent in the sectional survey by creating a community of people of one background. The country surrounding Cannington, looked at from a social point of view, was a wasteland of pioneer shacks. The contrast didn't escape John Donkin who, in his description of the village, indulged in a rare moment of sentimentality:

> *Towards evening we again entered a lovely country magnificent in rolling woodlands, with the blue range of the Moose Mountains rising behind. . . . At this place we were one mile and a half from Cannington, a flourishing English settlement. It is essentially a moneyed, aristocratic colony; in fact the village is a model one. . . . There is a mill, a pretty church, and an excellent hotel, well-furnished and possessing a most courteous host. It has also a club, a school, and town-hall. Captain Pierce, formerly of the Royal Artillery, is the moving spirit, and holds 2000 acres of land. Things are carried out to such perfection that there is a surpliced choir, and everything has a flavour of home. Flocks of Cotswold and Leicester sheep roam over the green slopes of this undulating country.*
>
> *When winding our way over an excellent trail through thickets, vocal with the music of birds, it did not take a very strong imagination to make one fancy we were moving through some fine old park in Merry England. A flourishing homestead stood on a gentle rise, with barns, and byres, and folds. Sheep and cattle clustered round the out-buildings, some plethoric ducks waddled down to a pond, poultry cackled round the doors, and a group of chubby children gazed in awe as the red-coated soldiers went jingling by. After passing the glimpse of comfort, so painfully suggestive of the dear land across the sea, we faced once more the desolate plains, with lonely, ugly log shanties standing in hideous solitude here and there.*

Chapter Seven

NOSTALGIA FOR THE HOMELAND

John Donkin's nostalgic response to Cannington was so predictable that it might have been programmed. Familiar objects in the landscape, familiar sounds and smells, frequently triggered memories of the homeland. Though settled, immigrants were far from "at home." Even contented settlers could be unmanned by the sight, sound, or smell of something familiar. The Scottish settler William Gibson, who was well pleased with his life in Saskatchewan, was disarmed by the sound of a cockerel crowing in the early dawn: "This was like sweet music to us. I could, when listening to this, almost forget my new home and its present surroundings, and conceive myself to be inside of an old-fashioned Scotch farmhouse, with a straw thatched roof away on the moorland borders of Ayrshire . . . sheltered by trees hoary with age, and which had been a shelter for these homesteads two hundred years."

In the chronically homesick, however, reminders of the homeland induced anguish rather than nostalgia. Erik Munsterhjelm found that the trees and lakes of northern Saskatchewan reminded him so strongly of his native Norway that he was felled by a violent attack of homesickness: "It tormented me like a physical pain; everything that reminded me of my home was like a fresh stab." Homesick Ukrainian immigrants were also undermined by the sight and sound of trees. One of them wrote:

> *Oh, do not whisper, my grove,*
> *You green grove,*
> *Do not give my heart more pain*
> *Because I am in a foreign land.*

Yet with time familiar objects in the landscape could ease the pain of being uprooted. Erik Munsterhjelm found that the feeling of intense homesickness eventually passed, and he felt more at home among the trees and lakes of northern Saskatchewan than anywhere else he had been since crossing the Atlantic.

There is no way of gauging the extent of homesickness among the immigrants, but the evidence suggests that it was endemic. Leaving the Fatherland and the place where the cradle stood was not, as one Norwegian remarked sombrely, "a small matter." Least affected by homesickness were the "pushful and determined," who quickly joined the ranks of the prairie boosters, and the English-speaking young, for whom the world seemed full of opportunity and hope. "No small town in Canada or elsewhere," wrote James A. Smart, "could possibly have contained a happier army of young men than did Brandon in its earliest years."

But older and reluctant emigrants, who had come to Canada to escape unacceptable or intolerable conditions at home, seem to have suffered acutely. Unlike the United States, Canada had no constitutional ideals of happiness and individual liberty to sustain immigrant morale. A Loyalist country that had remained faithful to the Crown was less a land of beginning again than a northern refuge from debilitating forces in other places. Canada could offer political safety and shelter, but not transcendent ideals. People came here not, as de Tocqueville said of immigrants to America, to be "born free," but to escape oppression, to preserve traditions and ways of life threatened at home and, like immigrants the world over, to improve their material lives. They arrived as quiet recipients of a land already won, not as potential conquerors: the Indians had been subdued, the land surveyed and subdivided, and lawlessness brought under control. Psychologically, it was a setting better suited to the transplanting of old worlds than to the making of new ones.

For European settlers in particular, the sense of homelessness was exacerbated by the absence in the new land of a culture or a history with which they could identify. Traders and settlers who came before the railway and the settlement survey had complemented native ways of life. Fur traders had provided the Indians with a market for furs and pemmican; by clinging to the rivers, long-lot farmers respected the old highways and did not impede Indian and Métis movements across prairie and parkland. Far from obstructing the hunters, the farmers frequently joined the chase. But mass European settlement simply obliterated native ways of life; Indian culture seemed so remote that it could never have occurred to the settlers that it might be learned from or aspired to. Immigrants suffered a double loss as a result: they were separated both from their own homelands and histories, and from the history and traditions of the country they had come to occupy. For immigrants from cultivated backgrounds there was also the fear, as Wallace Stegner noted, that they

Eastern Europeans on the deck of an emigrant ship, photographed by Page Toles, c. 1910. (Public Archives Canada, C 68842)

had given up a heritage of some richness to become part of a backwater peasantry incapable of the feeblest cultural aspiration.

Set down in an environment with neither a history nor a culture that held any meaning for them, the immigrants were assailed by nostalgia. They expressed it by homesteading in familiar looking settings, building houses of traditional European type, and naming features, towns, and villages after places or people in the homeland. The literate also wrote about their sense of loss. One Englishman remarked that feelings of homesickness were so intense and widespread that most of the immigrants would have walked home had there been a bridge across the Atlantic. "But there was no bridge and no money, so we stuck it out. What else could we do?" Even the Mennonites, who had no homeland to return to, and who were accustomed to the steppes, hungered for a familiar, lived-in setting:

> *With tears I look upon the place*
> *Where I have chosen to live.*
> *No house, no hearth, no chair, no bed,*
> *No horse, no cow, no meat, no flour,*
> *No dish, no spoon, no nothing at all.*
> *How unencumbered I am in this wide world.*

Mennonites who had elected to go south found just as little to comfort them in the Kansas prairie. There were "no inviting roads leading to well-known places, no friendly trees, no sociable herds of cattle; not a familiar sound except the chirp of a cricket." Just "barren prairie in every direction." In Russlaund (Russia) they had left behind "a land of beautiful villages where the *hundatjoasche letj* [hundred year oak] threw out its branches in the heart of Chortitza, a village in which everything was handier than anywhere else on earth."

The most poignant expressions of anomie, or the loss of place, came from those least capable of being uprooted: the peasants of central and eastern Europe. Place matters to everyone, but to peasants, as Oscar Handlin remarked, place was the centre of their being, the fixed point from which they gauged their relationships with the world and all humanity. "I was born in such and such a village in such and such a parish" was the refrain that opened the recital of all peasant lives. The village church, the inn, the houses, and the surrounding fields were their entire world, and they were bound to it by the rituals of work, prayer, and seasonal festivals. Unable to read or to travel — only migrant labourers would have journeyed more than twenty-five or thirty miles from home — they knew little of the world beyond the village, and they had almost no conception of global distances. Yet when Poles, Galicians, Ruthenians, and Bukowinans left for Canada, ignorance of geography

The huge oak in the village of Chortitza, Russia. It is said that the village children played hide-and-seek on its branches. (Mennonite Heritage Centre Archives)

was no shield against the intuitive knowledge that it was a journey from which few travellers would return. Therefore, they brought with them all that was most useful and precious: sickles, scythes, hoes, hatchets (all with handles removed); thimblefuls of grain; vegetable, herb, and flower seeds neatly tied or sewed into tiny pockets in each corner of a kerchief; small bags of native soil, and carefully wrapped roots of the revered *kalyna* bush. Some would also have carried a history of the Ukraine, a volume of the poems of Schevchenko, a prayer book, and a book of Bible stories.

On the eve of departure there were special church services and dances, but one suspects that the dances, like the "America wakes" held by the Irish, were masks for sorrow. The agony of the final leave-taking was described by the poet Maria Adamowska, who left the Western Ukraine, then in Poland, in 1899: "When we reached the hill on the outskirts of the settlement, we paused for a last look at our dear native village, nestled proudly in the midst of its cherry orchards as if decked with garlands. Overcome by grief, none of us had the strength to utter a single word. Only the weeping heart sang:

> *Farewell my village, my native village*
> *My native land,*
> *For God only knows whether*
> *I shall ever see you again."*

At a bend in the lane leading from a village in Hugh Brody's parish of Innishkillane in Western Ireland there was a large rock, known as the Rock of the Weeping of Tears, where the departing looked back for the last time at the assembled villagers.

As unworldly peasants, Galicians, Ruthenians, and Bukowinans had a more difficult passage to the new land than most. They were easy marks for money-changers and hawkers, who descended like locusts on the emigrant boats and trains, and they were convenient victims for the bullies amongst customs and immigration officials. Once free of officialdom they boarded trains that ran for a week through a land of rock, muskeg, lakes, and bush before being, in Vera Lysenko's bitter phrase, "hurled" at the prairie. To sympathetic observers they looked more like refugees than the bold pioneers of Whitmanesque fancy. The Ukrainian poet Ivan Franko saw them thus:

> *If in some railway station you should spy*
> *Like herrings in a keg, tightly packed, a crowd,*
> *Women so gaunt and pale you want to cry —*
> *Like wheat stalks hit by hail, broken, wilted, bowed —*
> *The children huddled close, without a smile,*
> *The men morose, of stern, fanatic glance,*

With care and thwarted dreams each forehead lined,
Their ragged, dusty bundles round them piled —
Those are the emigrants.

Once in Western Canada, Ukrainians, like all non-English-speaking immigrants, found themselves isolated linguistically as well as geographically, and even when they did learn to speak English — haltingly — they were frequently regarded as oafs. They suffered particularly from Anglo-Saxon condescension and hostility. "Galicians" (pronounced Galeecians), the Anglo-Saxon's generic term for all central and eastern European immigrants, were tolerated only as work-hardened farmers and labourers — "stolid and stunned and brothers to the ox," in one unsympathetic characterization — capable of clearing the heavy bushlands and building the railways. Repulsed by unfriendly Anglo-Saxons, dismayed by the harshness of the environment, they lost what they most needed and once had in abundance: a sense of belonging. Those unable to establish contact with the new environment suffered from what psychoanalysts now recognize as a stuporous depression that amounts to the emptying of the entire psychic apparatus. In early photographs they looked out at the world with the bewildered, uncomprehending eyes of refugees.

Though Ukrainian immigrants brought fifty new species of plant to Canada, and would in time transform the environments of their farm-

Uncertain Galician immigrants, in traditional costume, photographed by W. J. Topley, Quebec, 1911. (Public Archives Canada, PA 10401)

steads, they were at first distressed by the absence of familiar plants. Only the cranberry (*kalyna*) comforted:

> *All is different in you, Canada!*
> *The plants, the birds and all the animals —*
> *Sadness and dreariness, as in a grave.*
> *Nothing to see that is dear to me*
> *Save the lone cranberry, the only plant*
> *That took our roots — beloved cranberry!*

For all immigrants, the initial period of settlement was the most difficult. These were the "dog years" of the Scandinavian settlers, when to earn needed cash men often had to leave their families to work on threshing gangs, or as labourers on the railways and construction sites. Once the immigrants were established, the intense phase of their homesickness abated, but attacks could come at any time. Usually they were triggered by a specific event or incident: the onset of spring, the first snowfall, the death of parents in the homeland or, without fail, old age and imminent death. In one of the earliest recorded incidents of homesickness in Western Canada, a dying Highlander from the Kildonan district of the Red River settlement cried to her physician: "If only I could see a hill I think I would live."

Readers of Vilhelm Moberg's trilogy of novels about emigration will also be familiar with the aged Karl Oskar Nilsson's final preoccupation. In a drawer by his bedside Karl Oskar kept a coloured topographic map of his native parish in Sweden, tattered and worn thin from frequent handling. Every day he withdrew the map and, guided by an arthritic finger, walked again the roads of his youth. He noted the villages and crossroads, the fields and farm boundaries; he could almost smell the ripe crops, the sweet birch leaves, and the pungent pines. For Karl Oskar, as for all aged immigrants, the old country was the country of youth, and the new of crabbed old age. Yet nostalgia for the homeland wasn't just a longing for youth. When the Nilssons first came to North America, Karl Oskar's young wife Kristina made similar mental journeys. Prostrated by homesickness, she found some relief by retracing the ground that had brought her to a lonely cabin on the plains. She winged her way across the continent and the ocean, but when she approached her village she halted and covered the last few miles in a slow, lingering walk that allowed her to savour every detail of the scene.

The Nilsson rituals and the lament of the dying Kildonan Highlander suggest that memories of the homeland were rooted in landscape: memories require a local habitation and a name; they are soundest when fixed in space. Generalized longings for the homeland were usually fixed in space. Generalized longings for the homeland were usually expressed by listing the most pleasant features of the country: "I can almost see them

Travellers in hope. Prairie-bound Scottish immigrants, c. 1918. (C.P.R. Corporate Archives, 8454)

[the Carpathians] and hear the gentle whisper of their pine trees, the burble of the streams, the warble of the nightingale, and the trill of the lark." Pine trees, streams, and larks were symbols of longing for the homeland rather than objects missed in their own right. There were trees and streams on the prairies, but they were not Carpathian trees nor Carpathian streams. Longing for particular places usually centred on the childhood home and the native village, the intensity of this longing may be taken as a measure of the trauma of being uprooted. In traditional peasant societies, detachment from the parental hearth was a gradual process that seldom involved geographical dislocation more serious than a move to a neighbouring village. But for young emigrants to Canada, the separation was abrupt and the physical dislocation almost beyond comprehension. Distances between the old land and the new were insurmountable, so that "the frayed ends of the little heartstrings broken," as Guy Divet, the son of Red River colonists, delicately noted, "were never brought together again." Most immigrants felt so vulnerable in the bewildering new land that they couldn't resist journeying in spirit back to the land of "Motionless Childhood," in Gaston Bachelard's words, where they were able to relive memories of protection. Most, too, sensed that they would be unable to recreate in the dynamic new world the kind of family stability and continuity they had known in Europe. Immigrants might build substantial houses and raise families but, for many, home would always be the family home in the native land. Even in heaven, remarked a Ukrainian immigrant, you pine for a native land.

Nostalgia for the landscape of home was most acute in winter, when the prairie seemed most alien. Mary Brown recalled how a visiting Irishman would, on winter evenings, regale her entire family by reciting poetry, and by telling tales of Ireland that were mere vehicles for detailed descriptions of the Irish landscape. Winter, too, she noted, brought the most extreme expression of longing for the landscape of home. "The sun would set on a perfectly white plain, no dark object visible, everything covered with the white mantle of snow. After sunrise in the morning the plain seemed to be dotted with houses and trees, in one direction would appear a range of hills, in another a vast lake, and you would imagine you saw ships upon it, then the scene would change and when you looked again you would see the same old familiar prairie."

PART II

MAKING A COUNTRY

Chapter Eight

THE CULT OF THE TREE

Although familiar features in the landscape often caused immediate anguish by triggering memories of the homeland, in the long run the very strangeness of the new landscape was a major cause of distress. The least familiar characteristic of all was, of course, the treelessness of the dry south. Cleared of vegetation by the ice sheets, and then subjected to a climate niggardly with moisture, the southernmost parts of Manitoba, Saskatchewan, and Alberta had for millennia been unable to sustain a continuous tree cover. Seedlings that managed to root in the dry soils outside the river valleys were killed either by browsing buffalo or, more probably, by prairie fires set by lightning or by Indian hunters, who used fire to drive the buffalo in desired directions. The absence of trees was seen by Europeans as a deficiency, not as a characteristic of the landscape. The prairie they defined negatively, and inaccurately, by what it was not: featureless, treeless, waterless, and flat. In short, it was a landscape without validity, an accident of nature. The perception was standard among immigrants, and it determined the ways in which they ordered the environment and changed it to meet their needs.

Henry Kelsey, the first European to record his impressions of the region, set the pattern for subsequent perceptions. In his report to the Hudson's Bay Company in 1691 he described the grasslands as barren, by which he meant not a wasteland but a plain without trees. A century and a half later, John Palliser, adopting American usage, used the phrase "central desert" to describe the plains near the United States boundary. Like Kelsey, Palliser probably meant not desert proper — he referred specifically to pastureland — but dryland terrain of short grasses, without trees and without much surface water. Once the plains were earmarked for agricultural settlement the term "desert" was heard no more, but the idea of unfinished or unsatisfactory nature lived on.

As well as failing to meet biotic norms, the grasslands also fell short on aesthetic grounds. Europeans had been raised in the belief that trees in a landscape were necessary for comeliness and beauty. A landscape without trees was as unacceptable as a head without hair. Fashion and decency decreed that both should be covered, by a wig in one case and by trees in the other. Trees were "to the earth as the hairs of a man's head," Englishman John Smith remarked in 1670. Twenty-five years later Charles Marshall and Lord Kames reiterated the sentiment. Marshall noted that a place without trees appeared "disagreeably naked," and Kames that "a hill covered with trees appears more beautiful . . . than when naked."

The European love of trees dates from the Middle Ages. The dense forests had terrified at first, but as they were cut back they ceased to frighten and became instead valued sources of inspiration and visual pleasure. Monks had planted trees for the sake of their beauty since Anglo-Saxon times. Orchards, in particular, were thought to be places of delight, and in the reign of Henry VIII John Leland could write of the "pleasure of orchards." In the countryside, hedgerows and hedgerow trees had many admirers. They provided shade for cattle, demarcated property, and furnished wood for fuel and fencing. But the hedgerows, and the trees incorporated in them, as Leonard Meager conceded in 1797, were not just useful: they could afford "pleasant and delightful prospects to the eye." The view was shared by foreign visitors to England who thought that hedges made the whole countryside look like a beautiful garden.

By the eighteenth century the pleasure afforded by trees and woodland had turned to passion. Part of the emotion might be called religious. Christians could have no truck with sacred trees or sacred groves, yet remnants of ancient rituals survived. Green branches were carried in procession on May Day or at Midsummer, and in popular folklore many trees had associations of protection that made it unlucky to cut them down. "The love of woods," Addison pronounced in 1713, "seems to be a passion implanted in our natures." To Alexander Pope a tree was "a nobler object than a prince in his coronation robes," while for William Gilpin trees were "the grandest and most beautiful productions of the earth." Even the notably urban Samuel Johnson loved the sight of a fine forest, and detested the South Downs near Brighton because they were so bare. "Walking in a wood when it rained," recalled Mrs Piozzi, "was,

I think, the only rural image he pleased his fancy with." In the later eighteenth century, painters began to specialize in portraits of trees, and devoted much time to studying their silhouettes. It was said of John Constable, for example, that he would embrace a tree with as much feeling as he would a child. English gentlemen, observed the American Washington Irving, spent hours discussing the shape and beauty of individual trees, as if they were statues or horses. Between 1770 and 1850 books on handsome trees, famous trees, and ancient trees, and books on how to draw trees, poured off the presses.

Trees were also cherished as symbols of continuity and association. From Anglo-Saxon times trees had been essential landmarks, establishing local boundaries or serving as meeting-places for assemblies. Such trees were older than any of the inhabitants, and they symbolized the community's continued existence. The desire to associate particular trees with national or historic events was ubiquitous. English travellers to Italy were shown trees supposedly planted by St Francis or St Dominic. At home they could see the oak were Edward I had convened his parliament, the oak in the New Forest which had deflected the arrow that pierced William Rufus, and the Boscabel oak that protected Charles II after the battle of Worcester. In 1978 *The Times* carried a photograph of Queen Elizabeth's Oak in Hatfield Park, under which she was allegedly sitting when she received news of her accession, and to this day British trade unionists help to maintain the martyr's tree at Tolpuddle.

The Gospel of Trees

The cult of the tree inevitably crossed the Atlantic. Nineteenth-century American transcendentalists declared the forests to be "God's first temples." In the woods, thought Emerson, we return to reason and faith. John Burroughs reiterated the sentiment in 1912: "If we do not go to church as much as did our fathers, we go to the woods much more." Expressions of feeling for trees sometimes became ludicrous, as in the verse of George Pope Morris:

> *Woodman, spare that tree!*
> *Touch not a single bough!*
> *In youth it sheltered me,*
> *And I'll protect it now.*

There were, however, practical as well as sentimental reasons for saving trees. Although parts of America were much more heavily treed than Europe, after the Civil War there were cries of alarm for what was seen as an impending shortage of wood. The fear was expressed that the day was not far off when there would be no forest left east of the Rockies. There were in fact local (and often temporary) causes for anxiety. During the war the supply of wood for fuel in the eastern cities had run short, and branch railroad lines had been obliged at times to burn hay. Out West the settler was beginning to discover that wood for fencing, fuel, and construction took a good deal of money, and in the Midwest, where much of the original stand of forest had been destroyed, farmers complained that the face of the whole country was becoming denuded, and that winter winds and summer storms swept the farms with unprecedented fury. Sherry Olson in her book *Depletion Myth* has disposed of the notion that America in the 1870s was menaced by a "timber famine," but timber was nevertheless seen to be scarce, and the favoured solution to the problem was to plant more of it. It seems to have been generally appreciated that cultivated timber is usually superior to spontaneous or natural growth, so there was little support for the idea of preserving existing stands. The ideal forest was a planted one, with slopes artificially graded for greater control of the discharge or retention of water.

The cultivation of trees was seen to be most necessary where trees were fewest: in the Midwest and on the great plains. One of the strongest advocates of tree planting in the Midwest was the New England-born landscape architect Horace Cleveland, designer of the park systems of Minneapolis and St Paul, Indianapolis, Omaha, and Southside Chicago. Cleveland had been distressed by the absence of trees over large areas of the interior; he believed that systematic and widespread planting would increase the general welfare by beautifying the country, ensuring future supplies of wood for fuel and construction, improving the climate, and softening the outlines of the raw, new towns. His enthusiasm for tree planting, and his conviction that trees were an essential element in environmental design, were matched by his dislike of the grid system and his efforts to modify and soften it wherever he could. Trees he considered a necessary accompaniment to the good life: "Civilization and population cannot advance far beyond the protection and advantages of groves and forests."

The view that there could be no civilized life without trees and ornamental plantings was also advanced by Andrew Jackson Downing, Cleveland's contemporary and a fellow landscape gardener. Downing subscribed to the environmentalist belief, then widespread, that surroundings influence human character, and he reasoned that the more attractive the surroundings the more refined the character produced in them. Downing's views were endorsed by the universities and by government. In 1870 Professor William Baker of the University of Illinois denounced widespread tree-felling because the destruction of forests threatened the "health, habits and morals of men." In 1871 Julius Sterling Morton, a former Territorial Governor, delivered an encomium on trees and ornamental plantings in an address to the Nebraska State Horticultural Society: "There is beauty in a well ordered orchard which is a joy forever. It is a blessing to him who plants it, and it perpetuates his name and memory. . . . Orchards are missionaries of culture and refinement. They make the people among whom they grow a better and more thoughtful people. If every farmer in Nebraska will plant out and cultivate an orchard and a flower garden, together with a few forest trees, this will become mentally and morally the best agricultural state, the grandest community of producers in the American union. Children reared among trees and flowers . . . will be better in mind and in heart, than children reared among hogs and cattle. The occupations and surroundings of boys and girls make them, to a great extent, either bad or coarse, or good and gentle."

But it was not only men and landscapes who were thought to be improved by trees. Many also believed that by retaining moisture and discharging it throughout the year, trees moistened the atmosphere and modified the climate. As the frontier moved west it presented Americans with two climatically-related problems: low rainfall in the interior and, along the eastern seaboard, rainfall that appeared to be less and less reliable. In the east, floods and droughts seemed more frequent and stream flow more irregular. The offending mechanism, so it was thought, was the rapidly diminishing forest cover. The cutting down of too much timber in some parts of the country, remarked the Commissioner of Patents in 1849, "[had] in some degree changed the climate and rendered large districts more subject to alternate droughts and rainy seasons." The conviction grew that deforestation reduced rainfall and, by turning the coin, that reforestation increased it. "This vast region," Horace Cleveland said of the Midwest, "requires only forest culture to restore the humidity of the climate." Journalists who covered the building of the railroads across treeless sections of Nebraska and Wyoming reported that the few trees that had already been planted were modifying the climate. In a report on Nebraska (1868) the geologist F. V. Hayden remarked: "It is believed the planting of ten to fifteen acres of forest trees on each quarter section will have a most important effect on the climate, equalizing and increasing the moisture and adding greatly to the fertility of the soil." It was also being said that the Mormon practice of planting trees had increased summer rainfall in Utah and raised the level of the Salt Lake. There were, of course, no climatological records against which the supposed changes could be measured.

If trees were a remedy for the dryness of the plains, then the obvious course of action was to plant many of them. Hopes were high that nature would to some extent heal herself through a spontaneous regeneration of trees as settlement moved west. In places along the Missouri where settlement and the removal of the Indians had eliminated prairie fires, trees invaded the edges of sloughs and the uncultivated corners of farms. James T. Allan, an agent for the Union Pacific Railroad, reported: "I have watched the spontaneous growth of young elms, walnuts, oaks . . . cottonwoods along the Missouri, Wood, and other rivers in the West, since fires have been kept back. . . . I hardly think I am out of the way in setting it at double the amount of timber planted." Allan's observation and others like it suggested that a trail of trees would follow settlement westward to the Rockies. Bernhard Fernow, who was largely reponsible for organizing the American Forestry Association, saw the entire earth as a potential forest and maintained that, were there no men or animals, "arborescent growth would prevail" wherever there was a long enough growing season and enough soil for a root system.

Although Americans were the first to plant trees in the hope of modifying climate, the idea of a causal connection between tree cover and rainfall was far older than the European settlement of the Great Plains. Columbus tried to explain differences in rainfall between the Azores and the western parts of Jamaica in terms of variations in the amount of tree cover. He attributed the rains of Jamaica to the great woods of the island, and the lesser rains of the Canary Islands, Madeira, and the Azores to a thinner tree cover, the result of extensive cutting. Mistaking an effect for a cause, Count Buffon, the great eighteenth-century naturalist, declared that the absence of trees made for arid or desert conditions. The corollary of this was that the presence of trees would make the desert bloom, even the "burning sands" of Arabia: "A single forest, however, in the midst of these parched deserts, would be sufficient to render them more temperate, to attract the waters from the atmosphere, to restore all the principles of fertility to the earth."

The notion that trees are father to rain was part of American thought at least as early as 1820. On his journey from Pittsburgh to the Rockies in 1820-21, Major Stephen H. Long remarked that "forests attract rain and impeded evaporation." A few years later Josiah Gregg offered the hope that "the genial influences of civilization," which included cultivation and "shady groves," would temper the climate and increase rainfall. By the second half of the nineteenth century the idea of a causal relationship between trees and rainfall was so entrenched that it hardly needed the endorsement of one of the century's landmark studies: George Perkins Marsh's *Man and Nature* (1864). Marsh collected and organized observations from both Europe and the United States that linked trees to the supply of moisture. He listed examples of regions destroyed by deforestation, and he summarized what were then thought to be the links between trees and rain. Trees were thought to moisten the air through transpiration, and to increase rates of condensation by shading the ground and lowering general air temperatures. A belief held by many was that rain clouds, carried inland from the oceans, were often cooled to the point of condensation when they came into contact with cooler air above the forests.

On the other hand, air passing over treeless plains gained rather than lost heat, and so increased its capacity for holding water vapour.

Notably absent from these observations, to a twentieth-century student of weather, were comments on the convection of air, movements of air masses, and the role of cold and warm fronts in cyclonic storms. Although Marsh was sceptical of the larger claims made for the effects of forests on climate, his book triggered new speculation and a sizeable literature. Books, government publications, promotional tracts put out by the western railroads, and articles in local and national newspapers and in literary and professional magazines promoted the benefits of tree planting. Many of the claims were unproven, and a few were spurious. The editor of the Nebraska *Advertiser* declared that Egypt's rainfall had been increased from six inches to twenty-four as a direct result of planting trees. Others, seeking to extend the range of arboreal influences, suggested that trees and shelterbelts screened out miasmas in the air and reduced the incidence of malaria, instilled patriotism, and cured homesickness.

A doctrine that promised to dispel drought in dry places was so intoxicating that not even clear heads were proof against it. Dean Bessey of the University of Nebraska reassured the State Board of Agriculture in 1886: "Were these plains covered by forests from the Rocky Mountains to the Missouri river, with every other condition unchanged, the much-talked of dryness of the summer air would no longer exist. The plains are dry because they are treeless, because the summer air sweeps over the surface of the soil heated by the unbroken rays of the sun. Shade the soil with the spreading branches of forests and orchards . . . and the summer winds will no longer roll down these plains with the fierce, dry heat of the sirocco." Trees do reduce rates of evaporation, and so conserve moisture, but the plains were dry not because they were treeless but treeless because they were dry. The point was acknowledged in the same year by Bernhard E. Fernow, Secretary of the American Forestry Congress, but he still held that trees could increase rainfall: "The co-relation of forest and atmospheric moisture is such, that while the latter, to a certain degree, is a condition *sine qua non* for forest growth, at the same time the growing forest tends to increase the atmospheric moisture of its surroundings, creating the very condition which it requires for its development." Similar hopes were entertained of extensive tree-plantings during the 1860s and 70s on the steppes of southern Russia, and as late as 1935 Russian meteorologists were divided over the issue of trees as modifiers of climate.

By the last third of the nineteenth century, tree planting on the American plains had become wrapped in moral virtue. The transition from secular to quasi-religious activity crystallized in Nebraska with the institution of a day "set apart and consecrated" for planting forest, fruit, and ornamental trees. At sunrise on April 10th, 1872, the first Arbor

Day, devotees moved to the planting sites on foot, by wagon, and on horseback, and by sunrise they had planted over a million trees. The most fervent, not to say miraculous, work that day was done by J. D. Smith who, according to the *Nebraska Herald,* planted one tree per second for nearly ten hours, an incredible 35,500 trees. By the end of the century Arbor Day was an international institution celebrated in Canada as well as in every state of the Union except Delaware.

Hard on the heels of Arbor Day followed the optimistic and much abused Timber Culture Act (1873). The object of the Act, declared its chief proponent in Congress (Senator Phineas W. Hitchcock), was to encourage the growth of timber, "not merely for the benefit of the soil, nor merely for the value of the timber itself, but for its influence upon the climate." Optimists hoped that the Timber Culture Act would result in forestation of one third of the plains. The Act enabled any homesteader to acquire an additional quarter section by planting forty of the 160 acres to trees and tending them for ten years. Abuse was inevitable. Many a hard-pressed pioneer used it as a pretext for increasing his land holdings, following the grant of an additional quarter section with only a little desultory planting and care. Disturbed by the abuse, United States Land Commissioners repeatedly recommended repeal of the statute in their annual reports, but not until 1891 did Congress act on their recommendation. In mitigation of the settlers' behaviour, it should be said that in the drier areas not even the best will in the world could have produced timber.

Gospels are international, and the gospel of trees was as appealing to Canadians — who had their own dry West to settle — as it was to Americans. On his cross-Canada journey in 1880, Daniel M. Gordon reflected the popular wisdom by attributing the slow drying-up of prairie sloughs to the absence of trees. He predicted that unless trees were planted the prairies would in time resemble Palestine or parts of northern Africa, where lands once fertile had been reduced to desert by the destruction of woodland. Conversely, he noted that in places where groves and forests were multiplying, rainfall amounts were increasing. By shading the ground and cooling it, trees reduced rates of evaporation and — in ways not explained by Gordon — contributed to the formation of clouds. In Canada, as in the United States, the cultivation of trees had a moral as well as a practical dimension. H. C. Robey of the Brandon Experimental Farm wrote in the *Farmer's Advocate* in February, 1897: "We can . . . say . . . by the appearance of [a man's farm] that his moral, his intellectual, and we might almost say his religious character may be inferred."

By the end of the nineteenth century, sceptics, who found no basis in the accumulating weather records for the belief that trees affected climate, had begun to raise difficult questions, but the idea of a connection between trees and rain was so fixed in both the popular and the scientific mind that it would take years to eradicate. The level of belief in Canada at the turn of the century is recorded in a charming document, "William Silvering's Surrender," published under the auspices of the Canadian Forestry Association in 1901. Silvering is a truculent farmer from Ontario, deadset against "Arbiculterers," who is confronted at a gathering in "Bowerbank," Manitoba, by the gentle Minister Brown. Before entering the church proper, Brown had taken orders of a secular kind; he had received instructions in arboriculture at Guelph Agricultural College. He was also acquainted with the work of the "sturdy" Angus Mackay in the tree nursery of the experimental farm at Indian Head, then in Assiniboia. The evening at Bowerbank begins with a devotion, an observation from the writings of Oliver Wendell Holmes: "I have written many verses, but the best poems I have produced are the trees I planted on the hillside which overlooks the sinuous Hoosatonic River."

As in most moral tales, there is no real debate. After a vehement outburst at the beginning of the debate, the antagonist (Silvering) is reduced to uncertain expostulation, and finally to respectful silence by the irrefutable logic and gentle wisdom of the master (Minister Brown). Trees are characterized as reservoirs of moisture, the individual tree as a "pumping apparatus" that takes moisture from the ground and delivers it to the higher air. Moisture is brought up only when needed, so that there is no continuous loss of it, as in places which have no trees. Indeed, intones the Minister, the tree is "a mysterious workshop which builds up a thing of beauty and also supplies the air with a requisite and timely supply of moisture." If one tree is so useful, he continues, "what may be said of a plantation or a forest! It cannot but be a powerful regulator of climate. . . . [Trees] preserve the moisture to be used by the growing herbage in the warm weather of summer and prevent the droughts to which all prairie countries are at times subject." Silvering's petulant objection to the assertion that trees prevent drought is dismissed by a reference to Ontario, then said to be suffering from the loss of its trees. Seasons there, declared the Minister, "are much drier than they used to be" and, with fewer trees to check run-off, "floods more damaging."

To set the seal on Silvering's unconditional surrender, one of Minister Brown's supporters intercedes to inform the gathering that trees also help prevent late summer frosts and reduce the incidence of hail. Silvering is overcome. He is told that by insulating the ground, in the same way that a layer of clouds insulates the lower atmosphere, trees reduce the risk of frost and moderate winter temperatures. Evergreen forests were said to be particularly effective in conserving heat. Tree-planting was thought to suppress hail by attacking the causal mechanism. According to a theory current at the turn of the century, hail was formed in whirlwinds created by the mingling of currents of air of slightly different temperatures. Forest and prairie were thought to heat up at different rates and so generate thermals of different temperatures. The whirlwind hypothesis was suggested by the strong downdraughts that precede hail and thunderstorms. Surfaces that were largely or wholly treed, it was argued, would equalize the radiation of heat and so eliminate hail.

Most of the climatic benefits claimed for trees had no scientific foundation. Trees shade the surface and obstruct winds, but they can do little to affect general air temperatures, and they are no antidote to deep winter cold. Winters in the boreal forest are even colder than winters on the prairies. Through transpiration trees do inject some moisture into the atmosphere, but the amount is only a fraction of the total moisture content of the atmosphere. The rain-making powers attributed to trees ought to be seen, however, not simply in terms of the limitations of contemporary meteorology, and of public ignorance of what was known about the causes of rainfall, but of the pressing need for moisture in a dry region. On the plains men wanted rain more than they wanted anything else, and they were prepared to believe in any action or agency that promised to increase the supply of it. There seems to have been no general awareness that natural conditions themselves might be subject to change, although some observers were certainly aware of the cyclical nature of rainfall on the plains. The more popular belief was that the plains environment had been static until the arrival of Europeans in numbers, and that subsequent changes were wrought by the settlement. Temporary increases in rainfall sent plainsmen in urgent quest for a cause and, in a region where rainfall tends to be inadequate as well as cyclical, the searching never stopped.

At first, cultivation itself held out some hope for a permanent increase in the supply of rain. As the saying went, rain would follow the plough. The reasoning was simple: ploughed land would absorb more moisture than virgin prairie, rates of evaporation would increase, and a more humid atmosphere would produce more rain. It was also thought that cultivation would delay the onset of frosts in the fall and thus extend the growing season. "It appears to be fact," Aylmer Maude noted in 1904, "that as the country becomes more occupied and more ground is broken up and cultivated, more of the sun's heat is retained, and the climate modifies." Not only was the heat of the waning sun supposedly retained more effectively by cultivated ground, but the moisture released by cultivation was thought to give added protection against frost by changing moisture conditions and making the land less amenable to frost — so thought James Mavor in 1905. By logical extension, irrigation was considered an even more effective deterrent of frost than cultivation.

Australians were just as optimistic about the positive effects of European settlement. George Ranken maintained, in 1876, that "the consequence [of settlement on the dry, inland plains] is nearly always more grass and more water — the pasture thickens, dry creeks fill, and swamps become standing lagoons." When settlement alone failed to produce enough rain, either in Australia or North America, some hoped that explosions, loud noises, fire, or smoke would take up the deficit by forcing the air to give up its moisture. Noise and fire became standard weapons in the arsenals of professional rainmakers. When railroads and telegraph wires were first thrown across the plains, there was even speculation that electrical currents in the wires and — mysteriously — in the rails would tease the moisture out of the air.

In the Powell report on the arid lands of United States (1878), G. K. Gilbert warned settlers to be wary of speculation: "An increase in the water supply, so universal of late years, has led to many conjectures and hypotheses as to its origin. It has generally been supposed to result from increased rainfall. . . . Many have attributed the change to the laying of railroad tracks and construction of telegraph lines; others to the cultivation of the soil. . . . In what manner rainfall could be affected through the cultivation of the land, building of railroads, telegraph lines, etc., has not been shown." Gilbert attributed the speculation to ignorance of the laws that govern precipitation, and he warned that it would be foolish to hope that human works could have much effect on the climate of the plains: "The operations of man on the surface of the earth are so trivial that the conditions which they produce are of minute effect, and in the grand effects of nature escape discernment. Thus the alleged causes for the increases of rainfall fail. . . . The permanent changes of nature are secular; any great sudden change is ephemeral, and usually such changes go in cycles, and the opposite or compensating conditions may reasonably be anticipated."

But Gilbert's magisterial warning, which was confirmed by the growing body of statistics on weather and climate, had no discernible effect upon public faith in the power of trees to modify climate. In an address to the (American) National Irrigation Congress in 1904, one of the peak years for immigration to the Canadian prairies, William Little presented a grandiose tree-planting scheme that promised to solve the problem of semi-aridity on the plains. Little, who was a newspaper editor from Perry, Oklahoma, argued that, in windy conditions, evaporation on the leeward side of a grove of trees or windbreak is much less than on the exposed windward side. He estimated that the size of the area protected in relation to the height of the windbreak stood at a ratio of 16:1. In other words, a windbreak thirty feet high would protect an area 480 feet wide. On the Great Plains, said Little, where the prevailing winds blow from north to south, a series of board walls thirty feet high and 480 feet apart, built across the wind and across the plains from the Gulf of Mexico to Canada, would be "the alpha and omega of both sub-humid and semi-arid farming." Acknowledging that board fences would be impracticable, he suggested that windbreaks of trees would achieve the same effect. If ponds were built on the windward sides of the windbreaks, then the combination of high rates of evaporation from the ponds and reduced rates from the land would solve the problem of moisture deficiency.

In design, if not intention, Little's scheme was a scaled-down version of an earlier plan by the Italian-born inventor Joseph G. Konvalinka. To take full advantage of their geographical location in relatively low latitudes, Konvalinka in 1889 urged Americans to build a system of shelterbelts across the northern boundary of the country from the Atlantic coast to the Rocky Mountains. He argued that the shelterbelts would protect the United States from invasions of cold Canadian air in the same way that the Alps protect Italy from invasions of cold northern European air. By the time the last shelterbelt had been crossed, the exhausted Canadian winds would have been reduced to mere breezes, and the United States would luxuriate in a climate warmer than Italy's.

Chapter Nine

PLANT PROPAGATION AND CULTURE

The expectation, or at least the hope, that trees would increase rainfall and reduce winds and rates of evaporation was an important stimulus to tree planting. In a region where there were no convenient substitutes for wood as fuel and fencing material, trees also had great utility. The costs of fencing at the beginning of settlement, for example, were as much as a hundred times the value of the land. Yet, in spite of the pressing need for wood, the real impetus for tree planting came less from practical considerations than from the emotional and aesthetic needs of the settlers. Norman M. Ross, chief of the tree-planting division at the forest nursery station, Indian Head, conceded that the greatest value of trees lay not in their utility but in their aesthetic quality, in the beauty they added to the surroundings, and the general feeling of rest and comfort they lent to the home. Even people raised on the prairies could hunger for trees. Annora Brown recalled that in spite of her love of the prairie she had a great longing for a tree, urging her mother again and again to tell of a playhouse she once had in the limbs of a giant white poplar. "Could heaven hold anything more desirable than a playhouse in a tree?"

Feelings of isolation and loneliness, primarily the result of distance from neighbours or the homeland, were compounded by the absence of familiar or comforting objects in the landscape. For Europeans, as the painter Philip G. Hamerton remarked, a treeless landscape is a lonely one; insert a tree, noted Hamerton, and it is lonely no longer. His assertion was supported by the behaviour of an Ontario settler who from time to time walked to two solitary trees more than a mile from his homestead "just to touch them and stand in their shade." Shortly after his arrival at Didsbury, just north of Calgary, Lewis G. Dye, who had hardly seen a tree on the journey west from Winnipeg, sketched two birches that grew

A farmstead in Burbank, Manitoba. Europe, or Ontario, has been re-created in the west. (Public Archives Canada, C 80419)

beside a nearby creek because they reminded him of Chislehurst in Kent, where he sometimes used to sketch. In the prospectus designed to lure settlers to Red River, Lord Selkirk's far-from-scrupulous recruiting agent was careful to bait the trap with trees: "all kinds of fruit trees, even the most delicate, grow and thrive here in perfection."

Subsequent promoters were also quick to realize that without trees there could be no settlement. Promises of Eden held out by the settlement literature were clearly foolish, and it was soon evident that if immigrants were to be retained as well as attracted they would need to be reassured not only that the prairie could be farmed, but that attractive surroundings could be fashioned from the featureless landscape. In an address on aboriculture to the British Association for the Advancement of Science, at Montreal in 1884, Professor William Brown of the Guelph Agricultural College declared that there could be no great future for Manitoba and the North-West unless systematic tree planting preceded agriculture. "No methods of farming, no railway or water communication, no minerals, natural grazing, or any other advantages will ever 'make' a country without trees. I am not theorizing. A peopled agricultural country without trees is an impossibility." Professor Brown's assertion was endorsed by C. G. Patten, one of Iowa's horticultural pioneers. His ideal settler was an orchardist bent on surrounding his house with trees, shrubs, and flowers. "In his daily meditations and his night visions he sees arising around him a changed and beautiful landscape. . . . His home is surrounded by trees and orchards."

Farm beautification was central to government and C.P.R. programmes of instruction, and much of the time and money devoted to the programmes were applied to the problem of how to grow forest and fruit trees, ornamental shrubs and gardens, in an environment always ready to reject them. The importance of the programmes to the success of the settlement was confirmed by a letter from an Ontario immigrant to the government tree nursery at Indian Head: "When I first saw the Canadian West in 1902, I came with an open mind as to whether I should like to settle on the prairies. The deciding factor, after seeing the economic advantages, was the possibility of growing trees and making beautiful the home surroundings as indicated by the results obtained at the Experimental Farms . . . as well as in the plantings at the various stations along the Canadian Pacific railway."

Taking its lead from the American Timber Culture Act, the Canadian government introduced a Wood Culture Act in 1876. The Act enabled settlers in treeless areas to take out 160-acre tree claims, as an alternative to pre-emption, with the proviso that the homesteader plant and care for thirty-two acres of woodland. Patent to the land was not to be issued until six years after the planting. Fifty-one tree claims were entered before the end of 1878, and eighty-one before the system was abandoned in 1879, but only five patents were ever issued. Without the incentive of short-term gains, the work of planting and caring for the trees was too great, so most settlers simply converted their tree claims to pre-emptions and bought them.

Nevertheless, settlers had thought about tree planting from the outset, and many Ontarians brought seedlings with them. But most weren't hardy in the Western climate, and the few that were had no chance of survival without careful preparation of the soil. The general failure of unaided efforts to plant trees meant that a successful tree-planting programme would depend on the introduction of hardy species and careful culture. Most of the field and garden crops grown in North America had been introduced from Europe, and though their progeny had adapted well to conditions in the east, in the West they met conditions that were quantitatively different. The growing season was shorter, and it could be visited by lethal combinations of wind and heat. Winter's trials were extreme cold and drying winds and, because of relatively light snow cover, deep freezing and low soil temperatures. Winter, too, was a season of sudden and violent changes of temperature. Chinooks in southern Alberta could dispel sub-zero (farenheit) temperatures and snow-cover in a matter of hours; elsewhere, waves of frigid Arctic air could replace conditions that were merely cold with temperatures that tested the limits of standard thermometers. The prairie climate was not just dry and cold; it was also capricious.

In general the field crops, garden vegetables, and annual flowers of

A bird's eye view, by W. J. Topley, of the Experimental Farm at Indian Head. Before European settlement, the Indian Head country was bald prairie. (Public Archives Canada, PA 19377)

the middle and higher latitudes did well on the prairies. But forest and fruit trees usually succumbed to the drying winds and extreme cold. Deep-rooted trees also like water in the subsoil, but in the prairies the movement of soil water is dominantly upward. Conditions favoured shallow-rooted grasses; trees in the drier districts could find their heads in the sun and their roots in soil that was powder dry. Yet another hazard was the high alkaline content of much of the soil. Fruit trees in particular prefer soils that are a little on the acid side; when denied acidity they develop alkali chlorosis, whose tell-tale yellow foliage is a common sight on the prairies.

The paramount problem for tree planters and horticulturalists, then, was what to plant and how to care for and protect the things planted. Although the prairies posed particular difficulties, the problem was general in a country without established field and garden practices. To resolve it the Dominion government decided, in 1886, to establish a nation-wide system of experimental farms. The scheme called for a central experimental farm in Ottawa, and satellite farms in Nova Scotia, Manitoba, the North-West Territories, and British Columbia. Chiefly in response to a suggestion from George M. Dawson, the much-respected assistant director of the Geological and Natural History Survey of Canada, two farms were allocated to the prairies: one at Brandon, in Manitoba, and the other at Indian Head (Saskatchewan), which then was in the Territories. The farms were to conduct experimental work in horticulture, stock raising, dairying, and forestry. In the West the objective was to establish experimental farms in advance of settlement, so that farmers could get help, from qualified government officials, with problems particular to the locality. In practice, however, the farms sometimes lagged behind settlement; the decision to establish a farm at Swift Current in 1920 was largely a result of the failure of farmers to resolve the agricultural and horticultural problems of the dry south-west.

One of the victims of ignorance of growing conditions in the southwest was the father of James Minifie, the Canadian author, journalist, and broadcaster. When two beech trees bought from a travelling peddler for a Quebec nursery failed to survive their first winter, Mr Minifie sent to Indian Head for a bundle of two hundred mixed seedlings of Manitoba maple, ash, willow, pine, spruce, and caragana. All the trees were planted but, despite tender care, most of them died. When James Minifie returned to the homestead after World War 1, expecting to find a beautiful windbreak, he found instead a single pine about a foot high, a few half-dead spruce, some straggly willows, and a caragana hedge. He returned again in 1935 to find the pine twelve feet high and dying; the rest had fallen to drought and drifting soil. The only substantial trees on the homestead were two native cottonwoods that had grown from cuttings planted by the Minifies in 1919.

In agriculture, as in most aspects of the settlement of the West, Canada had the advantage of American experience. The American West had been settled without benefit of state experimental stations or a federal Department of Agriculture. Repeated failures to transplant eastern and southern species had led, in the absence of supporting government institutions, to the organization of state horticultural societies and fruit growers' associations that allowed settlers to pool their resources and learn from their few successes. The scale of the failure was spelled out in the thirteenth annual report of the Minnesota Horticultural Society: "Our efforts and trials in Minnesota began thirty years ago last spring by planting one bushel of apple seed, a peck of peach seed, and five hundred apple, pear, plum and cherry trees, and for eleven years thereafter planting each year enough apple trees to bring 1,000 trees, and in the time named made frequent additions to the orchard of old named varieties — all southern or eastern grown trees and seeds, and all kept as long as they could be made to live in Minnesota, and today only two trees remain. . . . Here is a lesson for those who would plant fruit trees here or endeavour to produce new varieties suitable to this climate. It took thousands of trees and bushels of seed, brought from the east or further south, to produce one or two apple trees suitable for the Minnesota climate." A Kansas farmer, W. M. Pennell, had no more luck with planting native cottonwoods: "In the spring of 1876 I made a united centennial effort, in which I transplanted 3500 one-year-old cottonwoods, planted a hedge of Osage (Orange) around the whole place, put in 10,000 cottonwood cuttings, and in May I planted two bushels of cottonwood seeds. Owing to a protracted drought in June, and poor cultivation, I lost the whole crop."

America began its systematic search for hardy species in the 1880s. Through the American consul in St Petersburg, the Department of Agriculture in Washington obtained from the Imperial Botanic Gardens seedlings of Russian apples that seemed hardy enough to warrant a systematic exploration of the interior of Russia. Agronomists at the Department of Agriculture began corresponding with the Agricultural College of Moscow and the Botanic Gardens at St Petersburg, and were persuaded that fruit and forest trees from the interior provinces of Russia might do well in the central and northern parts of the United States. In 1882 Professor J. L. Budd of the Iowa Agricultural College left on an investigatory tour of Russia. He was accompanied by Mr Chas. Gibb of Abbotsford, Quebec, one of Canada's most distinguished horticulturists. The two men spent several months travelling in the region between the Carpathians and the Urals. At Moscow they found a climate similar to Iowa's, while east of the Volga summers were more like the summers of Western Kansas and Nebraska. Winter temperatures were as cold as those of Minnesota. Farther east the winters were even more rigorous, matching the winters of the Canadian prairies. As the travellers moved inland they noted marked changes in the character of the fruit trees: foliage thickened and became leather-like, and the trees themselves were stunted. In northern Kasan, on the upper reaches of the Volga, the apple trees were mere bushes growing in clumps at roughly ten-foot intervals. Six hundred miles nearer the pole than Quebec City, northern Kasan was probably the coldest apple-growing region in the world.

By 1885 Professor Budd was growing Russian fruit, forest, and ornamental trees in the experimental grounds of Iowa Agricultural College. His progress was reported to the Canadian Parliament by Professor William Saunders, prospective director of the Dominion Experimental Farms, who thought that some of the species could be of inestimable value to the North-West Territories. Saunders, who had recently returned from a tour of state agricultural colleges and experimental stations, referred to a practical demonstration of the hardiness of Russian apples carried out by Professor Budd. Two adjoining orchards in the college grounds, similar in situation and soils, had been planted with apple trees five or six years earlier: one to trees from the hardiest American stocks and the other to trees from Russia. The winter of 1885 was a particularly severe one; by the end of it three quarters of the American trees had died, but in the Russian orchard there wasn't a single casualty. At the same time, Chas. Gibb was experimenting on his farm in Quebec with hardy species of apple, pear, plum, and cherry from Russia, Poland, and northern Germany. Like Saunders, Gibb was also convinced that many of the varieties of fruit and forest trees that he had seen in Russia and northern Europe would be useful to settlers in the North-West.

When Saunders became director of the Dominion Experimental Farms in 1886, his duty was clear. He began at once the search for hardy species. Within months of taking office he had made contact with the directors of Kew Gardens in London, the Imperial Botanic Garden at St Petersburg, and the Imperial College of Japan, and had ordered from Russia 200 varieties of hardy Russian trees and vines. Saunders's personal ambition was the common one among horticulturists on the prairies and the northern plains: to produce an apple that would grow in the cold North-West. Commonly accepted to be the first tree of the first garden, the apple was a symbol of great power in frontier regions. No other tree or crop could demonstrate as persuasively that wilderness had been dispelled and the land made safe. The symbolic power of the apple explains, of course, the near-apotheosis of such legendary figures as John Chapman ("Johnny Appleseed"), who bestowed apple seedlings and orchards on the American Midwest and Henderson Luelling, who braved deserts, mountains, and marauding Indians to take a wagon-load of apple seedlings to Oregon's Willamette valley.

From St Petersburg William Saunders obtained the seed of a small, wild crab-apple — the Berried Crab — which grew abundantly in Northern Siberia. He planted the seed in the apple orchards of the Central Experimental Farm; the seedlings, when large enough for transplanting, were sent to Brandon and Indian Head. They proved to be extremely hardy in both places. To improve the size and quality of the tiny fruit, Saunders cross-fertilized the crab with hardier varieties of apple from Ontario. A few of the hybrids proved to be as hardy as the parent, and one of them — the Osman — is now regarded as the hardiest edible crab yet developed. By crossing these first hybrids with commercial varieties, Saunders continued to aim for larger apples, and the products, "Saunders's Hybrids," became a byword for hardiness amongst fruit growers in all severe regions.

Saunders also promoted general tree-planting in the North-West. In 1889 the Central Experimental Farm sent 12,000 shrubs and forest trees, representing 118 varieties, to Brandon and Indian Head; 60% died by the following spring. A further 21,000 were sent in 1890, and many of these also failed to survive. Gradually, however, the less hardy species were winnowed out, and by the early 1890s the nursery at Indian Head had about 120,000 trees and the Brandon nursery 75,000. As an experiment, the Central Farm sent bundles of twenty-five trees of the hardiest varieties to C.P.R. station gardens between Moose Jaw and the Rockies.

And at the request of the N.W.M.P., bundles were also despatched to Indian agencies and to commanding officers at N.W.M.P. posts in Regina, Maple Creek, Fort McLeod, Fort Saskatchewan, Battleford, and Prince Albert. Other bundles were sent to public institutions in the West.

But the main work of distributing trees and shrubs in the West fell to the regional experimental farms at Brandon and Indian Head. Under ordinary circumstances, ornamental trees, shrubs, and fruit trees are propagated and supplied by the nursery trade, but in the pioneer West there were no nurseries, and those in the settled parts of the continent had no stock hardy enough to survive on the prairies, although most were prepared to ship tender plants to needful homesteaders. By the 1880s the work of tree planting had assumed such urgency that the experimental farms were eager to take over the role of supplier. Henry Patmore, one of the pioneers of Manitoba's nursery trade, worked at Brandon before starting his nursery business. Within months of their inception, Brandon and Indian Head were testing a wide range of forest trees, fruit trees, and shrubs for adaptability to prairie conditions, and they had started nurseries to produce planting stock for interested settlers. S. A. Bedford, the first superintendent of the Brandon experimental farm, was well acquainted with pioneer conditions, and was convinced of the import-ance of tree planting. Before coming to Brandon, Bedford had farmed in Manitoba and Assiniboia, and he had helped locate settlers for land companies.

At Brandon, Bedford experimented with species imported from the United States, Russia, and Siberia, as well as with native species. Com-mon sense suggested that native species had the best chance for survival, and they were practically free, but tree culture was so difficult in the West that not even the use of locally grown plants guaranteed success. Differences between valley and upland soils could be considerable, and even wild stock could be felled by droughts and sudden temperature changes in spring and fall. In 1888 Bedford seeded three-quarters of an acre with native ash, basswood, and maple, but all the seedlings were destroyed by frost in the spring of 1889. The station had as little success with apples until the arrival of the first of Saunders's hybrids in 1898. Fruit trees were particularly vulnerable to the extreme cold, the drying winds, and low soil temperatures. By 1894 none of the 300 varieties of apples tested had been found winter hardy. The same was true of imported plum and cherry trees. On the other hand, fruit shrubs such as currants, gooseberries, and raspberries proved to be at least moderately hardy.

Tree culture was just as prominent in the work of the experimental farm at Indian Head. The farm's first superintendent, Angus Mackay — "the sturdy Mackay" of Minister Brown's fulsome description — had farmed on open prairie near Indian Head for six years and he knew the value of trees. He was convinced that settlement would be permanent only if prairie farmsteads could be made comfortable and attractive. At Indian Head he set aside twelve acres for nursery and wind-break plantings. At that time most homesteaders managed to grow a supply of vegetables, but nearly all of them failed with trees, fruits, and ornamental shrubs. Seeds and plantings were frequently blown out of the ground, and those that managed to survive the dry, windy summers then had to contend with the severe winters. To protect fruit trees, ornamental shrubs, and flowers, both the Brandon and Indian Head stations experimented with hedging plants and wind-breaks. One of their important successes was the Siberian Pea Tree, *Caragana arborescens,* now just plain caragana. It proved both winter hardy and drought resistant, and it gave excellent shelter. With the native box elder, or Manitoba maple, it became the standard hedging plant of the West.

To demonstrate the effectiveness of hedges and tree shelterbelts, the tree nurseries and flower and vegetable gardens at both stations were surrounded by them. Yields of small fruits, such as currants and raspberries, increased by at least 50% when properly protected, and vegetables at Indian Head did well enough to win awards at the World's Columbian Exposition at Chicago in 1893. Farmers were encouraged to visit the experimental farms so that they might see which varieties of plants did best locally, and how effective shelterbelts were in protecting them. Here, too, they would see the well-maintained grounds of the farm super-

Saplings in treeless prairie in southern Alberta being watered from a barrel hauled by team and stoneboat. Settlers sometimes went to great lengths to establish trees. (Glenbow Archives, NA-3163-3)

intendent and the less showy, but neatly ornamented, homes of the farm labourers. These, it was hoped, would serve as an incentive to dispirited gardeners whose farmsteads might have supported only a few stunted saplings and a patch of brown grass.

By the end of the century the experimental farms were not only demonstrating the effectiveness of hedges and wind-breaks; they were also supplying settlers with seedlings, trees, and packages of seeds. So successful and popular were the two original prairie farms that others were started, between 1906 and 1914, at Morden (Manitoba), Scott (Saskatchewan), and Lethbridge and Lacombe (Alberta). By 1913 the farm at Scott had made the first prairie arboretum and demonstrated, in mixed plantings of deciduous and coniferous trees, that conifers such as white spruce and lodgepole pine outlived faster-growing deciduous trees. As a result, conifers began to supplement deciduous trees in shelterbelt planting on the experimental stations and on farmsteads. At Lethbridge and Lacombe the chief problem was to find species capable of withstanding sudden changes in temperature. Chinooks were a mixed blessing. They ate up snow and delivered humans and animals from numbing temperatures, but sudden increases in temperature combined with strong drying winds could quickly dehydrate plant tissue. Horticulturists claimed that growing conditions in the chinook belt of Alberta were probably the most difficult in the country. Of the hedging and shelterbelt plants, box elder in particular often failed to survive the chinooks, but caragana, willow, poplar, and spruce proved reasonably hardy.

In full production, the tree nurseries at the two original experimental farms, Brandon and Indian Head, produced well over a million plants a year. But production fell far short of demand, and tree culture on this scale clearly interfered with the functions of agricultural experimentation for which the farms had been designed. The tail was wagging the dog: a role meant to be incidental, or at most equal with others, had become primary. To restore balance to the activities of the experimental farms, and meet the demand for trees, the federal government added a forestry branch to the functions of the Department of the Interior. Two forest nursery stations were set up, one at Indian Head in 1903 and the other at Sutherland, a village then five miles east of Saskatoon, in 1913. The stations were designed to supply nursery stock for farmers and, through attractively landscaped, well-sheltered grounds, to demonstrate the value of tree planting. Like the experimental farms, the tree nurseries became venues for Sunday outings, picnics, and weddings. Wedding parties still resort to groves in town parks or on the experimental farms for the ritual photo-taking and, occasionally, for the wedding ceremony itself.

In treeless areas, where no seeds or seedlings were available locally, plant material was supplied free, or nearly so; most homesteaders were in no position to buy seedlings or cuttings in large enough quantities to set out effective shelterbelts. Every spring the tree nurseries filled railway cars — refrigerated to prevent budding before the trees could be planted — with bundles of seedlings whose roots had been dipped in water, wrapped in Spanish moss, and sewn inside pieces of burlap. The trees were then dropped at the stations, where they were collected by the farmers. The nurseries would eventually supply parks, schools, and hospitals in the towns, but householders, who needed only a few trees, had to find their own.

To reduce waste on the farms, the Forestry Department insisted that farmers prepare the ground for planting and that, once planted, the young trees be looked after. From Indian Head a team of inspectors ranged over the treeless regions of the prairie, instructing farmers in how to prepare the soil, how to select trees, and how to cultivate and care for the growing plants. The most exacting regulations applied to the preparation of the soil. Whereas forest soil is kept relatively open and porous by the action of tree roots, and is covered by several inches of loose, decaying vegetable matter, virgin prairie soils were compact and hard, and covered by an almost impenetrable layer of tough grass sod. Free seedlings were available only for land that had been thoroughly cultivated and left fallow for a summer. Thorough cultivation eradicated the couch and svelt grasses, the worst enemies of prairie plantations, and a season of fallow ensured that there was a reserve of moisture for the young trees. After planting it was essential to keep the land cultivated until the trees were established, and then maintain a permanently cultivated belt around the plantation.

As well as planting regulations, the field inspectors also carried standard plans for the lay-out of farmsteads and shelterbelts. The plans divided the farmstead into functional units, and the more elaborate ones called for a maze-like network of trees and hedges that enclosed barns, lawns, orchards, and flower gardens. To avoid accumulations of snow, trees had to be at least thirty yards from permanent buildings and planted at intervals of no less than four feet. Where shelter from wind was the principal object, belts five to seven rows deep were thought to be adequate. Wider belts were recommended only if the farmer wished to grow a small supply of timber for fuel and fencing. The tree nurseries supplied both deciduous and coniferous trees, and for farm shelterbelts they advised that rows of broad-leaved trees be strengthened with one or two rows of hardy evergreens. As well as giving year-round protection, the evergreens added a touch of green to the winter landscape and, being careful of plant moisture, they remained vigorous and healthy during the dry spells that might kill their broad-leaved neighbours.

The Efforts of the C.P.R.

Because of its vast land holdings and its need for traffic, the C.P.R. was as interested as the government in any scheme that would make the West more attractive to settlers. If trees, shrubs, and flowers would convert, as a government spokesman remarked in 1901, "a bleak and uninviting stretch of country into one in which newcomers will be anxious to settle," then it was obviously in the C.P.R.'s interest to plant them. American railroads had shown the way. The Kansas and Pacific Railroad began tree planting in towns and stations on the plains in 1870, followed by the Atcheson, Topeka, and Santa Fe in 1873. Railroads in Kansas and Nebraska, the great tree planting states, hired agronomists to determine which trees and crops would be best suited to their lands. By 1880 most of the railroad companies had established nurseries, the largest being the 640-acre tree farm at Farlington, Kansas.

C.P.R. folklore has it that the company's interest in horticulture was aroused in 1880s when W. S. Dunlop, one of its officials in eastern Canada, distributed flower seeds among the employees for planting along the lines. By 1890 many of the Western stations had gardens, and on the main line between Moose Jaw and the Rockies more than two dozen stations were growing trees supplied by the Central Experimental Farm in Ottawa. By 1907 the C.P.R. had its own tree nursery — at Wolseley, Saskatchewan — that supplied stations with trees and flowering shrubs. Bedding plants and perennials came from company greenhouses and nurseries in Springfield, Manitoba. To oversee the park and garden work, and promote development of railway gardens along the rights-of-way, the company created a forestry department in 1908. The main purpose of the Western plantings was to reassure settlers and travellers that the prairie could be improved, but there was a secondary one, of which Andrew Jackson Downing would have approved. It was — according to C.P.R. records — "to instill into the minds of employees a sense of beauty and cleanliness, and by creating pleasant surroundings make them and their families contented and happy."

Though employees were allowed some initiative in the design of the gardens, the overall pattern was prescribed. Lawns and flower beds open to view from the stations and trains were enclosed by borders of trees, ornamental shrubs, and perennials. Flowers with white blooms were discouraged; they showed the dust, and they weren't cheering. The object was to produce a "barrage of colour" that would obscure dust and cinders and hearten travellers and immigrants. For practical spirits there were also bountiful vegetable gardens that testified to the fertility of prairie soils. For passengers at Broadview station in Saskatchewan, who might have overlooked the message, the word PRODUCE was spelled out with large lettuce plants. The station gardens ranged in size from a few hundred

An "island of beauty:" the C.P.R. station garden, Portage La Prairie. (C.P.R. Corporate Archives)

square feet to several acres. Moose Jaw, with an eight acre garden, was exceptional, but the gardens at the city stations were often large enough to justify the hiring of full-time gardeners.

As well as tending the station gardens, employees who lived beside the line were encouraged to make private gardens from seed and plant materials supplied by the company. Prizes were awarded annually for the best private as well as the best station gardens within each district and region. Railway gardens embellished all the settled parts of the country, but nowhere were their civilizing touches appreciated more than on the prairies. As the Manitoba author Aileen Garland put it, they were "islands of beauty, tokens of gracious living, in a landscape often bleak and bare." Beyond the station the land may have looked forbidding, the prairie gumbo may have been sticky and almost impassable, and the village just a cluster of flimsy, unpainted shacks, but the garden, Garland noted, was a reality that renewed courage. Like the vegetable gardens, the flower gardens were also a reminder of the fertility of prairie soil: "Land that could nourish such a profusion of sunflowers, geraniums, pansies . . . and marigolds could surely nourish wheat."

Yet neither the attractiveness of the station gardens nor the richness of the prairie soils had any noticeable effect upon the staying powers of homesteaders. Most left within a few years of making their entries. Alarmed by the instability of the farm population, prairie chambers of commerce appealed to the C.P.R. to do whatever it could to make farm life more attractive. The company's response was to step up the campaign for tree planting by taking the message directly to the farm population. It converted one of its day coaches into a travelling lecture hall, theatre, and museum, and donated it to the Canadian Forestry Association. The Association provided a live-in lecturer equipped with lantern slides and sound films. Between April and November, the Tree Planting Car, known affectionately by schoolchildren as the "tree train," travelled without charge over the prairie networks of both the C.P.R. and C.N.R., playing to audiences of up to 75 adults and 100 children. The standard subjects were farm beautification, shelterbelts, and soil conservation.

Aside from the churches, most prairie settlements in 1918 had no meeting places of any kind, and few diversions. One senses from the daily reports of the first lecturer, Alan Beaven, that the arrival of the tree train was a signal event: "Devron, Sask.: No town here, only a box car station and a general store. But an audience of 180 turned out to meet the Tree Planting Lecture Car. First came the pupils from four rural schools, miles away. Then at night came the fathers and mothers from the homesteads, all deeply interested in the talks and pictures. Weather bitterly cold." From time to time belligerent prairie weather halted the train and tempered the enthusiasm even of Mr Beaven: "Adair, Sask.: One of the worst blizzards of the year howling outside our car. Our fires are roaring but the place can't be heated. We sit about in overcoats and galoshes, then shovel coal and dump ashes. From this deserted siding, the whole world is one dizzy cloud of snowflakes." In an average season the train pulled in at about a hundred prairie sidings; over the half-century of its existence it attracted about 1.5 million visitors.

Private Plant Breeders

The world-wide search for hardy species, and the work of culture and propagation on the scale required to supply the prairie farms, could only have been undertaken by the government and the C.P.R. But plant breeding and selection, which require no equipment beyond a plot of land, can be done by individuals. Before taking over the direction of the Dominion experimental farms, William Saunders, a trained pharmacist, had been a self-taught experimental fruit farmer near London, Ontario. In setting out to develop hardy apples for the West, Saunders set the pattern for much of the private, non-institutional experimentation. The experimental farms and government tree nurseries might clothe the prairie by producing and distributing forest trees for wind-breaks and shelterbelts, but individual plant breeders were determined to decorate it. For pioneer settlers, fruit trees, flowers, and ornamental shrubs were the true measure of habitable space; planting them, as W. A. Munro, the first director of the Rosthern Experimental Farm, intimated, was the settler's way of home-making: only when fruits and flowers have been planted, he once remarked, "does the place of abode become a home."

Fruit trees preoccupied A. P. Stevenson, one of the first horticulturists in the West. Stevenson planted his first apple trees, in about 1875, on what is now Portage Avenue, Winnipeg, and had repeated failures until he acquired varieties of hardy Russian apples from Professor Budd of Iowa. By 1900 Stevenson had established fruit-bearing orchards at Morden, Manitoba, and was so successful a producer of apples and general fruits that the choice of Morden as the site for an experimental farm in 1910 was largely due to his presence there. Other well-known private plant breeders early on the scene were Frank L. Skinner of Manitoba and Seager Wheeler of Saskatchewan. From seeds and seedlings acquired from the Central Experimental Farm in Ottawa and botanic gardens in Europe and America, both men produced many new varieties of hardy fruits and woody ornamentals. Skinner quickly discovered that the seedlings of a species sometimes vary greatly in hardiness, and from one particularly hardy seedling acquired from the Arnold Arboretum in Boston he cultivated what was probably the most winter hardy pear tree ever produced in North America.

Other horticulturists were noted less for their skill as plant breeders than as promoters of horticulture and tree planting. George F. Chipman, editor of *Country Guide*, experimented with fruits and vegetables on a small acreage at his Winnipeg home, but he made his most important contributions to horticulture through the columns of his popular magazine. Raised among the gardens and orchards of Nova Scotia's Annapolis Valley, he was convinced that fruit trees and flowers were indispensable accoutrements to farm life, especially to farm life on the prairies. He said so over and over in the columns of his magazine. Chipman also backed his exhortation with practical help. He published special bulletins on horticulture that were sent out to interested growers and, through *Country Guide*, he distributed large quantities of seed and seedlings donated by the experimental station at Morden.

If George Chipman was the most influential individual promoter of horticulture and tree planting in the West, the most prominent was William Pearce, the so-called Czar of the West. Unlike Chipman, Pearce was a public servant. He came West in the 1870s as one of the first Dominion land surveyors, and by 1884 he was Superintendent of Mines for the North-West Territories. In Pearce's hands the office was so prominent and its jurisdiction so wide-ranging — encompassing the lands, forests, and waterways of the West as well as its minerals — that its occupant acquired the imperial sobriquet. Pearce's interest in tree-planting dated from his boyhood in the Talbot settlement of Southern Ontario. Forest clearances for lumbering and farming had caused such widespread soil erosion by the middle of the nineteenth century that they were followed by a wave of replanting. By the time he had studied engineering in Toronto, and joined the Dominion Land Survey, governments in both the United States and Canada were drawing up policies designed to protect the remaining forest resources and so avert what they saw as a looming timber famine.

From his base in Calgary, Pearce agitated constantly for a tree-planting programme for the city's streets and parks. He recognized at once the need to protect the well-treed islands in the Bow River from land speculators, and he used the powers of his office to set aside the islands for future parkland. As a tree planter, Pearce was a devotee of the hardy and long-lived white spruce, and he prescribed its use on every possible occasion. At his instigation, and through the cooperation of the C.P.R., trainloads of spruce trees were brought to the city from the federal government's forest reserve in Banff and from the experimental farms at Brandon and Indian Head. To demonstrate the usefulness of trees, and of spruce trees in particular, Pearce grew them on the grounds of his large riverside house — Bow Bend Shack — that overlooked the Bow River flood plain on the eastern edge of the city. Part of his estate was a tree nursery in which spruce from several sources, and cultivated in varying ways, were carefully monitored. The rest of the property was a picturesque arrangement of shrubberies, flower-beds, extensive lawns, and curved gravel paths that was laced (after 1893) with irrigation ditches. Pearce was as devoted to irrigation as he was to the white spruce, and he used his estate to demonstrate that it could increase yields by as much as 70%. On part of the estate Pearce grew vegetables and crops and, always the meticulous surveyor, he kept careful notes of yields.

Beyond the river and the lush Pearce estate lay bald prairie.

Chapter Ten

GARDENS, PARKS, AND SHELTERBELTS

To describe the efforts of settlers from Europe and the east to reproduce at least the semblance of a humid landscape in the dry West, John Bennett, the American anthropologist, employed the phrase "symbolic adjustments." The adjustments ranged from gardens, shelterbelts, and ponds at one end of the scale to large reservoirs, urban parks, and landscaped settings for institutional buildings at the other. The standard adjustment was the garden and the shelterbelt. Alone in open prairie or parkland, pioneers were naturally anxious to create surroundings that were familiar and protecting. Most settlers probably sensed that a few scattered clumps of trees could not significantly affect the prairie climate, but a shelterbelt would at least reduce wind velocities and rates of evaporation, and provide some protection for the house, livestock, and garden.

Ideas of home and shelter are so inseparable that sometimes the first act of cultivation was to plant tree seedlings around the dwelling, even if the latter was only a tar-paper shanty or a sod house. In Europe, the deep woods may have intimidated people, but a grove was a recognized symbol of human habitation. Trees were planted around mediaeval churches to act as wind-breaks, and houses which, like the house of Chaucer's reve, "stood ful faire upon an heeth," were "with grene trees yshadwed." From Chaucer's time, trees that stood "in the defence and safeguard of the house" were protected by law. For European settlers on the prairies, a permanent house without a protecting belt, or clump of trees, would have been inconceivable. Trees, wrote one pioneer to the tree nursery at Indian Head, showed that "real homes" could be built upon even "bald-headed" prairie. And another: "I consider my grove the prettiest and nicest thing I have about my farm. Without it I don't think I would care to live on the farm. . . . The bigger [the trees] grow and the more I have of them they tie me stronger to my home. The birds build in them, and flocks of birds come to them that we never saw before the trees were there. I think the best thing of all about the trees is that they make a place look like home, while even fine buildings to me would not have their real worth without trees; so my trees are to start growing before I am to have many buildings."

As minimum shelter against the dominant winds, farming magazines and government publications recommended belts of trees five or six rows wide on the northern, western, and southern sides of the farmstead. But some went beyond the minimum and planted shelterbelts on all four sides of the property; some, too, doubled the recommended width of the belts. Within the shelterbelt, homesteaders were able to make comforting havens. As yet another of Indian Head's grateful correspondents remarked, shelterbelts "dispelled the barrenness of the prairie, broke the wind, . . . created joy in homemaking, and showed that our lives and surroundings were just what we choose to make them." Kristine Kaldor Gilbertson recalled the delights of her grandmother's garden, protected by trees brought from Minnesota to the Regina plain: "It still seemed like fairyland to me. . . . A gravel path led to a summer pagoda, built of latticework made from laths and covered in summer with wild cucumber vines. On top was a weather vane, like a little flag with the number 1905 cut into it. . . . On one side of the path were flower beds outlined with white-washed stones. . . . These were filled with old-fashioned flowers. Bachelor buttons, sweetpeas, and mignonettes. She had a rose bush, brought from Minnesota, which bore a profusion of bright, pink flowers. I wore a corsage of them on my confirmation day."

The world inside the shelterbelt, where homesteaders were able to approximate their former surroundings, bore little relation to the world outside: "You step," Frederick Niven noted, "from the great billiard-board, the expanse of rectangular fields and long straight roads into a grove where the birds are singing . . . into an oasis where the garden paths twist for a change, and there are green lawns, and the billiard-board at once seems remote." The contrast between the homeliness of the world within the shelterbelt and around the farmstead, and the anonymity of the world without is a familiar theme in prairie writing. Beyond the shelterbelt lay the imprisoning plain — a world of unlimited space, rigidly controlled, in which arrow-straight roads led nowhere and, the ultimate irony, there was nowhere to walk. Readers of Edward McCourt's *Home is the Stranger* may recall Jim Armstrong's exasperated response to his Irish wife's suggestion that they go for a walk: "But Norah, there just isn't anywhere to walk. This isn't like the Old Country." A few days earlier

Jim had explained to the uncomprehending Norah that on the prairies the world beyond the horizon was no different from the one in view.

The landscape that subservience to abstraction had produced outside the shelterbelt may have satisfied the settlers' desire for order and control, but it did nothing to gratify their need for familiar, lived-in space. To be loved, a place must have forms and arrangements that express custom and practice, not preconceptions of geometric order. The world inside the shelterbelt was also contrived, but it was of the homesteader's making and, like the prairie before settlement, it was seamed by paths that were an expression of necessary but unpremeditated movement. As accidental features, smoothed and packed firm by the passage of human feet, paths have about them, as John Updike remarked, "that repose of grace that is beyond willing." Updike's affection for the accidental or the unwilled was shared by the young Wallace Stegner. "In a country practically without landmarks," he wrote in his inspired memoir, *Wolf Willow,* "it might have been assumed that any road would comfort the soul. But I don't recall feeling anything special about the graded road. . . . It was our own trail, lightly worn, its ruts a slightly fresher green where old cured grass had been rubbed away, that lifted my heart."

As well as enclosing comforting, lived-in space, shelterbelts were also a shield against wind and sun. But ramparts of trees ten or twelve rows deep on three, and sometimes all, sides of the farmstead were obviously designed to do more than keep out prairie weather. They were also a shield against prairie space. In the absence of trees even a fence would do. "Under that immense black dome," wrote one homesteader, "I was glad even of the barbed wire fence that shut me in from those immeasurable distances." Annora Brown recalled how a garden surrounded only by small twigs two or three feet high could dispel the prairie. "The prairie," she remarked, "was shut away. We looked in upon ourselves."

From inside the more formidable shelterbelts, planted by Ontario settlers in Manitoba, the prairie could be seen only from the widow's walk at the peaks of the houses. When Beret Holm was stricken by loneliness and unbearable feelings of exposure in her North Dakota cabin, one of her most comforting memories was of the churchyard in which she played as a girl: "The churchyard was enclosed by a massive stone wall. . . . In the midst of the churchyard lay the church, securely protecting everything round about." Around the church stood not the meagre trees of the prairie, but "a row of venerable old trees, looking silently down on the peace and stillness within. . . . They gave such good shelter those old trees." After he had returned to his native Cardiganshire, Evan Davies recalled that his most pleasurable pastime was to stroll along the gentle country lanes. Their clipped, quickset hedges and neat banks always filled him with a special satisfaction. "The prairie," he said, "had seemed cruel because it was without them."

Had Evan Davies remained on the prairies until 1935, he would have seen the first plantings of, not hedges, but field shelterbelts. Unlike hedges, which were built to enclose or repel stock, field shelterbelts were meant to reduce rates of evaporation, and — in the dry thirties — discourage soil erosion and drifting. The simplest field shelterbelt consisted of a single row of trees or hedging plants: caragana, Manitoba maple, ash, or mixtures of these. A popular combination was caragana and Manitoba maple. In alkaline soils Russian olive, buffalo berry, and Manchurian elm were the most common species. For plantings along highways and near buildings, the forest nursery station at Indian Head recommended fruit-bearing and flowering plants, such as Nanking cherry, hawthorn, and wild plum. These would not only gladden the eye but also attract birds which would, in turn, reduce the numbers of injurious insects. On the American plains, "beautification" had a more explicit role in the field shelterbelt programme. Almost all the wider shelterbelts planted under the auspices of the United States Forest Service had a row or two of flowering shrubs and often, to add lines of green to the winter landscape, a row of pine or juniper.

Major Transformations of the Landscape

While individual settlers could make only token changes to the landscape, institutions and municipalities that wanted to recreate old world settings were able to remodel extensive areas. The grounds of the University of Saskatchewan, for example, were stripped to a depth of about two feet, then built up again with alternate layers of gravel and soil into which were laid flexible sprinkler pipes. Soil and pipes were then covered with a layer of grass sod. The reward for such effort is a sward of lush green grass thick enough to conserve its own moisture. The combination of lawns and limestone buildings, the latter in the college gothic style, is reminiscent of old England. Here, as in other institutional settings, prairie and dryland forms have been utterly banished.

Symbolic patterns of this kind can even be discerned in undertakings which appear to be wholly practical. A striking example is Diefenbaker Lake, and the dam that retains it, on the South Saskatchewan River. Designed for irrigation first and the generation of electricity second, the order of priorities has since been reversed, as the demand for irrigation water has fallen to levels far below original calculations. As the dam's practical value has declined, so have estimates of its recreational potential risen. A Royal Commission advised against building the dam, but the people of Saskatchewan were determined to have "A Lake for the Prairies" — the emotive title of a promotional film — no matter what the cost.

While Diefenbaker Lake is the most costly example of a symbolic adjustment to the prairie landscape, the most unequivocal is Wascana

The diminutive Wascana Creek in 1885. In the background is the N.W.M.P. barracks. (Saskatchewan Archives Baord, R-B4525)

Park, now Wascana Centre, in Regina. A broad swath of lawns, trees, gardens, and lake water running through the heart of Regina, the park is a defiantly humid landscape in a dry and intimidating part of the prairies. Regina lies in the middle of a plain so flat — the bottom of a former glacial meltwater lake — that early settlers described it as a billiard table. In the centre of the plain the only relief from unrelenting space was the shallow valley of a sluggish tributary stream — an "exaggerated ditch" to one acerbic English eye — that joined a larger system of rivers and lakes in the district of Qu'Appelle. Cree Indians called the stream *Oskunah-kasas-take,* or bone creek; buffalo killed in the fall hunt were skinned and butchered, and their bones neatly piled, at a crossing of the stream. Captain John Palliser described the creek and its uninviting setting on his reconnaissance expedition in 1857: "Our course was due west, and as far as the eye can reach nothing but desolate plains meet the view; at noon reached a small creek called The Creek Before Where The Bones Lie, here we found water and some little grass, also a few willow and cherry bushes, but no wood for fuel." With his Irish ear for the mellifluous, Palliser called the stream Wascana, lengthening the vowels of the native Oskunah to do so.

A quarter of a century later the crossing at Wascana Creek was chosen, against the strong claim of scenic Fort Qu'Appelle, as the setting for the new capital of the North-West Territories. Lying on the projected route of the C.P.R. and in the centre of what promised to be fine wheat-growing country, the crossing had tangible economic advantages. Even so, few capitals have been founded with less enthusiasm. Asked to comment on the setting, Sir John A. Macdonald, then Prime Minister of Canada, was torn between the desire for honesty and the necessity for tact. Honesty prevailed. He replied that he thought it would be improved by a little more wood, a little more water, and here and there a hill. To add difficulty to difficulty, the unsightly new settlement acquired an unfortunate name. That choice lay with Princess Louise, wife of the Governor General, Lord Lorne, who ignored the lilting Wascana to honour her mother, Victoria Regina. Neither the name nor the site pleased visiting members of the press. The reporter from *Forest and Stream* said he had never seen so wretched a site for a city, while his colleague from the *Brandon Sun* suggested, with unneighbourly asperity, that for such a setting Golgotha might have been a more appropriate name. Anxious to ward off potential English investors, the London *Advertiser* dismissed the entire capital scheme as a "huge swindle."

In spite of an unpromising start, the settlement survived; by 1906 it was permanent and prominent enough to be chosen as the capital of the new province of Saskatchewan. New legislatures need new buildings, and the search for a site began at once. In the Regina section of its course, Wascana Creek had been converted into a reservoir that lay just south of the city. The stream had been dammed in 1883 to provide water for stock and to raise the levels of surrounding wells. The site preferred by the new government, and the one finally chosen, lay immediately south of the creek on a slight elevation that overlooked both the reservoir and the city. Reginans objected on the grounds that the site was too far — about a mile — from the city centre; they offered the government a forty-acre block of undeveloped land that lay on the north side of the reservoir immediately opposite the government site. Satisfied with its location on the south shore, the government declined the offer. By way of compromise it offered to develop its own 168-acre site and the city land, which came to be known as Wascana Park, in concert.

To select a precise location for the legislative building and design the general setting, the government commissioned Frederick G. Todd, a prominent landscape architect from Montreal. Todd had been a student of Frederick Law Olmstead, the designer of New York's Central Park. His first decision was to locate the legislative building on a high point of land well back from the reservoir. He then recommended that the remainder of the property be ploughed to allow irregular plantings of trees and shrubs, and the replacement of native grasses with cultivated varieties. By planting along the shoreline of the reservoir and along the edges of the combined government and city properties, Todd aimed to create enclosed grassy spaces.

To provide seedlings in the numbers that would be required, and to acclimatize imported plants, Todd advised the government to build a nursery on the edge of the property. The government took his advice; between 1908 and 1912 it bought more than a 100,000 trees and shrubs from commercial nurseries in North America and Europe. Nurseries

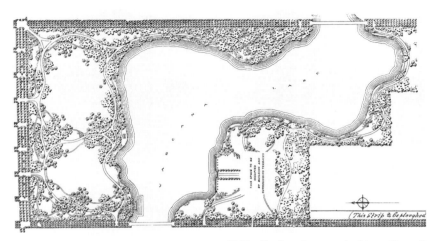

Frederick G. Todd's Plan for Wascana, 1907. (Saskatchewan Archives Board)

in Manitoba and the neighbouring American states had only limited stocks, chiefly of native species. More than 200 varieties of trees and shrubs were then known to be hardy in the region, but fewer than fifty of them were available in prairie nurseries; of the exotics on sale, not all were proof against the prairie climate. Distressed by the limited choice, Malcolm Ross, the Provincial Landscape Architect, predicted that without some increase in the variety of species available, all government-maintained parks and gardens would look alike.

To satisfy Ross's demand for variety, the Wascana nursery became an experimental plot. Seeds and plants were solicited from the Botanical Division of the federal government in Ottawa, from the American Bureau of Foreign Plant Introductions, and from botanical gardens and private collectors in Russia, Siberia, and Korea. By 1914 more than a hundred varieties of trees and shrubs had been grown from seed alone, most of them for the first time in Western Canada. Native species considered suitable for ornamental planting but unavailable in commercial nurseries were also planted. In the park, the main plantings were American elm, green ash, white birch, Manitoba maple, white and blue spruce, and the fast-growing cottonwoods and willows. Lilacs, Tartarian honeysuckles, Ginnalian maples, spiraea, cotoneaster, and highbush cranberry were the chief shrubs. About 11,000 trees and shrubs were planted in the spring of 1913 alone.

After the completion of the Legislative Building in 1912, the government commissioned, at the suggestion of George Watt, the chief gardener, a landscape architect even more prominent than Frederick Todd. Watt was frustrated with some of the details of Todd's plan, and he had heard of the forthcoming visit of the English landscape architect and civic designer

Thomas Henry Mawson. Mawson was a star. By 1912 his company had designed parks and gardens and planned towns on three continents, and Mawson himself had written two successful books on landscape gardening and town planning. His North American tours were promotional. He lectured on the principles of civic planning and design — usually inveighing against the iniquities of the grid plan — and then accepted design and planning commissions to be executed by the Vancouver office of his company. By the end of 1912 these included broad landscape schemes for the Universities of Dalhousie, Calgary, and Saskatchewan, general plans for Calgary and Banff, and plans for improvements to Coal Harbour and Stanley Park, Vancouver. In Calgary, Mawson's amanuensis was William Pearce.

At Regina Mawson was fêted. As a guest of the Lieutenant Governor, he was conveyed from the station to Government House in a horse-drawn coach attended by a footman and a cockaded coachman. His public lecture, on the principles of planning and design as they applied to the host city, was so effective that he was immediately offered three related commissions: to lay out the grounds of the Legislative Building and adjacent parklands, to select a site for a new Government House and design the setting, and to devise a scheme for the civic improvement of Regina. At the time of Mawson's visit Reginans were divided on such questions as ideal widths for sidewalks and the most desirable arrangement for avenue trees. The city, like the government, was in the grip of arboreal fever, having planted 40,000 trees in 1912 alone. The debate over sidewalks and trees absorbed the question period following Mawson's lecture and, though irritated by the preoccupation with details, Mawson understood the concern. He was a planner in the "City Beautiful" mould who believed that planning should attend to convenience and beauty. For Mawson, planning a city — a capital city in particular — was exclusively a problem in design or aesthetics. He dismissed the work of Dr Haggeman, a rival for the Regina commission, on the grounds that it was sociological.

The Regina commission gave Mawson an opportunity to practice two of his cherished principles: that gardens should complement the buildings they embellish, and that public gardens and parks should be integrated with their surroundings. In his report to the Regina city council, Mawson described the park system as a unifying chain designed to convert the city into an artistic whole by binding all the parts. He envisaged three connected zones of parkland: a protective belt of woodland around the city, a parkway of woodland and landscaped gardens running the length of Wascana Lake and creek, and a connecting tissue of small parks and boulevards within the city. His objective was to convert Regina into a "garden city" from which "the reproach of treelessness" would forever be removed. A system of linked parks and boulevards would make possible sylvan walks and drives and would provide, through trees, the vertical relief that the landscape adamantly did not.

For the grounds of the Legislative Building, art and nature dictated a regular or "architectural" layout. The axial symmetry of the building, its classical façade, the levelness of the terrain, and Mawson's insistence on a marriage of building and setting, made anything but a formal design unthinkable. A regular layout also complemented the symmetrical arrangement of boulevards and grand avenues that dominated his general plan for the city. For the remaining public lands around the lake, Mawson extended the Palladian scheme. Buildings were formally related in a grand scheme of civic design that was intended to focus the cultural and intellectual life of the city upon the shores of the lake. The Regina *Leader-Post* described it in retrospect as a "lofty and far-sighted blueprint for the planned development of the area." The blueprint contained government offices, two colleges, an auditorium, a library, and a new house for the Lieutenant Governor. Mawson's plan set the house in formal gardens on the city side of the lake due east of the Legislative Building. To open the legislature the Lieutenant Governor would sail regally across

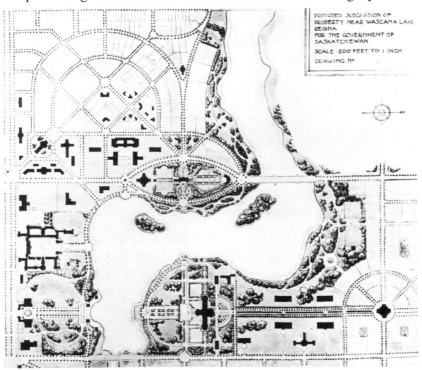

Thomas Henry Mawson's Plan for Wascana, 1912. (Saskatchewan Archives Board)

the lake in a royal barge, disembarking at a decorative landing-stage in front of the Legislative Building.

However far-sighted Mawson's recommendations, they were implemented only where the need was pressing: namely, in the grounds of the Legislative Building. A fine building standing on a treeless site overlooking a stock-watering reservoir was an incongruity that could not be tolerated for long. Mawson's recommendations for driveways, terraces, paths, and gardens were carried out promptly and to the letter. But his general plan for Wascana languished, as did his plan for the city. The outbreak of war in 1914 burst the bubble of Edwardian confidence, and at the war's end it was evident that Regina was no longer, in the embarassing rhetoric of 1912, the "City of Certainties." Rates of immigration slackened as the country filled up, and in the 1930s Saskatchewan suffered woefully from drought and economic depression. Chastened, Regina remained the small capital of a thinly populated agricultural province. Until 1920 a forlorn reminder of pre-war euphoria stood in the northwest corner of Wascana Park. Chateau Qu'Appelle, a large hotel begun by the Grand Trunk Pacific Railway, was never made flesh, figuratively speaking. Construction stopped at the steel-frame stage, and eventually the skeleton had to be dismantled.

Despite war, depression, and drought, work continued on the lands around the lake, but not on the visionary scale recommended by Mawson. Trees and shrubs were planted and grasses sown on the site for the new Government House, but the house was never built, and the grasses made hay for government work-horses, not lawns. In the grounds of the Legislative Building an ingenious underground sprinkler system was installed to protect grasses, trees, and shrubs from the intense summer heat. In the exceptionally dry summers of 1929 and 1930, two men had to be constantly employed to pump lake water to places beyond the reach of the sprinklers. In spite of the effort, so many poplars and maples died that the head gardener despaired of plantings in upland locations unless they could be watered regularly. To guarantee a supply of water, the lake was drained in the summer of 1930 and a well dug in its bottom. While dry, the lake was cleaned and deepened by 2,000 unemployed men. Earth from the lake bottom was shovelled into horse-drawn wagons and piled to make two small islands that had featured in the Mawson plan.

The final stages of the Wascana development date from the 1950s. The decision in 1959 to create a second campus for the University of Saskatchewan raised the question of whether to expand an existing college (Regina College) or to start afresh on a new site. The architects consulted recommended a new start on land offered by the provincial government: the site of a 300-acre experimental farm that lay south of the lake. Except for a few privately-owned patches, all lakeside land was now in public hands. The architects also recommended that the lake be the centre

A view of the Legislative Building taken in 1913 from across the Regina Plain. Bald prairie stretched for miles around. (Saskatchewan Archives Board, R-A2302)

of an educational, cultural, and recreational complex. The recommendation struck a responsive chord and stirred a memory — of the long-abandoned Mawson plan. Committees were formed, an architect/planner appointed, and the scheme given legal sanction by the smooth passage through the legislature of the Wascana Centre Act. Control of the 1,800-acre development was placed in the hands of an authority representative of the chief landowners: the provincial government, the municipality, and the university.

The buildings that make up the educational and cultural complex are set in a continuous swath of irrigated, undulating parkland that now dominates the southern half of Regina. Approached from the north, the park provides relief from city streets, and from the south, relief from a flat, featureless, and rigidly subdivided countryside. The pride that Reginans justifiably feel in the park was voiced by John W. Fisher in a C.B.C. radio broadcast, "Dust but never Despair," in March 1944:

> *Wascana Lake . . . is a terrific undertaking. Every tree imported. Your parks just grow . . . but this park, this Wascana Lake within it and indeed the whole tree-studded city of Regina is a tribute to the sweeter side of man. More planted trees per capita than any other city in the world, they claim. Out here trees just don't grow wild . . . everything must be planted and it will forever be a tribute to Farmer John Saskatchewan who wanted more than prairie about him — he wanted the softness of nature — the sweet smell of flowers and the comfort of trees. So, in his Capital he planted them.*

As an artfully maintained oasis in the centre of what was seen as a fig-

Rupert Brooke's "superb, great House of Parliament." Wascana Lake and Legislative Building, December, 1912. (Saskatchewan Archives Board, R-A3739)

urative desert, Wascana is a metaphor for prairie settlement. It is a symbol of both the farmer's and the townsman's collective triumph over ungenerous, intractable nature. The lush green sward and the park setting have obliterated the prairie. Wascana is Western Canada's most resounding answer to the reproach of treelessness.

But in the populous zones of the park there are no complexes of native plants, no dryland landscapes. Anthropologist John Bennett laments their absence, and sees the entire development as a design against nature that only unremitting care can sustain. His censure extends even to the Legislative Building, a towering, high-ceilinged structure in the English Renaissance style that answered the request for a building with imperial associations, but whose design was hardly suited to a cold, windswept plain. For Bennett, Wascana was less a triumph over difficult nature than an opportunity missed to promote an unfashionable environment that still lies outside the scenic canon.

Chapter Eleven

RANCHERS AND THE PRAIRIE LANDSCAPE

When awarding credit for Wascana, one is careful to single out the Saskatchewan farmer. Farmers had brought to Western Canada a romantic dream of European life; their vision was the vision of the garden plot, and Wascana was an extension of that vision. Ranchers, on the other hand, seem to have travelled without images of an ideal landscape; with no templates to guide them, they made little effort to change or "beautify" the prairie. They made gardens and they sometimes planted trees but, like nomads, they often dispensed with both. If they made reservoirs, they used them strictly for watering stock. Some were so indifferent to the traditional rural arts that they preferred canned milk to fresh — even though they might have owned thousands of cows — and bought hay from neighbouring farmers rather than put it up themselves. "Everything, even butter," wrote the Commissioner of the N.W.M.P. in 1888, "is generally purchased."

Symbolic changes to the landscape were uncommon in ranching districts, and nostalgia, though not unknown, never reached epidemic proportions. On the contrary, the rancher's most singular trait, according to the historian Lewis G. Thomas, was his evident satisfaction with his life and his place. While farmers wrestled with the environment and lamented the loss of home, ranchers revelled both in the ranching life and in the ranch country of southern Alberta and southwest Saskatchewan. So articulate were they, and so willing to voice their pleasure, that in 1883 the editor of the Fort McLeod *Gazette* had to turn away poetry in praise of ranching and the ranch country for fear of "getting mobbed" by unsolicited submissions.

136

Pioneer ranchers in the West began with several advantages. In scenic terms they had the best of the prairie landscape. The foothills of southern Alberta and the Cypress Hills–Wood Mountain region of Saskatchewan would have graced any scenic pantheon, and the ranchers knew it. Probably no pioneer country ever elicited so much praise from settlers and visitors alike. "The verdant, blooming landscape smiles, / Like Eden for a thousand miles" wrote one ecstatic contributor in a poem to the Fort McLeod *Gazette* a year before the editor's embargo. A. E. Cox of Pincher Creek thought southern Alberta "a lovely country" in which he felt the presence of God. Robert Stead, the novelist, offered more elaborate praise. He thought the foothills one of nature's minor masterpieces. They may have lacked the majesty of the mountains and the solemnity of the plains, but they offered in recompense the "friendship of hills that could be climbed, and trees that lisped in the light wind, and water that babbled playfully over gravel ridges gleaming in the August sunshine." In a region of generally brackish water, clear water streams fed by snow-melt or upland springs, and favoured by trout, were a delight. In the prospectus for the Bradfield College Ranche, Dr H. B. Gray regarded the plains as a mere foil for the foothills. "The exclusively wheat growing regions are generally situated in the monotonous and 'prodigious plains,' eastward of Calgary, and have often a depressing effect on the settler." But the Bradfield Ranche, located "in a high valley amid the scenery of an English park, with low trees and hills," lifted the spirits.

It was the foothills that appealed to Lord Lorne and his party on the Vice-regal tour of 1881. The rich soils of Manitoba and Saskatchewan inspired admiration and delight, but it was the park-like valleys of the foothills and the majestic snow-capped mountains beyond that thrilled. Lord Lorne declared southern Alberta "God's country," and the following year he remarked to a friend who visited him at Rideau Hall, Ottawa, that if he were not Governor General of Canada he would be a rancher in Alberta. His staff and the journalists accompanying the tour were just as affected by the beauty of the region. After trekking across dry grasslands, they were intoxicated by the champagne-like air, the many clear streams, and the wooded valleys. Unable to resist their siren-like appeal, several of Lord Lorne's aides did what their superior could not; they returned to Alberta and established ranches. One of them, Lieutenant Colonel Sir Francis de Winton, had a town — De Winton, Alberta — named after him.

But appealing surroundings were only part of the ranchers' bounty. In southern Alberta, in particular, they could add to it the advantages of life lived among people of like mind and background. Not for ranchers the linguistic and social mixtures of the polyglot and democratic plains. Ranch society in Alberta was predominantly English, middle class, and conservative — both socially and politically. The body of ranching may have been American, but its spirit, as the historian Lewis G. Thomas remarked, was British. The practice of raising cattle on open ranges spread northward from Mexico via the United States, and with it came the colourful dress, speech, and terminology of the American cowboy. But there the similarities between Canada and the United States ended. Albertan ranchers and ranch-hands may have worn boots and bandanas and used stock saddles and lariats, but in all other respects Albertan ranch society was law-abiding and decidedly Anglo-Canadian.

The earliest ranchers in southern Alberta were Americans who had trailed herds across the line from the occupied rangelands of Montana and Wyoming, but they were joined, and soon outnumbered, by Canadian frontiersmen and former members of the North-West Mounted Police. The Great March west of the N.W.M.P. in 1874 coincided with the north-ward spread of the American cattle industry, and when the first contingent of officers finished their three-year enlistment contracts, many took up ranching in the Bow Valley or in the country around Fort McLeod. As skilled horsemen accustomed to a life of movement, they slipped easily into the ways of ranching. Most of them were easterners from middle-class families and had the means, or the borrowing power, to acquire a herd of cattle. On their trips east in search of investment capital they were such effective ambassadors for ranching that, on the return journey, they frequently brought back the sons of well-to-do farmers and merchants. Many of these came, as did several of the first N.W.M.P. officers, from the Eastern Townships of Quebec. The Townships were then a stock-breeding area, and in the 1870s an infiltration of French Canadians had unsettled their English-speaking inhabitants.

After 1879 Alberta's budding Anglo-Canadian ranch community attracted recruits directly from the motherland. Buffeted by cheap foreign imports, British agriculture was badly depressed, and the younger sons of landed families in England and Ireland were forced to seek livelihoods beyond the family estate. Many emigrated. Those who came to Alberta, attracted by favourable press reports and the effusive praise of Lord Lorne, usually had enough capital to establish ranches and enough social confi-dence to write "gentleman" under the heading of "previous occupation" on their homestead applications. Several had the backing of influential and sometimes wealthy friends at home. Charles Inderwick and F. W. Godsal, for example, came with the personal recommendation of Lord Lorne.

Besides younger sons, Alberta also attracted former army officers who were as fond of the prefix "Captain" as civilians were of the suffix "gentle-man." According to Zachary Hamilton, editor of the *Calgary Herald,* the typical guests at the Alberta Hotel, which served men from the range, "were tall, lean Englishmen of the type supposed to denote Norman ancestry, some in riding breeches, the cut of which indicated Bond Street."

So prominent was the English presence that J. F. Fraser could write: "In Calgary you strike a new stratum of Canadian, distinct, unique. These men are hardly of the traditional bronco-breaking, cow-punching sort. They are Englishmen of the country class, younger sons who have taken to horse-ranching and cow-breeding on the foothills of the Rockies. You cannot start ranching with nothing but faith and muscle, as you can wheat-growing. . . . Ranching means money."

Money also meant mild eccentricity. W. E. Smith, who insisted on appearing in formal dress at every community gathering, was known by all as The Gentleman Cowboy, and Lionel ("Lord") Brooke of the Chinook Ranch was nicknamed "Window Pane Chief" by the Indians because of his ever-present monocle. Also fond of the monocle was the English painter Inglis Sheldon-Williams, who spent the summer of 1887 working on the Duthie ranch at Pincher Creek before homesteading in Cannington; he is said to be the only private in the British army ever to have worn one. But not everyone was amused by the British presence. The country was so overrun with expatriate Britons, complained one Canadian woman in 1884, that conversation was hopelessly confined to school, military tournaments, the opera, and Henley.

The ranch-hands, or cowboys, came from many different stables. Americans and half-breeds were probably the most numerous, but there were also experienced stockmen from the Eastern Townships, adventurous young Englishmen attracted to Western ranches by advertisements in British magazines, and former constables in the N.W.M.P. The typical police constable was the son of a respectable eastern farmer, or of a worker in the clerical or skilled trades. Under the watchful eye of the N.W.M.P. and a vigilant press, frontier Americans were never allowed to determine the ethos of ranching society. There was occasional rowdiness — attributed to youthful high spirits — but there were no range wars, shootings, or lynchings, and little rustling. "The rough and festive cowboy of Texas and Oregon," declaimed the editor of the *Calgary Herald*, "has no counterpart here. [There are] two or three beardless lads who wear jingling spurs and ridiculous revolvers, and walk with a slouch . . . [but] the genuine Alberta cowboy is a gentleman."

Because they were horsemen who arrived on the prairies at roughly the same time, there was a natural affinity between the police and the ranchers. The commanding officer of "E" Division was always granted honorary membership in the Ranchmen's Club, Calgary's oldest and most select fraternity. Social and commercial links developed quickly. In the early days of ranching, police forts provided the security that open range grazing required, and the forts and Indian reserves were the ranchers' first markets. The police forts were also centres of social life; the police dances were the great events of the social calendar. Ranchers were invited to the balls and, in turn, police officers dined regularly at the ranches.

At work or at play, it was far easier for the N.W.M.P. to identify with ranchers than with frontier squatters or American dryland farmers who in the 1880s moved into the southwestern prairies. Mounted police were adventurers, and most had no interest in farming.

The migration of American farmers northward into Alberta was seen as a threat to the British ways of life and British institutions. To counter it, a group of prominent ranchers struck on the idea — shades of Cannington Manor — of a ranch school designed to instruct young Englishmen in the ways of ranching. Ranches had accepted pupils since the early 1880s, but the idea of a ranch school was new. In a draft proposal circulated among the ranchers, the prospective school was described as a nonprofit organization that would prepare young Englishmen for ranch life through a three-year programme of instruction. To attract pupils, advertisements were to be placed in magazines such as *Field* and *The Country Gentleman,* and in the school magazines of Eton, Harrow, Winchester, and Westminster. English private schools then laid stress on the formation of character, not on the acquisition of knowledge. They prized the outdoor life, and pupils were prepared for it through vigorous exercise, membership in the officer cadet corps, and instruction in horse-riding and the handling of guns. But the ranch school for English private schoolboys that eventually materialized was more modest than the original conception. The Bradfield College Ranche, located near Calgary, catered primarily to boys from Bradfield School. But the annual complement of twenty-five to thirty pupils needed to make the school viable was beyond the means of a single institution. The school managed to survive until 1914, but not even a high valley in the Albertan foothills was as alluring as the fields of France; when war was declared, virtually all the boys went home to enlist. None returned.

Ranching in southern Alberta was generally so profitable that many of the wealthier ranchers lived exceptionally well. J. J. Young, editor of the *Calgary Herald,* noted that the more successful ranchers lived in "charming homesteads, surrounded by the same kind of comfort and refinement which Englishmen associate with the life of an English country house." In the fall of 1902 Young described a visit to the Cochrane ranch: "Seventy thousand acres of . . . choicest grasslands in a solid block, bounded on its two long sides by rivers [and] stocked with fourteen or fifteen thousand head of well bred cattle. . . . Nothing could exceed the splendour of the view from the broad verandah of the Bungalow, a name . . . which gives no idea of the fine stone mansion it really is, with its green lawns, beautiful flower beds and vines and rose bushes, and furnished as it is with all the refinement that wealth and taste can suggest — with its fine reception hall, its open fire places, its pictures, its flowers, its trained servants from the Old Country . . . and even a mocking bird in the conservatory."

In the pioneer West, establishments as large and sumptuous as the Cochrane ranch were possible only because of the nature of ranching an the special social and economic characteristics of the ranching country. Unlike the "hired men" of the farming districts, cowboys were no ordinary labourers. They were notorious for refusing to do farm work — cutting stove wood, haying, digging post-holes — and although they were given general instructions, the execution of them was left to the individual cowboy, who frequently worked alone and at some distance from the home ranch. Farm labourers had less independence, and in country where land was available for the taking, labourers and house servants were difficult to retain. But in the foothill country, where there was no real alternative to ranching, household staff and ranch-hands were more easily held on to. In addition to cowboys and a foreman, the wealthier ranches might have had a Chinese cook, a maid, and a governess to look after the children.

Ordinary ranchers, however, lived much more modestly. The standard dwelling was a comfortable, one-storey log house that had, as Lewis G. Thomas remarked, the charm that comes from native materials used functionally. In other words, it was a folk or species house and it was never alien or lonely. "All through the ranching country," wrote Thomas, "along the edges of the rivers and the streams, among the trees which grew there, lay these houses, simple, solid, comfortable, secure in the knowledge that they were pleasant places to live in and that they could, with suitable adaptation, grow old gracefully." Unselfconsciously, a style had developed that suited both the landscape and the climate. Buildings with long, low lines and large roof areas were consonant with the sweeping character of the terrain, and they did not fight the wind. Yet, as in the farming districts, the satisfaction that native materials and native designs can give was powerless against the onslaught of convenience and fashion. As soon as sawn lumber, house plans, and house-building kits that promised smooth surfaces and dust-free interiors, became available, the picturesque log ranch house went the way of the traditional European house in the farming districts. Its standard replacement was a two-storey frame house, in the late Victorian style, with balconies, some coloured glass, and, as Lewis G. Thomas put it, plenty of tortured woodwork to catch the prairie winds.

For the ranch-owners, ranch life wasn't all-demanding, and games were important, as in all English or quasi-English societies. Nothing revealed the group personality of the Alberta ranchers more frankly than their pastimes. Cricket and tennis were both popular and, until farmers put up barbed wire fences, there were occasional hunts in which the hunters, for want of foxes, chased the unglamorous coyote. Riding and horses were their passion. Their most distinctive game, and the one that gave southern Alberta society its greatest cachet, was polo. It was played in Pincher Creek in 1886, only fifteen years after it had been introduced to England from India; by the turn of the century there were clubs in every ranching centre. Standards of play were high, and Alberta produced a few internationally-known players. Tournaments were celebrated with house parties, balls, and week-end excursions to the mountains.

For ranchers in Saskatchewan, however, life was more workaday. Fewer middle-class Englishmen and N.W.M.P. officers, and larger numbers of American ranchers, meant that there was no fox hunting, cricket, tennis, or polo. Yet even without games and society, ranch life was still appealing. Its deeper satisfactions came, as John Bennett has so eloquently argued, from a life lived in harmony with the environment. Ranchers were the first permanent white occupants of the plains, and to survive without the supports of an industrial civilization they had to learn to live with the land. The first open range cattlemen in Saskatchewan and Alberta lived a life similar to the life of the Plains Indians. They were mounted and semi-nomadic, and their one-storey mud and log shacks weren't much more elaborate than the Indian's teepee. Even the more substantial dwellings built later often kept the character of the first rough shelter. The home ranch in a sheltered coulee was the ranching equivalent of the Indian's winter encampment. There are obvious similarities, too, between range cattle and buffalo. Ecologically speaking, range cattle were heirs to the buffalo, and they were able to succeed only after the buffalo had been eliminated. When buffalo were numerous, their bulls killed the range bulls, and the cows mingled with the buffalo herds. As guardians of the range cattle, ranchers and cowboys had to spend as much time on horseback as Indian hunters. The communal spring and fall round-ups, or "whoop-ups" as they were called on the northern plains, bore some resemblance to the Indian buffalo drives. There were parallels, too, between the carousals following the annual drives to market the cattle and the Sun Dance of the Indians.

As if responding to some intuitive rite of succession, ranchers took to old Indian and buffalo trails when they were searching for ranch sites, or simply for squatting places where they could live off the land without having to buy anything but a few clothes and shells to hunt with. The Indian trails led to campgrounds where there was plenty of grass, wood, and water; and the buffalo trails to spring water, salt licks, and well-sheltered coulees. Pioneer cattlemen in search of their first ranch site sometimes hired half-breed or Indian guides; once established, many of them hired Indians and Métis as ranch-hands. Ranchers seem to have been no more sympathetic to the condition of the Indians than were other settlers, but there is an occasional suggestion of a sensed affinity with Indian ways of life. Nina V. Grier, the daughter of a rancher at Fort McLeod, left this touching vignette: "I loved an Indian camp at night.

A ranch house in Alberta, 1880, photographed by Hanson W. Boorne. Early ranch houses were simple structures, scarcely more permanent than wigwams. (Notman Photographic Archives, McGill University)

The interior of a ranch house, 1880, photographed by Hanson W. Boorne. (Notman Photographic Archives, McGill University)

The smell of smoke and hot horse, and Indian, and rawhide — fires glowing — beef strips curing — squaws dodging in and out of teepees."

The most telling symbol of the greater spontaneity of the rancher's way of life was the cabin in the coulee surrounded by, not a shelterbelt, but a promiscuous growth of native aspen, willow, or box elder. Unrestrained by the sectional survey and the homestead laws, early ranchers, like the first farmers, were able to build their cabins or ranchhouses in places that gave shelter from prairie winds and storms and, for those who found it oppressive, from prairie space. The ranching settlement was an organic settlement, not a mechanical one. Marie Hamilton described her delight at exchanging a location on the Regina Plain for one in the Wood Mountain district of southern Saskatchewan where her father had decided to ranch: "The morning after our arrival the weather changed. . . . I was up early and rushed out of doors to enjoy the new scenes. There were many springs in the hillsides, and the water . . . made liquid music as it hurried through little channels to the valley below . . . all around were dark and wooded ravines, and the high level meadows of a wide valley stretched away for miles. . . . I ran about everywhere, peering into the dark mysteries of the ravines, racing down slopes and climbing the heights until a splendid scene of hill and valley, meadow and plain lay spread before me. After the years of convent, of loneliness

A horse ranch in the Cypress Hills. Scenically speaking, ranchers had the best of the prairie landscape and sometimes the ranches were in spectacular settings. (Public Archives Canada, PA 11480)

and homesickness, it seemed like an enchanted land. . . . In later years, I thought father had picked the most beautiful and convenient location in all the country."

Their beauty aside, the ranching districts of Saskatchewan and Alberta were rich natural pasturelands that had sustained millions of buffalo. American cattlemen who drifted north from Montana in the wake of the disappearing buffalo thought they had stumbled upon Arcadia: "We were only a few miles out of the old cow-town of Maple Creek," wrote Philip. S. Long, "when I could see this was great range country. There was grass everywhere, more of it than we had seen for a long time. The Cypress Hills to the south did not look very high to an old mountain man but, as we drew near them, we were impressed with their timber and beautiful scenery. . . . Winding our way through this timber we finally came out on a flat-topped bench. Here several years growth of grass rippled in the wind knee deep to a horse as far as the eye could see. What a cattle heaven this could be."

And a cattle heaven it was that could, into the bargain, be leased in tracts of up to 10,000 acres for a cent per acre per year. Coulees and spring-fed streams gave shelter and water, and the pastures were rich. Blue-joint, buffalo, oat, timothy, and other natural grasses that made up the short-grass prairie were highly nutritious, and in the dry winds and under the late summer sun the grasses cured on the stem to form the famed prairie wool. By fall, the southern prairie was a great natural hay-field and, thanks to chinooks, the snow-cover was seldom too deep to prevent cattle muzzling through to the grasses beneath. Heated dynamic-ally by their descent from the Rockies, the chinooks are zephyrs that can raise temperatures by sixty degrees in a few hours. Without them, open range ranching would not have been possible; when the chinooks failed or were short-lived, covering the range with a thin coat of ice, the conse-quences were as serious for prairie ranchers as the failure of the monsoon for farmers in India. Small wonder that the low roar of the wind as it came through the high mountain passes was music in the ears of pioneer ran-chers. It was, Charles Inderwick said plainly, "a wonderful wind."

Although the short-grass prairie of Saskatchewan and Alberta might have been designed for raising cattle, the cattle still had to be managed and controlled. Success at ranching depended on understanding the behaviour of cattle on open range, on "knowing cow." Ranchers prided themselves on their ability to think like the animals. But knowing cow was not just a matter of cattle psychology, of outwitting the animals. More important was the ability to predict how they would behave in parti-cular topography, in particular arrangements of grass and water. To pre-vent excessive movement and to ensure proper feeding, watering, and breeding, an understanding of ecologized behaviour was essential. Con-temporary ranchers believe it takes a generation of experience on a particular tract of land to produce a man who really understands the behaviour of cattle, and they maintain that this intimate knowledge of the animals and the environment distinguishes them from stock-raising farmers.

The rancher's greater understanding of the environment was expressed in a vocabulary more truly descriptive of the topography. He quickly dispensed with English topographical names. Water and shelter are vital to the ranching industry, and from the outset it was necessary to distinguish between different valley formations. Thus a valley became a coulee, a draw, a cutbank, or a bottom, depending on its particular configuration and whether it contained a stream. A draw, for example, is a shallow valley of no great size without a stream, a cutbank a steep-sided valley usually in clay formations, and a gulch a dry stream bed. A plateau became the simple and expressive bench, a steeply rising hill with a flat or rounded front became a bluff, and a large grazing area the range. Riders learned to "fix" the topography in their minds, recalled Mr Dayman of Fort McLeod: "They noted every butte, coulee, knoll, hill and outstanding rocks and their characteristics. All were named. . . . Prevailing winds were from the south west. Consequently, the grass which grew high lay to the north east. When a blizzard was raging a rider could get his bearings by dismounting, scraping the snow away, and noting the lay of the land. There is always something on the range you can strike which will serve as a guide."

From the rancher's need to know his range and the behaviour of his cattle developed an attitude to environment that was more tolerant than the farmer's. To the farmer, virgin prairie was a wilderness that had to be "tamed" and cultivated, but to the rancher it was an already productive milieu that needed only to be managed. The rancher felt that he and nature were partners, and he resented changes in the natural order. With time, ranchers themselves were forced to exercise control — they had to make fences and grow fodder once open range ranching was no longer possible or profitable — but their affections lay always in open, unculti-vated prairie. The preference is implicit in Jane Kramer's description of the entrance to the ranch overseen by Henry Blanton, the protagonist of her fine book *The Last Cowboy:* "The land on either side of the Willow gate was flat, irrigated land, planted in wheat for winter grazing . . . The path ran straight between those precious wheat fields. . . . But once the grassland started, the path began to dip and curve. It followed a fence here, circled a patch of burnt-out mesquite there, and veered off toward a windmill somewhere else. The land turned vivid and surprising then."

The ranchers loved making trails and, more than other settlers, they resented the loss of them. For farmers and townsmen, the loss of a trail meant the loss of a fragment of the past; it induced nostalgia. But for the rancher, the loss of a trail signalled a threat to his livelihood. Untramelled movement was the very essence of ranching life.

Photographed by Harry Rowed. Ranchers exulted in rapid, uninhibited movement. (Public Archives Canada, PA 134188)

Often, love of the ranching country amounted to a fierce loyalty. Robert Symons could hardly have been more bound to his native English heath than to the country around the Cypress Hills: "She is a land you sometimes feel you hate, yet deep down you know she is a land you cannot leave for long; for she will call you back — back to the hiss of the ground blizzard, back to the star-lit nights, back to the scent of wolf-willow and sage, back to the uplands of yellow grass where the horses gallop."

The ranchers' affection for wild prairie also extended to the animals who lived on it. To the prairie farmer wild animals were pests to be eradicated or controlled, but to the rancher they were, as they remain, vital symbols of uncontrolled nature. They reminded him of the days when the range was open and free and when men, cattle, and wild animals could roam at will. When animals threatened the stock or the range, ranchers were capable of killing them in large numbers, but their regard for them held. Antelope were admired for their speed and their ability to leap fences, and thus enjoy the range in the old way. Coyotes, too, were regarded with particular affection because they are elusive animals, touched with mystery, and — no small consideration — potentially dangerous to barnyard species.

To the rancher, the dryland farmer — who with Government encouragement began to invade the southwestern prairies after the completion of the C.P.R. — was a destructive and contemptible interloper whom he dismissed with the hard words "nester," "mossback," "landgrabber," and "sodbuster." Because they were the first Europeans in the southwest, and because they lived directly off the grasslands, ranchers saw themselves as the only authentic inhabitants of the prairie. Although ranches had boundaries, ranchers claim to have had only a weakly developed sense of property. They believed that ranching was a way of preserving the wilderness, and were dismayed when surveyors and homesteaders imprinted the hand of property on the surface of the prairie:

Their house has locks on every door,
Their land is in a crate.
These are the plains of God no more,
They're only real estate.

Homesteaders not only fenced and crated the open range but, in the eyes of the ranchers, they compounded the trespass by committing ecological abuse. Ranchers were no guardian angels of the prairie ecosystem — the larger operators frequently overstocked the range with "green" cattle from the east in the hope that winter storms would not kill off too many underfed animals — but they did not make "awful wounds" on the "beautiful" prairie, nor did they, in areas too dry for agriculture, turn the ancient sod "wrong side up." By not touching trees and shrubs, ranchers protected wildlife habitats and provided grazing animals with shelter from sun and storm. But homesteaders had come to build a civilization, not conform to a wilderness, and their settlement was a form of conquest. They changed the contours of the land, drove out the objectionable fauna and, in their desperate search for fuel and fencing material, felled the trees in the creeks and river bottoms.

Yet the hated instrument was the plough, not the axe. Once touched by the plough, so the ranchers claimed, grasslands failed to cure in the old way, even though the land might never be ploughed again. Extreme feelings about the plough were expressed in a mocking will and testament prepared by J. B. Henson, a veteran rancher of Saskatchewan Landing. He instructed his lawyer to sell the whole of his real estate and with the proceeds create a fund "for the extermination of that class of Vermin, commonly known as farmers," who were then "polluting" the country adjacent to the South Saskatchewan River. In 1922 he added a codicil that was even testier: "I leave to each and every mossback my perpetual curse, as some reward to them for their labours in destroying the Open Range, by means of that most pernicious of all instruments, the plow."

Although the prairie climate sometimes bore down on the rancher, cattle were less vulnerable than crops to wind, hail, and drought; it was an exceptional year when they didn't have a year-round supply of pasture and hay. Raising cattle could be demanding but, unlike homesteading, it was seldom toilsome. There were periods of intense activity during the spring and fall round-ups when cattle were branded and selected for beef, and in winter there could be long periods of exposure to wind and cold. Ranch women, too, were even more isolated than women on the homesteads, and they were sometimes as lonely. But on the whole the general routine of pioneer ranch life was not particularly onerous and, to survive, ranchers weren't compelled, as in that chilling homesteader phrase, to "root, hog, or die." If settling the prairie is compared to a military campaign, then ranchers were the mounted brigades and homesteaders the foot soldiers.

Like all cavaliers, ranchers and cowboys thought well of themselves; they had, in the modern phrase, a positive self-image. The image depended in part on the excitement and camaraderie of the round-ups, on working for outfits with names as irresistible as Turkey Track, Matador, and T-Bar Down, on a vernacular speech that was as dry and spare as the country they lived in, and on picturesque yet functional dress. Whereas the farmer's clothing came out of the eastern catalogues and was often inadequate, the rancher's was a gift of the southern plains. Bandannas were shields against dust and smells, stetsons protected against the sun, canvas jackets lined with sheepskin kept out wind and cold, and high-heeled boots kept feet from slipping through stirrups. Cowboys and ranchers inherited a tradition which gave them a ready-made identity. To this they could add personal identities endowed by nicknames — Bacon Rind Pete, Seven-up Jim, or the simple Windy and Slim — that highlighted traits of behaviour, taste, and appearance.

Even more sustaining than a colourful identity was the conviction that they belonged on the prairie. Elsewhere in North America, European settlement had advanced along the parallels of latitude, but on the dry, high plains it had spread northward along the meridians of longitude from Texas to Alberta. The counter movement suggested that ranching was the natural occupation of the grasslands, and the rancher their rightful occupant. A man with his horse under him and with the range spread out around him believed, so Jane Kramer remarked, that he was privy to truths and satisfactions denied to sedentary men. Certainty of position gave him a natural dignity. The cowboy/rancher was one of Nature's gentlemen, a knight of the frontier or, to paraphrase Jane Kramer, Rousseau's Emile with a lariat and a stock saddle. Like all gentlemen, he was guided by codes of conduct, not rules and regulations. Where other men signed contracts and exchanged bills of sale, cowboys shook hands. And where other men talked, cowboys acted.

The image was reinforced at every turn by journalists, storytellers, and painters. Almost from the beginning of the ranching industry on the American plains the cowboy had been seen as the embodiment of a profound masculine ideal; he was the antithesis of rooted, regimented, domesticated man. Thanks to a popular press and widespread literacy, the cowboy was already a mythic figure by the late 1880s. The "drover," "herder," and drifter of the 1860s and 70s, who could be on the trail for months at a time without anyone to miss him, had been exalted. To a witness of an 1886 Montana cattle drive, the typical cowboy was a "brawny fellow with . . . crisp, tight-curling yellow hair," a neck that rose "straight and supple" from the low collar of a loose flannel shirt, and a sun-browned face with "piercing gray eyes" looking out from under the broad brim of his hat.

The image had even presidential sanction. Theodore Roosevelt, who seldom failed to respond to physical attributes, wrote rhapsodically about the cowboy: "They are smaller and less muscular than the wielders of ax and pick; but they are as hardy and self-reliant as any men who ever breathed. . . . Peril and hardship, and years of long toil broken by weeks of brutal dissipation, draw haggard lines across their eager faces, but never dim their reckless eyes nor break their bearing of defiant self-confidence." He thought them much better fellows and pleasanter companions than small farmers or agricultural labourers, and compared with the "sleek city merchant" or the "miserable farmer [engaged in] a losing and desperate battle with drought, cold, and grasshoppers," the rancher was as dashing as an Arab shiek.

Canadian commentaries on the cowboy were just as fulsome as the American. For Robert Symons, cowboys were virtue made flesh, a special creation who "weren't spawned by accident [but] . . . are born that way." They loved freedom, stood up to a challenge, loved nature, animals, and wind-swept places, were loyal to the outfit, the range boss, and each other and they did all of these not from duty, necessity, or expediency, but from "inner compulsion." Robert Stead wrote of Dave Barr, hero of *The Cowpuncher:* "How straight he was and how bravely his footsteps fell on the hard earth." In the painter John Innes the Canadian rancher and cowboy had an admirer as ardent as Charles Russell or Frederick Remington. Innes had owned a stable and breaking corral in Calgary, and had ranched at High River before turning to journalism and painting. His monument is a series of historical paintings of the development of the Canadian West in which the cowboy figures prominently.

Just as the modern cowboy is nourished by his film and television image, so the pioneer cowboy was sustained by dime novels. Hugo Maguire, a cowboy in the Shaunavon district of Saskatchewan in the 1890s, used to come into the bunkhouse after a day on the range and read "a western story fiction magazine." Eighty years later Henry Blanton, curled up in his bedroll along the lonely breaks of the Canadian River, would shore up his courage by calling on images of John Wayne, Gary

Cooper, and Glenn Ford. Farmers, too, had their sustaining myths, but in the romance stakes a sturdy ploughman dreaming of home and family was no match for a fleet, unencumbered horseman with his eyes on far horizons. The farmer/rancher dichotomy has never been better expressed than in George Stevens's brilliant movie *Shane* (1953). Readers who may have seen the film will easily recall its taut, mounted hero, given exactly the right measure of reticence and gentle strength by the actor Alan Ladd, but the gallant homesteaders whom Shane defended against a marauding cattle baron may well have slipped from memory.

Ochnophils and Philobats

However enlarged the myth of the rancher, the assertion that he is a distinctive type, more adventurous than the farmer, might have scientific as well as popular sanction. After reflecting on differences in human needs for security, and how these are related to space, the psychoanalyst Michael Balint identified two basic personality types. He labeled them *"ochnophil"* and *"philobat."* The ochnophil is hesitant and fearful, and his world consists of friendly objects (refuges) separated by threatening spaces. The philobat's world is the negative of the ochnophil image: threatening spaces become friendly expanses interrupted by occasional hazards that have to be negotiated. Unlike the ochnophil, whose security depends on the proximity of refuges and helpful equipment, the philobat relies on his own resources and a limited amount of equipment. Provided the elements are not actively threatening, the philobat is confident of his ability to survive. The philobat's world, Balint concluded, is characterized by safe distance and sight, the ochnophil's by physical proximity and touch. Thomas Hart Benton, the American painter, made a similar distinction when writing about people's responses to the Great Plains. He remarked that on some people the plains have a liberating effect, whereas on others — "cozy-minded" people who like having "life's little knicknacks" around them — the effect of the plains is inhibiting. People for whom a sense of intimacy is necessary for emotional security, he declared, are likely to have their "familiar urges" stilled by the "brute magnitude of the plains country."

Although distinctions between ranchers and farmers are now blurring as ranchers plant crops and farmers raise cattle, pioneer farmers and ranchers on the prairies fit readily into Balint's and Benton's categories. Pioneer ranchers were adventurers who, arriving before the homesteaders, either valued isolation or were not particularly frightened by it. Self-reliance, endurance, and the ability to take command quietly and efficiently were the most admired traits in the masculine ranching culture; in a country of great distances and sparse population they were often prerequisites for survival. Early farmers were also adventurers, but those who came after the turn of the century were mostly family men anxious to create stable communities in an ordered, cultivated countryside. Raised on the farms, and in the hamlets and small towns of continental Europe, Britain, and eastern North America, they were accustomed to close social

"The Harvesters," M. Leone Bracker, 1931. Homesteaders dreamt of home, family, and modest prosperity. The painting was used as a poster by the C.P.R. (C.P.R. Corporate Archives, 8202)

contacts and community life. They brought with them the accoutrements of civilization: pots and pans, books, linen, furniture and, as Jane Kramer put it, a republican dream of modest property and the rules and rhythms of domestic law. As soon as it was practicable they built houses, roads, schools, and towns, planted trees, and set up the machinery of government.

Except for the well-to-do English, the rancher/cowboy travelled light. American cowboys arrived in Western Canada with nothing but their "gear": a stock saddle, a lariat, and (sometimes) a horse. "A cowboy," Robert Symons wrote, "has no home, no furniture, no fine chinaware. His saddle is his investment, his sole possession, his necessity." Like all nomads, cowboys and ranchers were not much interested in civilization, and required only minimal services, often just an annual trip to town to give them the supplies they needed. When ranchers thought about government and cooperative associations, they did so not with a view to minimizing the effects of isolation but to ensuring that their isolation would not be threatened. Early ranchers were opposed to school districts — for homesteaders the very icons of civilized life — and the provision of social amenities in general, because they would have encouraged settlement and increased taxes. The rancher's overriding concern was to preserve his physical independence and freedom of movement. His security lay not in shelterbelts, machinery, towns, and good government, but in understanding the prairie and being able to move across it at will. Fences and settlement were hated not only because they impeded the movement of stock but also because they restricted the horseman. Ranchers delighted in the spaciousness of the landscape and in the rapid, uninhibited movement it allowed. The ease with which they were able to ride over the prairie is a persistent refrain in ranching literature. Moira O'Neill, an accomplished poet and the Irish-born wife of an Alberta rancher, wrote: "I like the endless riding over the endless prairie, the wind sweeping the grasses, the great silent sunshine, the vast skies and the splendid line of the Rockies guarding the west." Apart from the exhilaration afforded by free movement, in the absence of protective cover the ability to move swiftly across the prairie in any direction was a primal form of defence.

But the horseman's real security lay in his understanding of the environment and his knowledge of the behaviour of cattle, not in his ability to escape potential enemies. Ranchers were so much at home on the prairie that they could, metaphorically, haul anchor and drift at will. "After being on the trail a day or two, the trailer ceases to regard time, distance, or the things of the civilized land. Home is where grass and water are abundant. Time is marked by three events, sunrise, meridian, and sunset. All else is needless division." Hamlin Garland's observation would strike a sympathetic chord in Henry Blanton's exasperated wife:

"People say that cowboys — that if they wanted to be at home, they'd be at home. But it's not true. Cowboys *forget* about home. If Henry would only call me when he's out there and say where he was, I wouldn't worry." In contrast to the footloose ranchers, farmers were more attached to the home, and they also like routine and order. One of John Bennett's interviewees, a grain farmer of nervous temperament who admitted to having a compulsion for order, said that his chief agricultural worry was wind. First, wind disturbed the soil, and then the trash cover that he was obliged to lay on his fields to protect the soil. The disordered trash cover made his fields look "messy." He didn't like cattle, which he bought only when he had surplus grain to dispose of, and the thought of them wandering freely over his fields was so disturbing that it woke him at night. He liked the immobility of crops, "when you plant 'em," he said, "they stay there."

The poet Charles Olsen, echoing the psychoanalyst Michael Balint, remarked that there are two modes of survival in a sea-like land. You can either ride the land or fasten onto it like a tent stake. The rancher rode and the farmer fastened. One yielded to the elements, and the other resisted them. These fundamental differences in responses to the landscape occur repeatedly in both the imaginative literature and in the various chronicles of pioneer experience. When an aged Alberta rancher felt death approaching he asked to be buried on the highest point of land in the community so that he might enjoy a clear view of the prairies and at the same time, he added, keep an eye on his neighbours. The stricken Beret Holm, *in extremis,* could think only of lying in an ancient churchyard surrounded by old stone walls and tall, protecting trees. Some require shelter even in death.

PART III

THE PRAIRIE AS HOME

Chapter Twelve

IMAGINATIVE INTERPRETATIONS OF THE LANDSCAPE

Accounts of pioneer life on the prairies usually focus on the material difficulties of the settlement. These were formidable. A short growing season, uncertain rainfall, and the risk of hail, wheat rust, and grasshoppers often reduced farming to a one-sided joust with the elements. And even if victory went to the farmer there was no guarantee of a fair return. Distance from suppliers and markets and fluctuating international prices, ate into and sometimes devoured profits. Yet, however great the problems that threatened the physical welfare of the settler, they were matched by those that troubled his mind and spirit. The pain of leaving a beloved home is tolerable only if the migrant can make a home out of the new land. No material gain can compensate for a life-time of anomie. Migration is an emotional odyssey as well as a physical one, and in many cases the quest for home was completed not by the migrant but by his children and his children's children.

The first stages of home-making are practical ones. The new land is mapped and surveyed, its prominent features named. The settlers build houses; they make roads, fields, and gardens. Knowledge of the surroundings and physical control over them increase confidence and reduce feelings of vulnerability, but by themselves they do not create the feeling of home. They orient but they do not realize. House, shelterbelt, gardens, cultivated fields — these are the beginnings of homemaking in a new land, but the sense of belonging and the state of heightened awareness that we normally associate with the home place are gifts of the imagination, not the plough and the hammer. No land is home, Northrop Frye remarked, until it has been imaginatively digested or absorbed.

As a country, Canada proved particularly intractable to the European imagination. Sensibilities nurtured in gentle European landscapes were repelled by the scale of the land, the rugged terrain, and the wintry climate. A large area of continuously cultivable land and rich soils might have been expected to appeal to European sensibilities, but the scale of the prairies coupled with the severity of the winters more than offset the advantages of cultivability.

Imaginations presented with strange settings can respond in one of two ways. They can find new means to express the new forms, or they can cling to the old means and tailor the new forms to fit them. If the work of pioneer poets, painters, and novelists can be taken as representative, then pioneer imaginations followed the second course. Instead of confronting the disturbing new land, they ducked the issue — hid under the bedclothes, as Northrop Frye put it — by replacing an alien and implacable nature with one that was tamer and more comprehensible. The landscape they described is scarcely recognizable today. Most poets were able to produce only muted European landscapes, in the tradition of Wordsworth and the Romantic poets. They are remembered today only for provoking the inspired satire of Paul Hiebert:

> *How changed and bleak the meadows lie*
> *and overgrown with hay,*
> *The fields of oats and barley*
> *Where the binder twined its way!*
>
> *With doors ajar the cottage stands*
> *Deserted on the hill —*
> *No welcome bark, no thudding hoof,*
> *And the voice of the pig is still.*

Subject and treatment were equally at odds in pioneer paintings. Painters painted what they knew rather than what they saw. The process, in its most crude form, was described by the niece of a Sunday painter in Manitoba. "Like many other Canadians of the time, my aunt saw little to interest her in the Manitoba landscape. She used pictures of the English landscape as her models, changing and adding colour to suit her taste." But even accomplished paintings looked English, or European: tones were dark, colours restrained, shadows heavy, outlines blurred. The subjects were traditional ones: valley farms, grazing animals, trails, lakes, and trees. There were few paintings of open prairie, and none

Colonial heroic: Inglis Sheldon-Williams's "The Fireguard," oil on canvas, 26×35", 1923. Representations of the pioneer as hero boosted immigrant morale. (Norman Mackenzie Art Gallery, University of Regina)

"The Road in the Valley," A. F. Kenderdine, 1922. The winding road, the wooden fence, and the farmstead tucked into a fold of the valley evoked the Old World, not the New. (Glenbow Archives)

that conveyed a sense of prairie light and space. Any figures in the land-scape were treated heroically. Pioneers either tilled the prairie to feed the world or fought David-and-Goliath battles with fire and storm. Australian painting went through a similar phase, named "colonial heroic" by the historian Bernard Smith.

The transformations of land and people are not difficult to explain. In strange settings, the imagination instinctively asserts the familiar and the conventional. In the near-featureless prairies, that instinct was over-whelming. Painters scoured the landscape for familiar features, and then treated them in conventional ways. Farmsteads were made to appear solid and substantial, trees were sometimes given a full and leafy look. Oc-casionally, too, painters introduced picturesque features — flocks of sheep and wooden fences, for example — that were either missing from the actual landscape or uncharacteristic of it. Through introductions of this kind, and through the selection of familiar features that were then treated conventionally, painters superimposed on the landscape a veneer of European sensibility and style.

The paintings now seem unrelated to their subject, yet at the time pioneers accepted them as true statements about the new land. The accep-tance was a measure of their insecurity and homesickness. In pioneer societies, art is an analgesic, not a stimulant; the insecure and uncertain prefer romance to reality, sustaining myths to searing truths. Paintings — or, for that matter, poems and novels — that cast pioneers in a heroic light lifted morale; and by setting the pioneers in Europeanized land-scapes they served pressing nostalgic needs. Images that suggested correspondences between the old land and the new comforted the homesick; by preserving the patterns and traditions of the art of the old world they also reassured settlers of the continuity of cultural ties. In a region where settlers found no familiar cultural patterns, these ties were lifelines.

Reminders of the old-world culture may have assuaged nostalgia, but in the long run they prolonged the sense of alienation by presenting images

"Moose Mountain from Cannington Manor," A. Thomas, c. 1895. Thomas, a Cannington resident, was a product of the English school of landscape painting. (Courtesy Mrs. B. Forsyth)

of a distant world. If painting, literature, and folk tales continually reflect other places, then people may be physically in one world but imaginatively in another, and they remain dislocated for as long as the world they inhabit is filtered through the lens of another culture. "Poems and stories about babbling brooks, towering mountains, soaring larks, apples in orchards, the glory of the crimson maple leaf," remarked an exasperated prairie-born Max Braithwaite, "were lost to youngsters who had never seen these things." As Braithwaite's frustration demonstrates, the sense of being in the wrong place affected not only the immigrants, but the children of the immigrants. Thus Margaret Atwood's laconic comment about Canada: "We are all immigrants to this place even if we were born here."

This sense of homelessness, or placelessness, is endemic to all pioneer societies. The broadcaster and journalist Eric Sevareid, who grew up in North Dakota, described the sense of frustration felt by the literate, imaginative child for whom real places were always elsewhere: "I remember studying the picture books of the seaside places, the mountains and the crowded cities. Somewhere they existed. I remember tracing the meaningless rectangle of Dakota in schoolbook maps and thinking: Why am I here on the cold, flat top of the country? What am I doing here?" Ivan Southall, a third-generation Australian, offers this illuminating anecdote: "The first time I ever felt properly at home was on a gloomy Autumn morning in 1943. . . . I pulled up the blinds onto early morning light as our train crossed the river Thames and for the first time in my life I saw the Tower of London downstream. I was twenty-two, a pilot in the Royal Australian Air Force . . . and, I was sure, very soon to die, but I cried inside because I was home. The landscape was right at last. Do you know what that means? I don't. Because London doesn't feel like home to me any more."

The answer to Southall's dilemma can be found in an autobiographical essay by the historian W. L. Morton. Morton (a Canadian, also of the third generation) grew up on a farm in Manitoba early in this century, and like all Canadians of British background, he was raised on Victorian English literature. There was little Canadian or prairie literature available, and most of this reflected the old world rather than the new. Through living in one world and reading, almost exclusively, about another, Morton inhabited two landscapes — one external, one internal. As a result, he experienced the tension of a mind that is not integrated imaginatively with its surroundings. In the absence of a regional art or literature to provide the images he required, Morton realized that to resolve the dilemma he would have to provide his own. "Nothing, no country," he wrote, "can really be owned except under familiar name or satisfying phrase. To be apprehended by the mind and made personal, it requires not only the worn comfort of a used tool or a broken-in shoe; it requires also assimilation to the mind, ear, eye, and tongue by accepted, or acceptable, description in word, or line, or colour. . . . The need to reconcile the actual and the mind's landscape . . . underlies the need, felt at least by the sensitive of a new country, to create its own literature and write its own history." For Morton, good history had not only to be true to fact; to possess the "truth of total vision," it also had to be imaginatively true.

To be useful in the process of home-making, the art and literature of a pioneer country must match the settler's experience of it, however painful that experience might be. Psychological adjustment to a new land can begin only when the bonds of memory that attach the settler to the old land have been loosened or broken. The need for this was demonstrated by the experience of a relatively recent exile in Canada: an American draft evader legally banished from the United States. To orient himself when travelling in Canada, the American had to refer to points south of the border. Southern Ontario, for example, was the Midwest because it was adjacent to Michigan, and Western Manitoba was the far West because it lay above North Dakota. America was his "inner space" of memory and associations, Canada his "outer space," for which he had neither personal nor cultural coordinates. For the young American, as for generations of schoolboys everywhere, Canada was "the big pink country" that disappeared off the top of the map. The habit of seeing where he really was by referring to points south was broken only when he climbed and photographed, with great discomfort and some risk, a small but previously unclimbed mountain in the Yukon. His intense experience of a particular locality gave him a much stronger sense of the country as a whole. On subsequent journeys he no longer had to look at the American part of the map to know where he really was. "Now somewhere inside me," he concluded, "is a new mental image . . . [which] is a more faithful reflection of my objective reality. I'm not sure," he said cryptically, "but I think this has something to do with art."

The inference of the American's concluding remark is that art derived from an intense experience of place can dispel or reduce the sense of homelessness by providing images of environment that match the newcomer's experience of it. Time alone may loosen attachments to the homeland, but as long as the new land is filtered through the forms of the old culture it can never be home. To feel at home, immigrants, or their descendants, had to acquire new ways of seeing. For Canadians as a whole, the new vision, equivalent to the crossing of an imaginative Rubicon, was the gift of a group of Toronto-based painters: the Group of Seven. Avowed nationalists, the members of the group were determined to provide Canadians with identifiable symbols of the country. "An Art must grow and flower in the land," Lawren Harris wrote prophetically in the introduction to the catalogue of the group's first exhibition in 1920, "before a country will be a real home for its people." Later, Arthur Lismer would tell a Regina audience: "art is not something imposed from without, and from another age, but . . . is something within an artist responding to the call of love and beauty. A love of one's environment is requisite."

Though not the first painters to offer Canadians an identity, the Group of Seven were the first to reach the public. To break the European hold on the Canadian imagination they rejected quiet, pastoral corners of the country in favour of the region they considered to be the most Canadian part of Canada: the Precambrian Shield. Bold colours, cold, clear light, hard edges, and rough, energetic brush strokes celebrated the primeval qualities of the Shield and at the same time rejected the traditional values of European landscape painting. The paintings were arresting, and they were immediately popular. From the safety of their cities in the south, Canadians embraced their new northern image.

Regional liberation movements quickly followed, and they affected all the arts. In the West, novelists such as Martha Ostenso and Frederick Philip Grove questioned the romantic characterization of pioneering and the naïve assumptions underlying it. In their novels of the mid-twenties they acknowledged the physical and economic achievements of the settlement, but they lamented what they perceived to be the settlers' spiritual alienation from the land. The prairie may have been productive, but it was not Eden. There were also detectable changes in paintings of the prairies. Painters who arrived after World War I were less influenced by studio-bound nineteenth-century approaches to landscape. In the habit of painting out of doors, and trained in the techniques of watercolour painting, they responded to the landscape with greater spontaneity. Watercolour, as Walter J. Phillips remarked, is the medium for impulse, not meditation. Like the novelists, the painters, too, sensed that man was out of step with the rhythms of nature, and in a few of the paintings there are suggestions of discord. By the twenties, therefore, changing approaches to the landscape itself, and changing assessments of the settlers' relationship with it, began to make prairie painting look a little less like English art transplanted.

But the drive for a more realistic view of the prairies was led by prairie-born painters, not by immigrants. Two were prominent: Lionel Lemoine Fitzgerald of Manitoba and Illingworth Kerr of Saskatchewan. Fitzgerald, the elder of the two, saw his first paintings that were neither English nor Scottish during a year (1921–22) spent with the Arts Students League in New York. When he returned to Manitoba, he realized that a landscape without scenery would always defeat "mere picture-makers," and concluded that before he could paint the prairie convincingly he would have to understand it. To concentrate his vision, he narrowed his geographical range. Except for occasional visits to British Columbia, Fitzgerald remained in Manitoba. As John Constable would have said admiringly, he was a "stay-at-home" painter. Fitzgerald's reward for a

An unflattering view of Main Street by Western Canada's first realist painter: "Behind False Fronts (Back of Main Street)," Illingworth Kerr, 1928. (Mendel Art Gallery, Saskatoon)

lifetime of patient observation and painstaking work was a collection of lasting images of a still, often cold landscape covered with a delicate tracery of grasses and trees. In 1932, one year before they disbanded, the members of the Group of Seven invited Fitzgerald to join them. Stylistically, Fitzgerald had little in common with the group, but they recognized in him a kindred spirit who shared their desire for a land-based Canadian art.

Although not as rooted as Fitzgerald, Illingworth Kerr was cut from similar cloth. He was taught by members of the Group of Seven in Toronto, and when he returned to Saskatchewan in 1927 he was as determined as Fitzgerald to see the prairie anew — "with eyes unprejudiced by European influences." In Toronto, Kerr had renewed an acquaintanceship with Charles W. Jefferys, the first painter to appreciate prairie light and colour, and the fragile, shimmering qualities of prairie trees and shrubs. "Wolf Willow," he once said to Kerr, "lovely stuff to paint." Jeffreys had studied Scandinavian painting and learned the techniques of French Impressionism, so he was able to paint the bright colours of the summer landscape, the brilliant light, and the sharply defined forms. One of his halting places on his many visits to the West between 1901 and 1924 was Lumsden, Kerr's home town in the Qu'Appelle valley.

Like Jefferys and Fitzgerald, Kerr also sketched and painted out of doors, braving sub zero (farenheit) weather, blinding sunlight, wind, dust, and mosquitoes. The effort endangered his sight, but it produced the first uncompromising portraits of the prairies. Kerr's paintings of the prairie in winter were the first to register the stark quality of its light and lines and convey its essential hostility. During the droughts and depression of the late twenties and early thirties man's hold on the prairies seemed particularly tenuous, and Kerr chose, as the symbol of uneasy occupancy, the small prairie town. "Gap-toothed," "loose jointed," and "sloppily put together," it was out of tune with both the landscape and the climate. Kerr's small towns are all sisters to "Horizon," the town of Sinclair Ross's *As For Me and My House,* the most severe of the Depression novels.

For Mrs Bentley, the heroine of *As For Me and My House,* the vast simplicities of the prairie are the ultimate test for the imagination: "I used to think that only a great artist could ever paint the prairie, the vacancy and stillness of it, the bare essentials of a landscape, sky and earth." Elsewhere in the novel she remarks that the outlines of the uncluttered surface are so strong and pure "that they're just like a modernist's abstractions." The abstract tendencies in the landscape hadn't escaped Lemoine Fitzgerald or Illingworth Kerr. To fix them, Fitzgerald developed a "sort of shorthand" that allowed him to get down the essentials "in the fewest possible lines." Frustrated by the great dome of often cloudless sky and the Saskatchewan plain — "the least interesting environment for a painter" — Kerr also concluded that the painter of flat, open prairie must settle for an equation for nature. Noting that realism must "throttle" the prairie painter, he concluded that "abstract was the only answer to western space with its vast scale, its power of mood, rather than tangible form."

Although Fitzgerald and Kerr both pointed the way to painting the plain, Fitzgerald's abstract phase didn't occur until the 1950s and Kerr left Saskatchewan for England in 1935. Mastery of the plain was left to an unschooled but determined English painter named Robert Hurley. Hurley came to Western Canada in 1923 and, like many an immigrant before him, reacted to the prairie with Old Testament vehemence: "a desolation — an abomination of desolation." He began painting in the thirties. Like his English predecessors, he took to the river valleys. Hurley's valley paintings were commonplace, but when he came out of the valleys onto the plain he produced paintings of striking originality. To convey a sense of the spaciousness of the landscape and its geometric simplicities, Hurley used a ruler, pen and ink, and watercolour washes.

"Spring Thaw," Robert Hurley, 1954. Hurley's austere paintings of the cold, still plain dispelled comforting European interpretations of the prairie. (Courtesy of Dr. Jessie Caldwell)

Watercolour is translucent; when applied in broad washes it is an ideal medium for rendering prairie space and light. The effects of shadow and perspective Hurley mastered by using cardboard models of grain elevators and houses.

A typical Hurley painting is a distillation. He pared an already spare landscape down to its bones: usually, to a flat foreground empty except, perhaps, for a road, a railway, or a line of telegraph poles and, in the distance, the silhouettes of grain elevators or a town. The paintings are without figures, or movement of any kind. Hurley's vision was shared, some years later, by the writer Fredelle Bruser Maynard: "There were no 'prospects' on the prairies — only one prospect, the absolute, uncompromising monotony of those two parallel infinities, earth and sky. I draw it in my mind's eye, with a ruler — road and tree, farmhouse and elevator, all spare and simple and hard-edged, with a line of telegraph poles slicing the distance. Movement in this landscape has no more consequence than the leap of a jackrabbit across a dusty road. The stillness is the reality."

Hurley's compositions are now a familiar stereotype, but in the late thirties and forties they were a revelation. They sold and sold. Hurley kept no record of sales or gifts, but he reckoned that he produced five paintings a week for thirty years — a total of 7,800. The popularity of the paintings, which was immediate, seems to have been a classic example of the "shock of recognition." Tempered by time, pioneering, and the hardships of the Depression, prairie people no longer needed the buffering effect of the pastoral and the picturesque. Yet to be fully realized, feelings or emotions must be articulated and located outside ourselves. Hurley's gift to people on the prairies was to anchor those feelings in the clarifying images of his art. It was as if, wrote columnist Percy Wright, "they had been waiting for an interpreter who would point out to them the realities of their environment." Hurley, as Ivan Southall would say, had made the landscape right at last.

THE NEW LANDSCAPE

To "absorb" the prairie, painters and writers had to replace imaginative patterns imposed by eastern and European sensibilities with others that acknowledged the austere character of the land. The effort produced an aesthetic based on scarcity, not, as in the case of the picturesque, on fullness. Prairie farmers also had to replace old patterns with new. Government planners had been just as blind to the limitations of the prairie as the early poets and painters. The planners' vision of a landscape of quarter- or half-section farms, each with its flower and vegetable garden, and a dense network of small towns and villages, was as inappropriate as the imaginative constructions of the early poets, painters, and novelists. The plan was a dream of the east, or of Europe, that could never be realized in the West. It was more successful in the park belt than in the dry south, but even in the parkland the way was difficult. The farm population has declined steadily in all parts of the prairies since the 1920s, and evidence of the outflow lies all around. Dead or dying shelterbelts, decaying barns and machinery, abandoned houses, elevators, and railway stations are strewn across the landscape. Old artifacts rot or rust so slowly in the dry air that the prairie, seen through antiquarian eyes, is a great open-air museum.

Since the twenties a new landscape, more austere than even Hurley could have envisaged, has broken through the chrysallis of the old. The elaborate, picturesque farmstead of shelterbelts, lawns, and gardens proposed by government, the C.P.R., and rural reformers in general, had as little hope of becoming a standard feature of the prairies as the quarter- or half-section farm. The experimental farms were staffed by teams of well-trained horticulturalists and, in spite of the simple planting formulas they recommended — shelterbelt, native shrubs, wide expanses, bold massing, and few details — the results they were able to achieve went far beyond the skills of the average farmer and his wife. Even more serious — for devotees of Andrew Jackson Downing — than the failure to make a bower of the prairie was the general disregard for the belief that a life lived close to nature was improving. Although most farmers approved of the doctrine of agricultural fundamentalism, which held that life on the farm was more fulfilling than life in the city, few farmers could name even the common birds, wildflowers, and shrubs. To counter the indifference to nature, the Country Life Commission in the United States and the Commission of Conservation in Canada early in this century urged the teaching of natural history in the schools, and recommended the establishment of school gardens as places where the lessons of a moral life could be taught.

But as the century advanced a more powerful doctrine, based on technology and ideas of control, supplanted the old. The romantic notion that surroundings should be visually pleasing and morally uplifting lost ground to the belief that they should be designed chiefly for work. Gospels of efficiency replaced sermons on the good life and the role that an attractive environment could play in it. Even the kitchen garden had to submit to a new order. The old compartmentalized method, that had been both utilitarian and ornamental, was abandoned in favour of long, straight rows, placed far apart, that could be drilled, seeded, and tilled by machine. In technical journals the farm itself came to be described as a collection of "confinement facilities for the production of eggs, meat, and milk." Popular farm literature still encouraged the farmer to beautify, but it became more and more difficult to reconcile the picturesque world of house, garden, lawn and ornamental plants within the shelterbelt with the mechanistic world of feedlots, dugouts, irrigation ditches, and great open fields that lay beyond. To keep faith with the new order and abreast of changes in agricultural technology, the experimental farms were renamed "research stations" and subjected to repeated reorganization.

Although carrying remnants of the old landscape, the new landscape is now visible. Its distinguishing features are light, pre-fabricated buildings, fields swept clean of bluffs and sloughs, and large, expensive machines worked by unseen operators from within enclosed cabs. There are no figures in the modern prairie landscape. Clearly, the aim of the men who work the machines is efficient production through manipulation of soil, plants, and animals. Soil is treated with a complex series of additives to ensure the proper balance of nutrients, and to control insects and weeds. Thanks to advances in genetic engineering, crops will become more convenient to grow, care for, and harvest. Barns, where they still exist, have also changed. Once comfortable catch-alls of animals, feed, and equipment, they are now controlled environments in which light, heat, feeding, and reproduction are carefully regulated. For the most up-to-date farmers, home is now the nearest village or town; where the farmhouse and outbuildings once stood there is an office and a machinery shed. The landscape is slowly emptying. Smaller, struggling farms are bought up by individuals, cooperatives, corporations, or foreign investors, and the surviving farms become ever larger. This is the pared down, energy-intensive landscape of agro-industry that bears little relation to popular notions of how a countryside ought to look.

For the pioneers, changes in farming technology and in the landscape were doubly confusing. They had crossed an ocean or a continent only to land, figuratively speaking, on a shifting plain. Sudden changes in technology and society required them to adapt to changing conditions of life and work as well as to a new physical environment. No sooner had people begun to settle than machine farming began to thin out the rural population. Homesteads that might have supported a family under a horse-powered technology now had to bear the costs of new machinery, and many were too small to do so. As the farm population declined, social life suffered; to intensify the distress, the landscape itself began to change. The textured landscape of bluffs, barns, fences, hayfields, and oatfields made by the pioneers was quickly reduced to one of large, unbroken wheatfields worked by combine and tractor. "I remember," recalled one pioneer, "our farm had been a patchwork of bush, pasture, and plots of ground cultivated here and there. Now a tractor pulls a four-bottomed plow almost a mile of field without turning." Although the uniform, seemingly undifferentiated new landscape is distressing to old-timers, antiquarians, and lovers of traditional countrysides, it is consistent with the mechanistic spirit of the original settlement plan. For the realist, the new landscape is simply the most recent phase in a process of landscape rationalization that began with the rectangular survey and the mechanical planning and placement of the towns.

The reorganization of farming has inevitably affected the character of social life. No longer restrained by the limitations of horses, and with fewer bluffs and sloughs to negotiate, farmers work with greater intensity and for longer hours. Old-timers complain that there is less time for visiting, and because there are fewer people, social occasions are less frequent. Hardest hit are the elderly, many of whom now have no physical connection with their past. The original homestead may be part of a larger unit, the house abandoned, the children gone from the district. The sense of loss, which isn't limited to the old, is reflected in the folk art of the region. Once the undisputed icon of the prairies, the elevator now has to compete with symbols of earlier and, in memory, gentler times: weathered, abandoned farmsteads, broken fencelines, rusting machinery, overgrown woodlots, and scenes of communal life — threshing days, country weddings, grain hauling, and journeys to and from the country school.

However popular these images, they should not, of course, be mistaken for an earnest desire to return to rural life. Nostalgia for the past has as much to do with an unsatisfactory present as with a desire to return to a former way of life which has been idealized in memory. Farm life was seldom as communal or as satisfying as it is now supposed to have been. The popular belief is that the prairies were emptied by an insensate technology and the depression and droughts of the thirties. But none of these can be blamed for the movement from the land. The exodus was greater in the prosperous forties than in the destitute thirties and, on balance, technology ought to have prevented displacement, not caused it. Offsetting the displacing effects of larger tractors and combines were other inventions — such as telephones, radios, and rural electrification — that made rural life more tolerable than it had ever been. Not even the automobile, the greatest single antidote to rural isolation, was able to stem the outflow.

Richard du Wors, the Saskatchewan sociologist, saw the exodus as nothing less than a "panic flight" from the land, and he attributed it to the attraction of the towns and cities and the repelling effects of the plain. He argued that in a pleasure-loving age, when people in general are attracted to areas of "low discomfort," life on an isolated farmstead in an emptying plain can only be a minority taste. Du Wors also made the point that, physically, the prairie in some ways is more threatening than it was in the past. Technology has made us careless of what he called "passive defences" — heavy underwear, warm hats, stout boots — so that when our machines break down we are more than ever at the mercy of the elements.

The decline in the number of farms and in the number of farmers who live on the land is usually lamented, and a commitment to explore ways and means of reducing the losses is still a standard prop in the platforms of most political parties. But the concern may be unwarranted. In the context of world settlement, prairie settlement is conforming to an age-old pattern that is found throughout much of the old world. The grain farmer with no stock to care for can now, like a farmer in Italy or Spain, live in a village or a town and go out to the land to work. If crops are good and prices reasonable, he may even winter in the south or west. By living away from the farm he has eliminated many of the social costs of farming on the plains, and his presence may help to revive a small town. He is, in effect, a modern version of the once-despised "suitcase farmer," who showed up for spring ploughing and left after the fall harvest.

Only the sentimental now see rural life as a good, in the moral sense;

farming today is generally regarded as a way of making a living, not as a way of life. Whether he lives on or off the farm, the entire adaptive effort of the modern farmer is directed at efficiency in agriculture. The austere character of the prairie, which early promoters and settlers were at such pains to soften, is now less disturbing. Wives who live on the farms spend their money on home decoration and modern kitchens, not on gardens and shelterbelts. Modern farm-houses, say old-timers, "jump onto the road." The maintenance that trees require, and the short life of even adapted species in the rugged climate, makes many a farm family regard growing them as not worth the effort. Natural gas is plentiful and cheap, and the modern house tight, so there is less need of shelterbelts to cut the wind. Western Canada may lead the continent in the design of energy-efficient housing, but while gas supplies last, house design on the prairies can ignore the elements. Provided the shell of the house can prevent the well-heated interior from blowing away, the farmer can now have the house of his dreams: a Spanish villa, a California split, or a Greek revival mansion with pillars and portico.

The prairie may no longer intimidate, but it remains a difficult environment. As a group, only the ranchers remain completely at home. They seldom consider other ways of life or alternative habitats; on retirement, they are much less inclined than farmers or townspeople to head for the sunbelt or the west coast. In spite of the popularity of Hurley-like images, the picturesque maintains its hold on the collective mind. The art of hotels, motels, and calendars is more likely to be by Constable than Kerr or Hurley, and streets, suburbs, and shopping malls are wistfully named after faraway plants and places. Every city has its Green Acres and its Wildwood, or equivalents. City people, now the overwhelming majority, occasionally speak of the prairie as "out there," which suggests that they have not taken to the landscape of agribusiness and that the garrison mentality still holds. As a species we are remarkably adept at seeing in our surroundings only what we wish to see, and there is some evidence that prairie people may block out the harsher features of the environment, preferring to hold on to more comforting images. A friend reports that during a showing of the movie *Dr Zhivago* on a winter evening in Saskatchewan, a young woman was heard to exclaim to her companion, at the sight of a Siberia-bound train snaking its way darkly across a snow-covered plain, "Oh, I wouldn't like to live there!" That particular scene had been filmed in Alberta.

But the last word on the difficulties of making a home of what is, by any measure, one of the world's more difficult environments, should go to Edward McCourt, dean of prairie writers until his death in 1972. McCourt was the first post-war writer to address the problem of how to adapt to an environment that, as he put it, overwhelms the newcomer and haunts the native, however far he may wander, until he dies. At the end of his book on the treatment of the Canadian West in fiction, he suggested that the prairie might be too austere an environment for the common sensibility ever to absorb completely and that, like Thomas Hardy's Egdon Heath, it would always be a minority taste, appealing, at the deepest levels, only to "subtler and scarcer" instincts than those which respond to the sort of beauty called charming and fair.

BIBLIOGRAPHY

Introduction and Chapter One

Billington, Ray Allen. *The Westward Expansion*. New York: MacMillan, 1967.

Butler, William F. *The Great Lone Land*. London: Sampson Low, 1872.

Commager, Henry Steele. "The Literature of the Pioneer West." In *Selections from Minnesota History,* eds. Rhoda R. Gilman and June D. Holinquist. St Paul: Minnesota Historical Society, 1965.

Dunbar, Gary S. "Isotherms and Politics, Perception of the Northwest in the 1850's." In *Prairie Perspectives II,* eds. A. W. Rasporich and H. C. Klassen. Toronto: Holt, Rinehart and Winston, 1972.

Friesen, Gerald. *The Canadian Prairies: a History*. Toronto: University of Toronto Press, 1984.

Gilbert, Bil. "The Cry Was: Go West Young Man and Stay Healthy." *Smithsonian,* March, 1972.

Grant, George Monro. *Ocean to Ocean*. Toronto: Belden Bros., 1873.

——*Picturesque Canada*. Toronto: Beldon Bros., 1882.

Hall, D. J. "Clifford Sifton: Immigration and Settlement Policy 1896–1905." In *The Prairie West, Historical Readings,* eds. R. D. Francis and A. W. Rasporich. Edmonton: University of Alberta Press, 1985.

Hedges, James B. *Building the Canadian West*. New York: MacMillan, 1939.

Hiemstra, Mary. *Gully Farm*. London: Dent, 1955.

Hogarth, Paul. *Artists on Horseback, the Old West in Illustrated Journalism 1857–1900*. New York: Watson-Guptill, 1972.

Jackel, Susan. *Images of the Canadian West*. Unpub. Ph.D. Thesis, University of Alberta, 1977.

Jahn Evelyn, Hertha. *Immigration and Settlement in Manitoba 1870–1881*. Unpub. M.A. Thesis, University of Manitoba, 1968.

Lehr, John C. "Propaganda and Belief, Ukrainian Emigrant Views of the Canadian West." In *New Soil — Old Roots: the Ukrainian Experience in Canada,* ed. J. Rozumnyj. Winnipeg: Ukrainian Academy of Arts and Sciences in Canada, 1983.

Owram, Doug. *The Promise of Eden: The Canadian Expansionist Movement and the Idea of the West 1856–1900.* Toronto: University of Toronto Press, 1980.

Orwell, George. *Such, Such Were The Joys.* New York: Harcourt and Brace, 1953.

McDonald, Norman. *Canadian Immigration and Colonization 1841–1903.* Toronto: MacMillan, 1970.

Moodie, D. W. "Early British Images of Rupert's Land." In *Man and Nature on the Prairies,* ed. Richard Allen. Regina: Canadian Plains Research Centre, 1976.

Roper, Edward. *By Track and Trail through Canada.* London: W. H. Allen, 1891.

Spry, Irene M. "Early Visitors to the Canadian Prairies." In *Images of the Plains: The Role of Human Nature in Settlement,* eds. B. W. Blouet and M. P. Lawson. Lincoln: University of Nebraska Press, 1975.

Shortt, Adam. "Some Observations on the Great North West." *Queens Quarterly II,* January 1895.

Stich, Klaus Peter. "Canada's Century: The Rhetoric of Propaganda." *Prairie Forum,* I, April 1976.

Thomas, Lewis H. "British Visitors' Perceptions of the West, 1885–1914." In *Prairie Perspectives II,* eds. A. W. Rasporich and H. C. Klassen. Toronto: Holt, Rinehart and Winston, 1972.

Warkentin, John. Ed., *The Western Interior of Canada, a Record of Geographical Discovery 1612–1917.* Toronto: McCelland and Stewart, 1964.

West, John. *The Substance of a Journal during a Residence at the Red River Colony.* Republished Winnipeg: S. R. Publishers, 1966.

Chapter Two

Begg, Alexander. "Early History of the Selkirk Settlement (1894)." Reprinted in *Historical Essays on the Prairie Provinces,* ed. Donald Swainson. Toronto: MacMillan, 1978.

Berry, Virginia. "Washington Frank Lynn: Artist and Journalist." *The Beaver,* 24, Spring 1978.

Dempsey, Hugh A. "Blackfeet Place Names." *Alberta Historical Review,* Summer 1956.

Donkin, John G. *Trooper and Redskin.* London: Sampson Low, 1889.

Gilman, Rhoda R., Carolyn Gilman, and Deborah M. Stultz. *The Red River Trails.* St. Paul: Minnesota Historical Society, 1979.

Giraud, Marcel. "Métis Settlement in the North-West Territories." *Saskatchewan History,* 7, Winter 1954.

Gunn, H. G. "The Selkirk Settlement." *North Dakota Historical Quarterly,* 1,4. Fargo: July 1927.

Jackson, James A. *Centennial History of Manitoba.* Toronto: McClelland and Stewart, 1970.

Johnston, Alex. "Blackfoot Indian Utilization of the Flora of the Northwestern Great Plains." *Economic Botany,* 24, July-Sept., 1970.

—— "Uses of Native Plants by the Blackfoot Indians." *Alberta Historical Review,* 8, 1960.

—— *Man's Utilization of the Flora of the Northwestern Plains.* Unpub. manuscript, Glenbow–Alberta Institute.

Martin, Sandra and Roger Hall. Eds., *Rupert Brooke in Canada.* Toronto: P. M. A. Books, 1978.

Morton, W. L. *Manitoba: A History.* Toronto: University of Toronto Press, 1957.

—— "The Significance of Site in the Settlement of the Canadian and American Wests." *Agricultural History,* XXV, July 1951.

Pritchett, John. *The Red River Valley 1811–1849.* New Haven: Yale University Press, 1942.

Spry, Irene M. "The Great Transformation: The Disappearance of the Commons in Western Canada." In *Man and Nature on the Prairies,* ed. Richard Allen. Regina: Canadian Plains Studies Centre, 1976.

Warkentin, J. H. "Western Canada in 1886." Historical and Scientific Society of Manitoba, *Transactions,* Series III, 20, 1963–64.

Chapter Three

Appleton, Jay. *The Experience of Landscape.* New York: Wiley, 1975.

Bachelard, Gaston. *The Poetics of Space.* Boston: Beacon Press, 1969.

Bailey, Leuba. *The Immigrant Experience.* Toronto: MacMillan, 1974.

Bernhard, Iver. "Nyveien til Fevatn," *Ved Arnen,* 59, Feb. 1933.

Cather, Willa. *My Antonia.* Boston: Houghton Mifflin, 1949.

Clark, Georgina Binnie. *Wheat and Woman.* London: Heinemann, 1914.

—— *A Summer on the Canadian Prairie.* London: Edward Arnold, 1910.

Dahlman, August. "Homesteading in the Willow Bunch District." *Saskatchewan History,* II, I, 1958.

Davies, Evan and Aled Vaughan. *Beyond the Old Bone Trail.* London: Cassell, 1960.

Ganzevoort, Herman. Ed., *A Dutch Homesteader on the Prairies: the letters of Willem de Gelder 1910–1913.* Toronto: University of Toronto Press, 1973.

Grove, Frederick Philip. *Over Prairie Trails.* Toronto: McClelland and Stewart, 1922.

Gruchow, Paul. "This Prairie, This Terrible Space." In *The Minnesota Experience,* ed. Jean Ervin. Minneapolis: Adams Press, 1979.

Hamilton, Zachary and Marie. *These Are The Prairies.* Regina: School Aids and Text Book Publishing Co., 1948.

Herklots, H. G. G. *The First Winter.* London: J. M. Dent, 1959.

Hoffer, Clara and F. H. Kahan. *Land of Hope.* Saskatoon: Modern Press, 1960.

Kostash, Myrna. *All of Baba's Children.* Edmonton: Hurtig, 1977.

McCourt, Edward. *Home is the Stranger.* Toronto: MacMillan, 1950.

Minifie, James. *Homesteader: A Prairie Boyhood Recalled.* Toronto: MacMillan, 1972.

Moorhouse, Myrtle G. *Buffalo Horn Valley.* Regina: Banting, n.d.

Niven, Frederick. *Canada West.* Toronto: J. M. Dent, 1930.

Roberts, Sarah E. *Alberta Homestead.* Austin: University of Texas Press, 1971.

Robinson, Elwyn B. *A History of North Dakota.* Lincoln: University of Nebraska Press, 1966.

Rolvaag, O. E. *Giants in the Earth.* New York: Harper, 1927.

Savage, Candace. *A Harvest Yet to Reap: A History of Prairie Women.* Toronto: 1976.

Stegner, Wallace. *Big Rock Candy Mountain.* New York: Duell, Sloan and Pierce, 1938.

—— *Wolf Willow.* New York: Viking, 1966.

Stevenson, John A. "Prairie Memories." *Beaver,* Winter 1959.

Tennyson, Bertram. *The Land of Napoia.* Moosomin: Spectator Printing and Publishing, 1896.

West, Edward. *Homesteading: Two Prairie Seasons.* London: T. Fisher Unwin, 1918.

Chapter Four

Campbell, Marjorie Wilkins. *The Soil is Not Enough.* Toronto: MacMillan, 1938.

Dawson, C. A. *Group Settlement: Ethnic Communities in Western Canada.* Toronto: MacMillan, 1936.

England, Robert. *The Central European Immigrant in Canada.* Toronto: MacMillan, 1929.

Hiemstra, Mary. *Gully Farm.* London: J. M. Dent, 1955.

Kaye, Vladimir J. *Early Ukrainian Settlements in Canada.* Toronto: University of Toronto Press, 1964.

Keywan, Zonia. *Greater Than Kings.* Montreal: Harvest House, 1977.

Lehr, John C. *The Process and Pattern of Ukrainian Rural Settlement in Western Canada 1891–1914.* Ph.D. Thesis, University of Manitoba, 1978.

Maynard, Fredelle Bruser. *Raisins and Almonds.* Toronto: Doubleday, 1972.

Mitchell, Elizabeth. *In Western Canada Before the War.* London: J. Murray, 1915; reprinted Saskatoon: Western Producer Prairie Books, 1981.

McCarthy, Mary. "One Touch of Nature." In *The New Yorker,* Jan. 24, 1970.

McGregor, J. G. *Vilni Zemli.* Toronto: McClelland and Stewart, 1969.

Moberg, Vilhelm. *Unto a Good Land.* New York: Simon and Schuster, 1954.

Panchuk, John. *Bukowinan Settlements in Southern Manitoba.* Battle Creek, Michigan, 1971.

Piniuta, Harry. *Land of Pain, Land of Promise.* Saskatoon: Western Producer Prairie Books, 1978.

Rees R. and C. Tracie, "The Prairie House." *Landscape,* 22, 3, Summer 1978.

Richtik, James M. *Manitoba Settlement 1870–1886.* Unpub. Ph.D. Thesis, University of Minnesota, 1971.

Roy, Gabrielle. *The Fragile Lights of Earth.* Toronto: McClelland and Stewart, 1978.

Taggart, Kathleen M. "The First Shelter of Early Pioneers." *Saskatchewan History* II, 3, Autumn 1958.

Trotter, Beecham. *A Horseman and the West.* Toronto: MacMillan, 1925.

Turek, Victor. *Poles in Manitoba.* Toronto: Polish Alliance Press, 1967.

Van Cleef, Eugene. "Finnish Settlement in Canada." In *Geographical Review,* 42, 2, 1952.

Young, Charles H. *The Ukrainian Canadians: a Study in Assimilation.* Toronto: Thomas Nelson, 1931.

Chapter 5

Adams, Thomas. *Rural Planning and Development, Commission of Conservation, Canada.* Ottawa: Commission of Conservation of Canada, 1917.

Bicha, Karel Dennis. *The American Farmer and the Canadian West.* Lawrence: Coronado Press, 1968.

Drache, Hiram M. *The Challenge of the Prairie: Life and Times of the Red River Pioneers.* Fargo: North Dakota Institute for Regional Studies, 1970.

Garland, Hamlin. *The Joys of the Trail.* Chicago: Bookfellows, 1935.

Johnson, Hildegard Binder. "Rational and Ecological Aspects of the Quarter Section." *Geographical Review,* 47, 3, 1957.

——— *Order Upon the Land.* London: Oxford University Press, 1976.

Moodie, D. W. "Alberta Settlement Surveys." *Alberta Historical Review,* Autumn 1964.

Shepard, Paul. *Man in the Landscape.* New York: Ballantine Books, 1967.

Smalley, E. V. "The Isolation of Life on Prairie Farms." *Atlantic Monthly,* 72, Sept. 1893.

Tyman, John L. *By Section, Township, and Range: Studies in Prairie Settlement.* Brandon: Assiniboine Historical Society, 1972.

Warkentin, John and Richard I. Ruggles. *Manitoba Historical Atlas.* Winnipeg: Historical and Scientific Society of Manitoba, 1970.

Chapter Six

Dunae, Patrick. *Gentleman Emigrants: from the British Public Schools to the Canadian Prairies.* Vancouver: Douglas and McIntyre, 1981.

Dufferin and Ava, Marchioness of. *My Canadian Journal 1872–'78.* New York: D. Appleton., 1891.

Epp, Frank H. *The Mennonites in Canada 1786–1920.* Toronto: MacMillan, 1974.

Foster, Keith. "The Barr Colonists: Their Arrival and Impact on the Canadian North-West." *Saskatchewan History* 35, 3, Autumn 1982.

Francis, E. K. *In Search of Utopia: The Mennonites in Manitoba.* Altona: D. W. Friesen, 1955.

Hewlett, A. E. M. "England on the Prairies," *Beaver,* December 1952.

Hill, Douglas. *The Opening of the Canadian West.* New York: John Day, 1967.

Kloberdanz, Timothy J. "Plainsmen of Three Continents: Volga German adaptation to Steppe, Prairie, and Pampa." In *Ethnicity on the Great Plains,* ed. Frederick C. Luebke. Lincoln: University of Nebraska Press, 1980.

Martynowych, Orest T. *The Ukrainian Bloc Settlement in East Central Alberta, 1890-1930.* Alberta Culture Historic Sites Service, Occasional Paper No. 10, 1985.

Rasporich, A. W. "Community Ideals and Community Settlements in Western Canada 1890-1914." In *Prairie Perspectives II,* eds. A. W. Rasporich and H. C. Klassen. Toronto: Holt, Rinehart and Winston, 1972.

Rees, R. "Eccentric Settlements in the Canadian West." *History Today,* 27, 9, September 1977.

Smith, C. Henry. *The Coming of the Russian Mennonites.* Berne, Indiana: Mennonite Book Concern, 1927.

Tanner, Henry. *The Canadian North-West and the Advantages it Offers for Emigration Purposes.* London: 1885.

Vaughan, Walter. *The Life and Work of Sir William Van Horne.* New York: Century, 1920.

Warkentin, John. "Mennonite Agricultural Settlements of Southern Manitoba." *Geographical Review,* July 1959.

Woodcock, George and Ivan Akumovich. *The Doukhobors.* Toronto: McClelland and Stewart, 1977.

Tracie, C. J. "Ethnicity and the Prairie Environment: Patterns of Old Colony Mennonite and Doukhobor Settlement." In *Man and Nature on the Prairies,* ed. Richard Allen. Regina: Canadian Plains Research Centre, 1976.

Zacharias, Peter D. *Reinland: An Experience in Community.* Altona: D. W. Freisen, 1978.

Chapter Seven

Aberle, George P. *From the Steppes to the Prairies.* Dickinson, North Dakota: 1964.

Brody, Hugh. *Inishkillane: Change and Decline in the West of Ireland.* London: Allen Lane, 1973.

Healy, W. J. *The Women of Red River.* Winnipeg: Women's Canadian Club, 1923.

Handlin, Oscar. *The Uprooted.* Boston: Little, Brown, 1951.

Klymasz, Robert B. *Ukrainian Folklore in Canada: An Immigrant Complex in Transition.* Ph.D. Thesis, University of Indiana, 1970.

Kostash, Myrna. *All of Baba's Children.* Edmonton: Hurtig, 1977.

Lysenko, Vera. *Men in Sheepskin Coats.* Toronto: Ryerson, 1947.

—— *Yellow Boots.* Toronto: Ryerson, 1954.

Marunchak, Michael. *The Ukrainian Canadians: A History.* Winnipeg: Ukrainian Free Academy of Sciences, 1970.

McCann, Willis. *Nostalgia: A Descriptive and Comparative Study.* Unpub. Ph.D. Thesis, University of Indiana, 1936.

Moberg, Vilhelm. *The Last Letter Home.* New York: Simon and Schuster, 1961.

Munsterhjelm, Erik. *The Wind and the Caribou.* Toronto: McClelland and Stewart, 1955.

Skardal, Dorothy Burton. *The Divided Heart: Scandinavian Immigrant Experience through Literary Sources.* Lincoln: University of Nebraska Press, 1974.

Zwingmann, Charles and Maria Pfister-Ammende. *Uprooting and After.* New York: Springer-Verlag, 1973.

Chapter Eight

Canadian Forestry Association. *William Silvering's Surrender, A Story of Western Experience.* Winnipeg: 1901.

Droze, Wilmon H. *Trees, Prairies and People: A History of Tree Planting in the Plains States.* Denton: Texas Women's University, 1977.

Gordon, Daniel M. *Mountain and Prairie.* Montreal: Dawson Bros., 1880.

Gregory, Annadora F. "Creating The Fruited Plains." *Nebraska History,* 49, 3, Autumn 1968.

Jackson, J. B. *American Space, The Centennial Years 1865-1876.* New York: W. W. Norton, 1972.

Kollmorgen, Walter, and Johanna Kollmorgen. "Landscape Meteorology in the Plains Area." In *Annals of the Association of American Geographers,* 63, 4, December 1973.

Mirov, N. T. "Two Centuries of Afforestation and Shelterbelt Planting on the Russian Steppes." *Journal of Forestry,* 33, 12, December 1935.

Olson, Sherry. *Depletion Myth: a History of Railroad Use of Timber.* Baltimore: Johns Hopkins University Press, 1971.

Ross, George W. *Patriotic Recitations and Arbor Day Exercises.* Toronto: Warwick Bros. and Rutter, 1893.

Shelford, V. E. "Deciduous Forest Man and the Grassland Fauna." *Science,* 100, August 1944.

Thomas, Keith. *Man and the Natural World: A History of the Modern Sensibility.* New York: Pantheon, 1983.

Williams, Burton J. "Trees But No Timber: The Nebraska Prelude To The Timber Cultural Act." *Nebraska History,* 53, Spring 1972.

Chapter Nine

Alderman, W. H., Ed., *Development of Horticulture on the Northern Great Plains.* St Paul: Inst. of Agriculture, University of Minnesota, 1962.

Brown, Annora. *Sketches from Life.* Edmonton: Hurtig, 1981.

Brown, William. "The Application of Scientific and Practical Arboriculture to Agriculture." *Canadian Economics.* British Association for the Advancement of Science, Montreal Meeting, 1884.

Buchanan, D. W. *Horticulture in the North.* St Charles, Manitoba: 1907.

Donaldson, Sue Anne. "William Pearce: His Vision of Trees." *Journal of Garden History,* 3, 3, July–Sept 1983.

Fry, Harold S., Ed., *Development of Horticulture on the Canadian Prairies: An Historical Overview.* Edmonton: Western Canadian Society for Horticulture, 1956; reprinted 1986.

Garland, Aileen. "Gardens Along the Right of Way." *Manitoba Pageant,* 22, 2, Winter 1977.

Minifie, James M. *Homesteader: A Prairie Boyhood Recalled.* Toronto: MacMillan, 1972.

Pellett, Kent. *Pioneers in Iowa Horticulture.* Des Moines: Iowa State Horticultural Society, 1941.

Pomeroy, Elsie. *William Saunders and His Five Sons.* Toronto: Ryerson, 1956.

Ronald W. G. Ed., *The Development of Manitoba's Nursery and Landscape Industry.* Altona: Manitoba Nursery and Landscape Association, 1983.

Ross, Norman M. *Trees Free to Farmers.* Ottawa: Dept. of the Interior, 1907.

—— *Tree Planting on the Prairies of Manitoba, Saskatchewan, and Alberta.* Ottawa: Dept. of the Interior, 1923.

Walker, John. *Planning and Planting Field Shelterbelts.* Ottawa: Experimental Farms Service, Dept. of Agriculture, June 1951.

Wessel, Thomas R. "Prologue to the Shelterbelt." *Journal of the West,* 6, 1967.

Chapter Ten

Brown, William. "The Application of Scientific and Practical Arboriculture to Agriculture." *Canadian Economics.* British Association for the Advancement of Science, Montreal Meeting, 1884.

Bennett, John. *Northern Plainsmen: Adaptive Strategy and Agrarian Life.* Chicago: Aldine, 1969.

Berton, Pierre. *The Great Railway.* Toronto: McClelland and Stewart, 1972.

Fisher, John W. CBC radio broadcast, March 1944.

Gilbertson, Kristine Kaldor. *From Mouldboard to Metric.* Altona: D. W. Friesen, 1978.

Kraenzel, Carl. "Trees and People in the Plains." *Great Plains Journal,* Fall 6/1, 1966.

Mawson, Thomas H. *The Life and Work of an English Landscape Architect.* London: The Richards Press, 1927.

Niven, Frederick. *Canada West.* Toronto: J. M. Dent, 1930.

Rees, R. "Wascana Centre: a Metaphor for Prairie Settlement." *Journal of Garden History,* 3, 3, July–Sept 1983.

Ross, Norman M. *Success in Prairie Tree Planting.* Ottawa: Forestry Branch Bulletin No. 2, 1922.

Stoeckeler, J. H. "Psychology and Aesthetics as Factors in the Evolution of Farmstead Windbreaks and Field Shelterbelts." In *Symposium on the Great Plains of North America,* eds. Carle Zimmerman and Seth Russell. Fargo: North Dakota Inst. for Regional Studies, 1967.

Thomas, Greg and Ian Clarke. "The Garrison Mentality and the Canadian West." *Prairie Forum,* 4, 1, 1979.

Chapter Eleven

Balint, Michael. "Friendly Expanses — Horrid Empty Spaces." *International Journal of Psycho-Analysis,* 36, 1955.

Bennett, John W. "Attitudes toward Animals and Nature in a Great Plains Community." *Plains Anthropologist,* 9, 1964.

Benton, Thomas Hart. *An Artist in America.* New York: 1937.

Breen, David H. *The Canadian Prairie West and the Ranching Frontier 1874–1924.* Toronto: University of Toronto Press, 1983.

Edwards, Yorke. "Man and the Prairie Landscape." *Canadian Audubon,* 32, 4, Sept–Dec 1970.

Ference, Ermeline Ann. *Literature Associated with Ranching in Southern Alberta*. M.A. Thesis, University of Alberta, 1971.

Kollmorgen, Walter M. *The Woodman's Assault on the Domain of the Cattleman*. Association of American Geographers, 59, 2, June 1969.

Kramer, Jane. *The Last Cowboy*. New York: Harper and Row, 1977.

Long, Philip S. *Seventy Years a Cowboy*. Saskatoon: Freeman Publishing Co., 1965.

Loveridge, D. M. and Barry Potyandi. *From Wood Mountain to the Whitemud: An Historical Survey of the Grasslands National Park Area*. Ottawa: Parks Canada, Dept. of Indian and Northern Affairs, 1977.

MacInnes, C. M. *In the Shadow of the Rockies*. London: Rivingtons, 1930.

Jameson, Sheilagh S. "The Era of the Big Ranches: The Romantic Period of Southern Alberta's History." *Alberta Historical Review*, 18, 1, 1970.

McGowan, Don C. *Grassland Settlers*. Regina: Canadian Plains Research Centre, 1975.

MacGregor, James. *Lord Lorne in Alberta*. Alberta Historical Review, 12, 2, Spring 1964.

Olsen, Charles. *Call Me Ishmael*. New York: Grove Press, 1947.

Roosevelt, Theodore. *Ranch Life and the Hunting Trail*. London: T. Fisher and Unwin, 1904.

Symons, R. D. *Many Trails*. Toronto: Longmans, 1963.

—— *Where the Wagon Led*. Toronto: Doubleday, 1973.

Shepard, George. *The West of Yesterday*. Toronto: McClelland and Stewart, 1965.

Thomas, Lewis G. *The Ranching Period in Southern Alberta*. Unpub. M.A. Thesis, University of Alberta, 1935.

Sharp, Paul F. *Whoop-Up Country*. Minnesota: University of Minnesota Press, 1955.

Stead, J. C. Robert. *The Cowpuncher*. Toronto: Musson, 1915.

Tiessen, Hugo. "Old-Style Prairie Ranching Gives Way to Intensive Crop-and-Cattle Farming." *Canadian Geographical Journal*, 88, 4, 1974.

Webb, Walter Prescott. *The Great Plains*. Boston: Ginn and Co., 1931.

Chapter Twelve

Atwood, Margaret. *Survival*. Toronto: Anansi, 1972.

Braithwaite, Max. *Why Shoot the Teacher?* Toronto: McClelland and Stewart, 1965.

Frye, Northrop. *The Bush Garden*. Toronto: Anansi, 1971.

Harrison, Dick. *Unnamed Country: The Struggle for a Canadian Prairie Fiction*. Edmonton: University of Alberta Press, 1977.

Hiebert, Paul. *Sarah Binks*. Toronto: Oxford University Press, 1947.

McLeish, John A. *September Gale: A Study of Arthur Lismer of the Group of Seven*. Toronto: J. M. Dent, 1955.

Morton, W. L. "Seeing an Unliterary Landscape." *Mosaic*, 3, 1970.

Rees, R. *Land of Earth and Sky: Landscape Painting of Western Canada*. Saska-
toon: Western Producer Prairie Books, 1984.
Sevareid, Eric. "You Can Go Home Again." In *Readings of the Geography of
North Dakota*. University of North Dakota, Grand Forks, 1968.
Smith, Bernard. "Art and Environment in Australia." *Geographical Magazine*,
19, 9, 1947.
Southall, Ivan. *One Ocean Touching*. Papers from the first Pacific Rim Con-
ference on Children's Literature, ed. Sheila A. Egoff. Metuchen, New Jersey:
Scarecrow Press, 1979.
Tayen, Eric and Joe Bodolai. "Borderlines in Art and Experience." *Arts Canada*,
31, Spring 1974.
Winks, Robert W. *The Myth of the American Frontier* (Sir George Watson Lec-
ture). Leicester: Leicester University Press, 1971.
Woodcock, George. "Possessing the Land." In *The Canadian Imagination*, ed.
David Staines. Cambridge: Harvard University Press, 1977.
Wright, Percy H. "The Robert Hurley Vogue." *Star Phoenix*, Saskatoon: February
1, 1952.

Chapter Thirteen

Gray, Ian D. *An Ethno-historical Approach to the Pioneer Farmers of Saskatch-
ewan*. Unpub. M.A Thesis, University of Saskatchewan, 1977.
Leacock, Stephen. *My Discovery of the West*. Toronto: Thomas Allen, 1937.
McCourt, Edward. *The Canadian West in Fiction*. Toronto: Ryerson, 1949.
Zimmerman, Carle D. "Socio-Cultural Changes in the Plains," and Richard
E. DuWors. "Prevailing Life Perspectives and Population Shifts in the Cana-
dian Prairie Provinces." In *Symposium on the Great Plains of North America*,
eds. Carle Zimmerman and Seth Russell. Fargo: North Dakota Institute for
Regional Studies, 1967.

INDEX

Adamowska, Maria, 90
Adams, Thomas, 63, 69–70
Advertiser, Nebraska, 101
Advertiser, London, 128
Advertising. *See* Promotion
Americans, desirability of, 11; land selection, 45–46; rates of defection, 67
Anderson, Aquina, 47
Apple tree, symbolic power of, 113
Arbor Day, 101–102
Arnold Arboretum, 121
Artist-reporters, 12
As For Me and My House, 164
Atcheson, Topeka, and Santa Fe Railroad, 118
Atlantic Monthly, 65
Atlas of Western Canada, 17, 19, 22
Atwood, Margaret, 160
Austin, Charles, 12

Bachelard, Gaston, 41, 93
Baker, Professor William, 98
Balint, Michael, 151, 154
Ballantyne, R.M., 2, 5
Barr Colonists, 58; settlement in Saskatchewan, 79–80

Barr, Isaac, 79
Battleford, 7, 80
Beaven, Alan, 120
Bedford, S.A., 114
Begg, Alexander, 17
Bennett, John, 123, 135, 142, 154
Benton, Thomas Hart, 151
Bernhard, Iver, 38
Bessey, Dean, 101
Bicha, Dennis, 67
Billington, Ray Allen, 4
Blanton, Henry, 150, 153
Block settlement, 50–52
Blodgett, Lorin, 15, 16
Bow River, 122, 138
Bradfield College Ranche, 137, 140
Braithwaite, Max, 160
Brandon Experimental Farm, 113, 114, 115, 122
Brandon Sun, 128
Brandon Times, 37
Broadview, Saskatchewan, 118
Brody, Hugh, 90
Brooke, Lionel, 139
Brooke, Rupert, 13, 42, 43
Brown, Annora, 107, 125
Brown, Mary, 94

Brown, Professor William, 108
Budd, Professor, J.L., 112, 121
Buffon, Count, 100
Bulletin, Edmonton, 64
Burroughs, John, 97
Butler, William F., 5, 6, 12, 35
By Track and Trail, 13

Calgary, 122, 139
Calgary Herald, 138, 139, 140
Campbell, Marjorie Wilkins, 46
Canadian Forestry Association, 120
Canadian Pacific Railway, promotional work, 8–11; station gardens, 118–119; tree planting campaign, 120
Cannington. *See* Cannington Manor
Cannington Manor, Saskatchewan, 80–85, 139, 140
Caragana Arborescens, 115
Cather, Willa, 35
Catlin, George, 5, 30
Central Experimental Farm, 113, 118
Chapman, John, 113
Chateau Qu'Appelle, 132
Chaucer, Geoffrey, 123
Chinooks, 109; effects on planting, 116; on snowcover, 145
Chipman, George F., 121
Chornlesky, William, 64
Clarke, Georgina Binnie, 38
Cleveland, Horace, 98, 99
Climate, efforts to change image of, 7–8, 14–18
Climato-therapy, science of, 16
Climatology of North America, The, 15
Cochrane ranch, 141
Colony settlement. *See* Block Settlement
Commager, Henry Steele, 2
Cooper, James Fenimore, 5
Country Guide, 121
Cowboys. *See* Ranching
Cox, A.E., 137
Cypress Hills, 137, 145, 147

Daily Telegraph, London, 24
Davies, Evan, 35, 37, 48, 125
Dawson, G.M., 6, 110
De Gelder, Willem, 43
De la Blache, Vidal, 81
De Tocqueville, Alexis, 87
De Winton, Alberta, 137
Dennison Grant, 70–71
Denny, Sir Cecil, 31
Department of Agriculture, 10
Department of the Interior, 8, 11, 12, 18, 116
Depletion Myth, 98
Diefenbaker Lake, 126
Divet, Guy, 93
Donkin, John, 26, 30, 44, 63, 85, 86
Doukhobors, 35, 47, 48, 77–79
Downing, Andrew Jackson, 98, 118, 168
Dufferin, Lady, 77
Dunlop, W.S., 118
DuWors, Richard, 69, 170
Dye, Lewis G., 107

Edmonton, 28
Emerson, Ralph Waldo, 97
Emigrant letters, 13–14, 51
England, Robert, 58
Evolution of the Prairie by the Plow, 20
Expansionist movement, 7
Experimental farms, establishment of, 109; locations, 116

Farlington, Kansas, 118
Fernow, Bernhard E., 101
Fertile belt, 6
Field, 140
Fish Creek, 52, 68
Fisher, John W., 134
Fitzgerald, Lionel Lemoine, 162–164
Forest and Stream, 128
Fort Carlton, 28
Fort McLeod, 40, 138, 142
Fort Qu'Appelle, 127

Fowke, V.C., 67
Franko, Ivan, 90
Fraser, J.F., 62, 139
Frye, Northrop, 156
Funk, Harold, 74

Galicians. *See* Ukrainians
Gardens, 58, 81, 124; C.P.R. station
   gardens, 118-119
Garland, Aileen, 119
Garland, Hamlin, 64, 153
Gazette, Fort McLeod, 136, 137
Genyk, Cyril, 71
Germany, attitudes to emigration,
   11
Giants in the Earth, 36
Gibb, Chas., 112, 113
Gibson, William, 86
Gilbert, G.K., 105
Gilbertson, Kristine Kaldor, 124
Globe, Toronto, 6
Goetzmann, W.H., 5
Gordon, Daniel M., 102
Grand Trunk Railway, 62, 132
Grant, George Munro, 12, 13, 19,
   20
Graphic, London, 12, 22, 24
Gray, Dr. H.B., 137
Great American Desert, 5, 7
Gregg, Josiah, 100
Greig, Robin, 40
Grier, Nina V., 142
Group of Seven, 161, 162, 163
Grove, Frederick Philip, 40, 162

Hall, Sydney Prior, 12, 22, 24
Hambley, G.H., 39
Hamerton, Philip G., 107
Hamilton, Zachary, 138
Hamilton, Marie, 35-36, 43, 65,
   144
Handlin, Oscar, 89
Hardy, Thomas, 172
Harris, Lawren, 161
Hawes, Ben, 6
Hayden, F.V., 99
Heimweh. *See* Nostalgia
Herklots, W.G., 41

Hiebert, Paul, 156
Hiemstra, Mary, 8, 47, 58
Hind, Cora E., 77
Hind, Henry Youle, 6, 7, 8, 14
Hippocrates, 1, 16
Hitchcock, Senator Phineas W., 102
Holm, Beret, 37, 125, 154
Holmes, Oliver Wendell, 103
Home is the Stranger, 124
Hudson's Bay Co., 5, 28, 46, 52,
   95
Humphrys, James, 81
Hurley, Robert, 164-166 167, 171

Imperial Botanic Gardens, St
   Petersburg, 112, 113
Imperial College of Japan, 113
Inderwick, Charles, 138, 145
Indian Head Tree Nursery, 1, 107,
   109, 111, 113, 114, 115, 116, 117,
   122, 123
Indians, 142, 144; adaptation to
   prairie environment, 30-31
Innes, John, 150
International Boundary Survey, 6
Iowa Agricultural College, 112

Jefferys, Charles W., 163, 164
Johnny Appleseed, 113
Johnson, Lucy L., 38
Johnston, Alex, 31

Kane, Paul, 5, 30
Kansas and Pacific Railroad, 118
Kelsey, Henry, 95, 96
Kenderdine, Augustus, 48
Kennedy, John, 47
Kerr, Illingworth, 162, 163, 164,
   171
Kew Gardens, 113
Kipling Rudyard, 13, 65
Konvalinka, Joseph G., 106
Kostash, Myrna, 43
Kramer, Jane, 146, 149, 153

Lacombe, 116
Landscape, efforts to soften image
   of, 18-24

Langley, George, 80
Leader Post, Regina, 131
Legislative Building, Regina, 129, 130, 131, 132
Lethbridge, 116
Lismer, Arthur, 161
Little, William, 105–106
Long, Major Stephen H., 100
Long, Philip S., 145
Lorne, Marquis of, 7, 17, 128, 137, 138; Vice-regal tour of Western Canada, 12; views on ranching, 137
Luelling, Henderson, 113
Lynn, Washington Frank, 13, 16, 29, 42
Lysenko, Vera, 90

MacDonald, Sir John A., 80, 127
Macoun, John, 7, 8, 16, 45
Maguire, Hugo, 150
Mair, Charles, 17
Man and Nature, 100
Manitoba and the Great North-West, 7
Manitoba Free Press, 69
Maple Creek, 145
Marsh, George Perkins, 100, 101
Martin, Chester, 67
Maude, Aylmer, 104
Mavor, James, 104
Mawson, Thomas Henry, 129–132
Maynard, Fredelle Bruser, 165
McCourt, Edward, 26, 35, 42, 124, 171
McDougall, John, 12, 20
McGregor, J.G., 48
Meager, Leonard, 96
Mennonites, 18, 20, 35, 88, 89; in Manitoba, 71–77
Métis, 28; way of life, 31–33; reactions to rectangular survey, 63
Minifie, James, 37, 111
Minnesota Horticultural Society, 111
Mitchell, Elizabeth, 57, 65
Moberg, Vilhelm, 47, 92
Moorhouse, Myrtle G., 40
Moose Jaw, Saskatchewan, 118

Moose Mountain Trading Company, 82
Morden, Manitoba, 121
Morris, George Pope, 97
Morton, Julius Sterling, 98
Morton, W.L., 160–161
Mumford, Lewis, 79
Munro, W.A., 120
Munsterhjelm, Erik, 86

Narrative of a Journey to Manitoba, 73
Nation, 14
Nilsson, Karl Oskar, 92
Niven, Frederick, 38, 124
North Atlantic Trading Company, 12
North-West Mounted Police, 26, 33, 114, 138, 142; affinity with ranchers, 139–140
Nostalgia, 1; for the homeland, 86–94; for pioneer days, 169–170

O Emigratsii, 24
O'Neill, Moira, 153
Ocean to Ocean, 13, 19
Ochnophils, 151–154
Oleskow, Josef, 24, 50
Olmstead, Frederick Law, 128
Olsen, Charles, 154
Olson, Sherry, 98
Orwell, George, 27
Osmond, Dr. Henry, 37
Ostenso, Martha, 162

Palliser's Triangle, 6, 7
Palliser, Capt. John, 6, 7, 14, 127
Parks. *See* Wascana Park
Patmore, Henry, 114
Patten, C.G., 108
Pearce, William, 16, 121–122, 130
Pennell, W.M., 111
Phillips, Walter J., 162
Philobats, 151–154
Picturesque Canada, 13, 20
Pierce, Edward Michell, 80–81, 82, 83, 84

Pillipiw, Ivan, 35
Pincher Creek, Alberta, 142
Plant breeding and selection, 120–122
Potts, Jerry, 37
Promotion of settlement, by C.P.R., 8–10; by Canadian Government, 10–12; by Great Britain, 12; by individuals, 13–14

Qu'Appelle Valley, 38, 47, 127, 164

Ranching, beginnings of, 33–34; as adaptation to prairie environment, 136–154
Ranken, George, 104
Red River settlers, 17, 29, 93, 108; farming practices, 29–30
Regina, 43, 69, 128, 132, 134; terrain, 127; tree planting in, 130
Regina Plain, 144
Rigby, Captain John, 40
River lots, 29, 64, 68, 70; as cultural symbol, 63
Roberts, Sarah E., 37
Robey, H.C., 102
Rolvaag, O.E., 36
Romanchych, Dmytro, 48
Roosevelt, Theodore, 150
Roper, Edward, 13, 18, 24, 38
Ross, Malcolm, 129
Ross, Norman M., 107
Ross, Sinclair, 164
Roy, Gabrielle, 47
Rupert's Land, 5
Russell, A.J., 6, 7
Ryan, W.J., 40

Saskatchewan, University of, 126, 132
Saskatoon, 43, 79
Saunders, William, 112, 114, 120; as plant breeder, 113
Schantz, Jacob, 73
Schell, F.B., 20
Selkirk, Thomas Douglas, fifth earl of, 28, 45, 108
Settlement plan for prairies, 61–63

Sevareid, Eric, 160
Shane, 151
Sheldon-Williams, Inglis, 139
Shelterbelts, preparations for planting, 117; benefits of, 123–125; field shelterbelts, 126
Shepard, Paul, 64
Shortt, Adam, 26
Siberian Pea Tree, 115
Sifton, Clifford, 10, 11, 13, 14, 17, 19, 20, 26; immigration policy, 11–12
Simpson, Sir George, 5
Sippa, importance to Norwegians, 47
Skinner, Frank L., 121
Smalley, E.V., 65, 68, 71
Smart, James A., 50, 84
Smith, Bernard, 158
Smith, John, 96
Smith, W.E., 139
Southall, Ivan, 160, 166
Speers, C.W., 50, 52
Spence, Thomas, 55
Springfield, Manitoba, 118
Stead, Robert, 71, 137, 150
Stegner, Wallace, 38, 57, 87, 125
Stevens, George, 151
Stevenson, A.P., 121
Stoughton, A.A., 69
Stuartburn, 52
Survey, Rectangular, 60–63; criticism of, 63–65, 69–70
Sutherland tree nursery, 116
Symons, Robert, 147, 150, 153

Tanner, Henry, 68
Tennyson, Bertram, 40, 84
The Country Gentleman, 140
The Cowpuncher, 150
The Great Plains, 2
The Great Lone Land, 5, 6
The Last Cowboy, 146
The Times, London, 12, 14
Thomas, Lewis G., 136, 141
Thomas, William Luson, 12
Timber Culture Act, 102
Todd, Frederick G., 128, 129

Towns, lay-out and distribution, 62–63; reactions to, 41–43, 164
Trails, appeal and utility of, 64, 125, 142, 146, 153
Tree claims, 109
Tree Planting Car, 120
Trees, aesthetic appeal of, 96–97, 107; as symbols of continuity, 97; effects on character, 98–99; effects on climate, 99–106; difficulties of tree planting, 109–112; search for hardy species, 112–113; propagation and distribution, 114–117
Trooper and Redskin, 26
Trotter, Beecham, 47
Trow, James B., 73
Truth, London, 14

Ukrainians, recruitment of, 11–12; predilection for woodland, 48–50; block settlements, 51–52; housing and settlements, 55–59; homesickness, 89–92
Updike, John, 125

Van Cleef, Eugene, 47
Van Horne, Sir William, 15, 16, 18, 69

Verner, Frederick, 5

Walter, John, 12
Warkentin, John, 77
Warre, Henry James, 31
Wascana Centre. *See* Wascana Park
Wascana Creek, 127, 128
Wascana Park, development of, 126–135
Watt, George, 129
Webb, Walter Prescott, 2
Wheeler, Seager, 121
Whitman, Walt, 58, 90
William Silvering's Surrender, 103
Willoughby, Gerald, 38
Windscheigl, Peter, 39
Winnipeg, 20, 42
Wolf Willow, 125
Wolseley, 118
Wood Culture Act, 109
Wood Mountain, 40, 47, 144
Wooff, J., 67
World's Columbian Exposition, Chicago, 115
Wright, Percy, 166

Young, J.J., 140

Zacharias, Peter, 74